BOOKS BY BILL GLEASON

Footsteps of a Giant (*1966*)
The Liquid Cross of Skid Row (*1966*)
Daley of Chicago (*1970*)

DALEY
of Chicago

The Man, the Mayor,
and the Limits of Conventional Politics

BILL GLEASON

SIMON AND SCHUSTER · NEW YORK

First printing

SBN 671–20697–4
Library of Congress Catalog Card Number: 77–130474
Designed by Edith Fowler
Manufactured in the United States of America
By H. Wolff, New York

For Joe Gleason, who is gone,
and for Helen O'Brien Gleason.
They helped me to understand
that the city belongs to the people.

CONTENTS

The generations to come will care nothing for our warehouses, our buildings or our railroads, but they will ask, what has Chicago done for humanity; where has it made man wiser or nobler or stronger; what new thought or principles or trust has it given the world?

—JOHN PETER ALTGELD, 1893

THE PLACE

CHICAGO is the name—Chicago, a calculating city that conceals the truth about itself because it prefers to be misunderstood. Chicago strives to conceal its realities from those who see the city infrequently. Chicago doesn't want to know the stranger on his first day in town, and Chicago doesn't want the stranger to know the city on his fifth day in town. Chicago has a need to awe a visitor, and Chicago is convinced that familiarity breeds contempt. This is why those who profess to know Chicago best know Chicago least. Chicago is not a woman, not a "she" as so many cities are. Chicago is the "he" among cities. Chicago is always the seducer, never the seduced. Chicago does not lie there at the western turn of Lake Michigan waiting for things to happen. Chicago moves, moves, making things happen.

Chicago is, has been and will be violent. When Chicago heard that Abraham Lincoln had been shot and gravely wounded, a man who was standing in the crowded lobby of the Matteson House said that Lincoln had got what was coming to him. Almost immediately the Lincoln critic was shot to death. The reaction of the witnesses to the Matteson House murder? Most in the huge crowd applauded. The killer stepped over the body of his victim, strolled from the lobby and walked into the street. Free? More than free. A hero. The police neither pursued him nor looked for him later. He merely had done what others would have done.

11

Almost a century later, after John Fitzgerald Kennedy was destroyed by an assassin, another Chicagoan put his gun into his pocket and went to the jail in Dallas. Jack Ruby, well remembered by refugees from Chicago's West Side as a hustler, a slugger, a tough guy with a marshmallow heart, is part of the legend now—a folk hero.

Chicago is violent. Five phases of its history have brought to it conditions that inspire violence and individuals who incite to violence. Chicago was a frontier fortress-outpost. Chicago was a river village. Chicago was a canal town. Chicago was a railhead city. Chicago was a Prohibition metropolis. In each of those phases violence was a way of life or of death. Citizens killed and citizens were killed.

Chicago is conservative. Rooted in history, as is the violence, the conservatism has been the reaction to the violence. The violent and the conservative are the contradictions that analysts from other places rarely comprehend. Chicago has had a reputation as a wide-open town, but this renown is based on misconceptions from the past. The illegalities of Chicago exist, and have existed, for the visitors from out of town and for those who promote the illegalities and profit by them. Chicago now may be one of the few large cities in the world that do not have a whorehouse that operates with the sanction of elected officials, and it is a city in which a person cannot make a wager on the outcome of a horse race in surroundings conducive to dignity and serenity.

Chicago misses its bookmaking establishments, which were closed during the administration of a reform mayor and have remained closed for almost twenty years, but when the can houses were flourishing on Federal Street in the swiftly receding past, Chicago did not provide the revenues that made them profitable. Chicago provided the protection and shared the profit. Chicago was too conservative to pay the two dollars. Chicago took its share off the top.

Chicago is conservative, but Chicago is not cheap. If you

need money for any purpose Chicago will lend it to you, but Chicago will not pay for a lay. Chicago stays out in the neighborhoods on Friday and Saturday nights and leaves Old Town, Rush Street and State Street to those visitors from other places. Chicago may covet its neighbor's wife in the corner tavern just after closing on Sunday morning, but Chicago will not go downtown to pay for what it can get free.

The monolithic Tribune Tower, the first building north of the Chicago River, has become the anachronism of North Michigan Avenue's "Magnificent Mile," but the presence of the ersatz Gothic tower is proof that Colonel Robert R. McCormick read the mood of the city. If Chicago had not been conservative, publisher McCormick would have gone the other way.

Marshall Field III, a liberal who organized the Chicago *Sun* to compete with McCormick's journal, was deceived by the city. Field, a modest, introspective man, was unaware that Chicago's liberals, a spineless lot, were not worthy of his glorious crusade. His son, Marshall Field IV, even more withdrawn than the father, read the mind of Chicago. The younger Field—now gone, as are his father and McCormick —comprehended that Chicago applauds liberalism in others but prefers conservatism in itself. Field IV moved his newspaper off left, toward center, and the city now has two enormously successful publishing corporations.

The city says, "If you can't make it in Chicago, you can't make it anywhere." What the calculating city means to say is, "If you can make it in Chicago, you can make it anywhere." Natives of other places may see themselves with similar confidence, but Chicago's men and Chicago's women, children of the man-city, reject the premise that any other city and the residents of any other city are comparable to Chicago and Chicagoans. The citizens of Chicago know, beyond any doubt, that they could slow their speed to three quarters of the pace they move at when at home and lead the field in other places.

The Tribune Tower overlooks the place where Chicago's first non-Indian inhabitant made his home. This first settler was a black man in the eyes and in the minds of those who accept Chicago's premise that a person who is half Negro, or any fraction thereof, is all Negro. Chicago's conscience prefers to skip over this black man who lived on the riverbank and think instead of the man who bought the Negro's property. The purchaser was "the first white settler," and those few words explain all that is wrong with Chicago.

Chicago's slogan of a generation ago—"I Will"—is laughed at by older citizens and is unknown to the younger. Chicago's authentic, unwritten slogan is "I'm with you," which is pronounced "I'm witchoo."

An easy air of conspiracy permeates day-to-day life outside the home. Chicago is a city of alliances. Those who stand apart from one another by tradition and background become allies when they are thrown together. The Pole and the Negro who work side by side in a machine shop confide in one another with the motto of a brotherhood that does not run as deep as blood. "I'm witchoo."

They work together, conspire together, laugh together and drink together. When the working day is done each returns to the sanctuary of the tavern in his neighborhood and tells ethnic jokes about the other.

The Pole and the Negro in the machine shop. The Irishman and the Lithuanian on the police force. The Jewish merchant and the Bohemian janitor. The Wasp stockbroker and the hillbilly waitress.

They understand one another and the understanding is complete. Each knows that the other will be "witchoo" until a more profitable alliance can be worked out. Today's ally may be tomorrow's enemy. The ritual is a big-city square dance in which the original partners "go on to the next" but rarely "come on home." Chicago is the caller.

The most skillful dancers are Chicago's politicians. Alliances, like campaign promises, are made to be broken. *I'm with you.* The unsaid part of this affirmation of loyalty is "We're against everybody else."

THE MAN

DALEY is the name—Richard J. Daley, a secretive man who
has managed to keep himself from being known to the millions who have watched him and listened to him and been
governed by him for more than fourteen years. Richard J.
Daley is like a king of olden times who daily came down
from his castle into the town to walk among his subjects, to
touch them and to be touched by them; but when the king
returned to the castle at dusk his subjects realized that he
had learned much about them and they had learned nothing
about him.

Richard J. Daley is a private man in a public job. He is at
least as calculating and as complicated as Chicago, his city.
He also makes a deliberate effort to be misunderstood. Nobody asks him, "How do you feel about this?" Instead the
question invariably is, "What do you think about this?" His
feelings are kept under lock in the strongbox of his soul except on rare occasion when he turns the lock with the key
that is temper. Then he says, "Shoot to kill," and the millions
who admire him realize that he does feel.

According to one who studies the derivation of surnames,
Daley means "He who goes to meetings." If this name did not
have that meaning, Richard Daley would have brought the
meaning to it. He goes to meetings and to wakes. It has been
said of him that he has attended more wakes than any politician in Chicago history. To this chore, which even a few

among Irish-Americans find to be onerous, he brings genuine respect for the dead and practical compassion for the mourners. In his quiet, diffident way he is saying, "I'm with you."

He is elderly now, but he remains charged with the energy of youth. He is a born walker, a parader, a marcher. Even when he is standing, he looks as though he is in motion. When he enters the Council chambers at City Hall to preside at a meeting of aldermen, he moves so quickly it seems as though he will stride through the large room and exit at a far door before he can stop.

When he arrives at a funeral home, he whirls through the entrance door, members of the retinue taking large steps to keep pace, and if it is not a Catholic wake and there is no kneeler upon which a man can say a prayer beside the casket, he looks to be in motion even when he is talking earnestly and comfortingly to the widow. He moves, moves, moves, making things happen.

His carriage and his posture, carefully cultivated, are magnificent. Chins in, abdomen tucked up. Because he looks so much like the politicians of the editorial-page cartoons, he does everything possible to avoid the stereotype. He is not a tall man. He is not a slim man. But he walks tall and slim. This is a trick he learned well from others. He has disciplined his body, but his face got away from him. It is a good face, but instead of having been stretched it was folded and piled. Just as he has an extra chin, he has a profusion of jowls. There are, within the jowls, great dimples and small crevasses. At times students of his face see Mr. Pickwick there; at other times they see Santa Claus; and at still other times the character portrayed so often by Sidney Greenstreet, the late movie villain. In 1955 critics made fun of the clothes worn by Daley. Now he makes "best-dressed men" lists, an accomplishment that amuses him.

His malapropisms, tautologies and syntactical errors are

collector's items. But he is not the "dese, dem and dose" mis-pronouncer that some among the literati have made him out to be. His basic speech impediment is one shared by most Irish-Americans, even to the third and fourth generation. There is something in the Gaelic language that makes the sounding of *th* all but impossible. For Richard J. Daley and millions like him *thanks* becomes *tanks* and *think* becomes *tink*. Even *the* is difficult—it usually emerges sounding like *tuh*—and *these, them* and *those* are more so.

For a very long time he infuriated his constituents by speaking as though he were sure that Chicago's major air-port, O'Hare Field, actually was O'Hara Field. The explana-tion offered and accepted was that Daley knew many O'Haras and hardly any O'Hares. The true explanation may very well have been buried in the subconscious of this man who has an aversion for anything that reflects upon the fair name of Chicago. Daley knew that the airport had been named to honor the deed and the memory of a young man who had been one of the great heroes of the dismal days early in World War II. Daley also knew that the hero's father had been a powerful associate of Al Capone, the boss of Chi-cago's crime syndicate, and that the elder O'Hare had been shot to death in a Chicago street, another victim of the con-tract killers of the Syndicate that contributed so largely to giving Chicago a notorious name.

It has been said that his approach to press relations is abominable, that he does not know how to handle the ques-tions volleyed at him by the men from newspapers, television and radio. The fact is that he uses a press conference or an interview for his purposes and that he loses control only on those rare occasions when his short temper routs his good judgment. One of his first major interviews was a question-and-answer session with a reporter from a news weekly. That was Daley's first opportunity for a national demonstration of a skill he had learned from masters—the knack of pretending to answer a question by talking away from the question. These are examples from that interview:

Q. Is there any organized crime remaining [in Chicago]?

A. Well, you have crime always, whether it's the large city or the village or the neighborhood.

Q. But what about the Syndicates, like the Capone gang—do they exist?

A. Well, whether it's organized or unorganized, it's still crime and it has to be met on all the various levels by very rigid law enforcement.

Those answers were accepted by the reporter in 1955, and the editors printed them. Reporters and editors have been taking and publishing similar answers from Daley ever since.

In 1955 Richard J. Daley became the fortieth mayor of Chicago. His opponents were certain that he would be a very bad mayor. His supporters hoped that he would be a mediocre mayor who would not disgrace his city, himself or his party. He was reelected in 1959, in 1963 and in 1967. He has been mayor of Chicago longer than any other man, and many contend that he is the best mayor the city has had. When he came to City Hall in 1955 his task, as he saw it, was to "restore, revitalize and rebuild the spirit of Chicago." His successes are unparalleled. His failure is singular. His failure is the failure of all of us, of the nation. Race. He is good with buildings, but he is poor with people—and deplorably poor with people who are black.

He is The Mayor.

Part One

THE WALK

1

Cast in Bronze

HE MIGHT have walked. The Mayor of Chicago might have walked to his home from this intersection of the street that he had dedicated, moments before, to the memory of Dr. Martin Luther King Jr. Fate had provided the coincidence and the juxtaposition, a combination that a man sometimes can take for his own and make of it a moment in history.

Richard J. Daley, the fortieth mayor of Chicago, had come here to Thirty-fifth Street and South Parkway on this August afternoon to participate in the ceremonies that changed South Parkway to "Dr. Martin Luther King Jr. Drive." In other circumstances "King Drive" would have been sufficient, but these were not other circumstances. These were rites to commemorate the complex mystic who was called "martyr" by millions, called "saint" by a few, and called "troublemaker" by other millions. The emotion he had aroused demanded a fullness of name, and the city's street-sign designer had been equal to the challenge. The signs were printed this way:

DR. MARTIN LUTHER KING JR. DR.

Those few Chicagoans, black and white, who loved Martin Luther King would be offended by the ostentation of those street signs. Those few Chicagoans, white and black, who hated Martin Luther King would be moved to ugly laughter

23

by the vulgarity of those signs. Those many Chicagoans, black and white, who had been indifferent to King, who never had heard what he was saying, would not care. The Mayor cared about the signs and about the ceremony, just as he cared deeply about all of Chicago. And in his way The Mayor cared about Martin Luther King.

Not so many days before, during a debate in Chicago's City Council to choose the street that would be renamed for Martin Luther King, a debate that was equal parts anguish and cynicism, The Mayor had been on the verge of tears when he pleaded for an end to the hatred and the divisiveness. Some Negro aldermen had demanded, in King's name, a street that would begin in the Loop—Chicago's central business district—and run west through Lawndale, the ghetto community that had gone up in flames on the April afternoon that followed the assassination of the black leader. Those streets had been named, however, for heroes who would not be willingly surrendered by white aldermen. Some of those streets are Washington, Madison, Randolph, Monroe, Adams, Jackson, Van Buren. Those street signs are sacred.

South Parkway had been selected by the city administration because it ran through the heart of the established black community on the South Side of the city and because no citizen could be expected to defend a point of the compass. Changing the name of South Parkway would offend nobody, the administration believed. The administration had been wrong, as it often was when it made decisions for its black constituents during these puzzling times.

At the most inflammatory moment of the debate, The Mayor rose to make a speech that was passionate, disjointed and at times incoherent. Admirers and detractors in the Council chamber feared that he was near the point of collapse. But at the end he brought himself back to himself and he won the day.

The broad intersection of Thirty-fifth Street and South

Parkway is a place of remembering. South of Thirty-fifth Street there is a monument to other black men whose lives were given in months of violence. The monument is topped by the familiar statue of the World War I doughboy running into battle with bayonet outthrust. This doughboy represents the soldiers of the 370th Infantry, 93rd Division, who died in 1918.

Below the figure of the Infantryman, a heroic representation of a woman holds a tablet on which are inscribed the names of the battles in which the 370th Infantry offered its dead to America. St. Mihiel, Argonne, Mont des Singes, Ailette Canal, Oise, Aisne.

From those places some of the men of the 370th came back to Chicago and the race riots of 1919. Richard Daley had been seventeen years old during that frightful week forty-nine years ago. He remembered. And at every side of him now, at Thirty-fifth and Dr. Martin Luther King Jr. Drive, there were elderly black men and women who also remembered.

A black boy had ventured, accidentally or daringly, across the line of demarcation that separated Negro swimmers from white. Words were exchanged; blows were struck; rocks were thrown. The blacks had fought back in that long-ago time, too. Power was not something that their grandchildren had discovered. Before the hatred had run its course, thirty-eight had been killed—twenty-three Negroes died; fifteen whites died, including one policeman. Twenty men were held to the grand jury for murder or manslaughter. A soldier was bound over to a court-martial on a murder charge.

Because he is part of the environment, The Mayor knows that this section of the South Side, west on Thirty-fifth Street through the ghetto and into the white communities beyond, still is affected by the wounds of that 1919 riot. The scars long since have been covered by nature and by building projects, but they remain deep within the people on both sides of other lines of demarcation between black and white. The Mayor also knows, as do the elderly Negroes staring into his eyes, that a riot of unimagined destruction is possible in the Chicago of their present time.

In his brief speech at the street dedication, The Mayor said that he and Dr. King had held a belief in common. The conviction they shared is that "hate accomplishes nothing."

The response to The Mayor's declaration of spiritual kinship with King had been polite but not empathetic. Too many in the crowd knew too well that The Mayor had said other things about Dr. King. In July of 1967 The Mayor had said of the civil-rights leader that he "comes up here from Atlanta for only one reason . . . to cause trouble in our city and in every city he visited." In August of 1966 The Mayor, speaking of Dr. King and his followers in the Southern Christian Leadership Conference, had said, "We don't want any people who come into our city for the purpose of agitation, regardless of who they are. We could do well without them. And we hope they'll go back to the place they come from."

Dr. Martin Luther King Jr. had gone back to the place he had come from. If The Mayor of Chicago had, in fact, discovered the meaning of the man from the South, the discovery had come too late to be helpful to discoverer or discovered. But The Mayor was not alone in his belated realization of what King had been doing and saying in Chicago. In this crowd at the statue of the Black Infantryman, there were too many whose veneration of the Black Evangelist had not begun until that April night when news of his death was flashed around the world. In March, February, January and December, he had been, in the eyes and ears of many, a face seen fleetingly on a television screen, a voice heard briefly. The analysts said that his doctrine of nonviolence no longer was relevant and the violent of all races corroborated the analysts.

The ceremony had ended. Chicago had a new name for an old street. As the throng began to move out, a spectator had an opportunity to move closer to the statue. He found very small letters that said the statue was cast in bronze in 1928. The spectator looked up to the Infantryman running to immortality. The Infantryman is the same color as every other doughboy atop every other World War I statue in Chicago. He and they are bronze. And this is Bronzeville.

2

Where Did They Go?

THE Mayor can remember when this attractive and spacious thoroughfare was called Grand Boulevard. Then the name was changed to South Parkway. Now it was Dr. Martin Luther King Jr. Drive. Thirty-fifth and King Drive always had been an important intersection in the Black Belt that was known as Bronzeville in a day when "ghetto" was synonymous with "Jew." It was not "the" intersection, however. That was at Forty-seventh Street and South Parkway, the heart of what insiders sardonically referred to as "The Spooks' Loop." Forty-seventh and South Parkway had been to the Black Belt what State and Madison meant to the rest of Chicago.

From 1919, when the men of the 370th came home to a hero's welcome and to blood in the streets, until 1950, when a new group of war veterans were filling the basements and attics, the geographical boundaries of the Black Belt had been extended hardly at all. Federal rent controls of the World War II years had been a major factor in keeping the Belt in place. Under rent controls Negroes were unable to outbid whites for rental of apartments on the periphery of the Belt. For three decades Bronzeville was involved in a municipal trick similar to the circus act in which fifteen clowns emerge from a tiny car. The nonwhite population of Chicago, which had been 109,525 in 1920, had become 277,731 in 1940, and had soared to 519,437 in 1950.

There had been a tremendous problem here, right here at Thirty-fifth and King Drive and south to Forty-seventh Street. The Mayor understood that problem. He understood it then, in 1950, when it was not his to solve, and he understood it now, in 1968, when the burden of it threatened to crush him and the city he loves.

It went back to the years immediately after World War II, when the flight of Negroes to the Black Belt from their homes in the South had become as inexorable as a troop movement from a Southern training camp to a combat zone in Europe. Nothing could stop that movement. No man dared to attempt to stop it. The Negroes had a name for the trains from Mississippi and Louisiana that brought the blacks to the Illinois Central's South Side station by day and by night. They called them "Freedom Trains."

The passengers had come to Chicago, as had the ancestors of The Mayor, to escape oppression and to seek opportunity. Chicago was the place. The great city of the American heartland. The Mayor understood that many white residents of Chicago were disturbed by what they considered an invasion of their city, but the whites could not bring their complaints about that to him. The great surge from the South, the quest for a better life, had begun long before he was elected mayor in 1955. Some whites, he was all too aware, lacked perspective. They did not know the history of their city. The Mayor had perspective.

The blacks poured out of the trains by the countless thousands and headed for the homes or tenement flats of relatives and friends, and as each migrant entered the Black Belt another blade of grass was crushed underfoot. "They're always asking me, 'Where are the lawns?'" a young black follower of Martin Luther King had said not long ago. "And I tell 'em there's a kid standing on every blade of grass."

The breakout from the Belt began in 1950. Room had to be found elsewhere in the city for the tens of thousands who could not be contained and for the few hundreds who would not be contained. Traditionally, room had been made a block at a time, door to door, in the white areas adjacent to the Belt. Sometimes this operation could be almost as bloody and surely as fiery as the street fighting during the World War II battle for Aachen. And when that happened there would be more hatred in the streets of Chicago than there had been in the streets of Aachen.

The city had needed housing in 1950 for blacks and for whites. It had been estimated that Chicago had 140,000 housing units that should be razed because they no longer were habitable. The Congress of the United States had done something about this problem that was shared by all the major cities of the nation. On July 8, 1949, Congress passed the General Housing Act. And on that same day the Chicago Housing Authority presented to the mayor of the city a proposal to build 40,000 public-housing units over the next six years.

The question that had to be answered by the mayor, whose name was Martin Kennelly, by the Housing Authority, by the City Council and by the citizens was "Where?" Would the projects be built on vacant land in the outlying communities as well as on cleared land in the Belt?

Professors Edward C. Banfield of the University of Chicago and Martin Meyerson of the University of Pennsylvania had emphasized the importance of that question in *Politics, Planning and the Public Interest,* which was published in 1955, the year Richard J. Daley was elected mayor of Chicago. Banfield and Meyerson wrote, ". . . whether one liked it or not and whether one ignored it or not, the housing problem and the race problem were inseparably one."

To begin his walk to his home from Dr. Martin Luther King Jr. Drive, the Mayor would have moved north to Thirty-fifth Street. There he would have looked around him to the Rexall Drug Store on the southwest corner, the Standard Oil service station on the northwest corner, the Supreme Life Insurance Building on the southeast corner, and the Lake Meadows Shopping Center on the northeast corner.

Beyond the shopping center are the sparkling high-rises and the green lawns of Lake Meadows, another of Chicago's good intentions that became a symbol of all that is wrong. For the very few whites and the great many blacks who live there, this private development that was begun by the New York Life Insurance Company in 1948 is an oasis in the ghetto. But for the blacks who still live in the nearby ghetto, it is a mirage.

To make way for the buildings and the lawns of Lake Meadows, a large section of a terrible slum was uprooted. This seemed to be a splendid idea. It was applauded by the urban-renewal specialists, by the City Council, by the local newspapers, by the national magazines and by some of the people. It was not applauded by those of the people who were uprooted from their hovel homes and from their tenement apartments. No provision had been made for them. They had drifted away and it is said that only the uprooted know where they have gone. Whether one liked it or not and whether one ignored it or not, the problem of The Mayor and the race problem were inexorably one.

3

Quiet Zone

SOME members of the crowd would have dispersed after the rites at the statue. For one reason or another they would not have followed The Mayor had he walked west on Thirty-fifth Street. They would have gone back to their working, their cooking, their talking, their loving, their hating. But for each one he lost, others would have joined the procession. Would it have been a somber walk? Who really knows? There might have been singing and dancing and Dixieland, as in the recessionals from funerals in New Orleans.

There at Calumet Avenue, a half block west of South Parkway (make that Dr. Martin Luther King Jr. Drive), is a supermarket of the A&P Food Stores chain. The supermarkets of the ghetto have become part of the battle for Black Power.

"How many stores you got in the ghetto?" the spokesman for the black militants had asked the chairman of the board.

"We have one hundred and thirty-four," the chairman said.

"And how many black managers you got?"

"Let's see now . . . we have, yes, we have thirty-one black managers."

"Hmmmm," the black leader said. "Don't you think you could have a hundred and thirty-four black managers by, say, January 1?"

These men were talking of more than the stores in Chicago. All the ghetto stores in the Midwest were under discussion, and it was not necessary for the militant to outline his strategy. The board chairman understood that the strategy would include boycott, harassment and, if negotiation failed, burning.

This was terribly unfair to the white store managers who must be displaced, but as somebody once said, life is unfair.

"Look, baby," the black spokesman explained, "we're not asking for black managers in your neighborhood. You've got plenty of spots for white managers. We want black managers here."

Across Thirty-fifth from the A&P, on the southeast corner of Calumet, is the Alex Loan Bank. During this momentous march, Mr. Mayor won't see Alex's customers drop in, but come past here another morning or afternoon and you can watch men and women darting in and sidling out. Pawnshops still are important to the economy in this part of town.

There's a poolroom, Your Honor. Not a Cue-for-Two, family billiards center, but an authentic dark and dingy poolroom of the type you were advised to avoid when you were a young fellow. Next is Giles Avenue, one of the few streets that share a common fate with the Chicagoans who live along it. Giles never escapes the ghetto. It begins at Thirty-first Street and runs south to Thirty-ninth, and disappears after that city mile. (North and south in Chicago there are eight blocks to a mile; east and west there are usually sixteen blocks to a mile.)

A few dozen yards south of Thirty-fifth, on the east side of the street, is the ancient armory which once was the home of the old 8th Infantry, the black unit that became the 370th when it was federalized for World War I. The Mayor is not unfamiliar with the history behind those dirty, broken and boarded-up windows. How could he be? Many great athletes came out of that place.

In late July of 1967 another crowd had marched here at Thirty-fifth and Giles, a crowd of 250 that had shouted that strange cry—strange then—for "black power." Seventeen persons had been arrested for throwing stones at the police. But in the terrible days of April, 1968, this area had been quiet. The Mayor had many reasons to admire these good people and to be thankful for them.

4

‖‖‖‖‖‖‖‖‖‖‖‖‖‖‖‖‖‖‖‖‖‖‖

Passion Week

By the streams of Babylon, we sat and
wept when we remembered Sion.
    —Offertory Psalm of the Mass
    for Thursday in Passion Week

THE anguish of April began, far away, on Thursday, the fourth. It was a day that had started with Mass for the faithful in Nativity of Our Lord Church, at 653 West Thirty-seventh Street. Nativity is the parish of The Mayor. It has been his parish all the days of his life. The church is only a few blocks from the ghetto, but it is a world apart. The Mayor tries to attend Mass there every day, to pray for the living and the dead.

Before this day ended, another man known well to The Mayor would make the trip from living to dead. Before this day ended, tears would be shed in the ghetto. Tears of sorrow. Tears of compassion. Tears of fear. Tears of rage.

That evening The Mayor attended a dinner of the Chicago Medical Society in the fashionable Drake Hotel at the northern end of Michigan Avenue's "Magnificent Mile." The Mayor must appear at many banquets, but he rarely dines. Unless his schedule rules otherwise, The Mayor blocks out time to have dinner with his wife, Eleanor, and those of their seven children who still are at home at 3536 South Lowe Avenue. Non-Chicagoans who make a rubberneck tour of

Lowe Avenue south from Thirty-fifth are surprised to discover that The Mayor's residence is a bungalow, renovated and enlarged to its present seven rooms.

While The Mayor sat at the speakers' table in the large dining room at the Drake, the sniper moved to a window in the sleazy rooming house. The sniper fired. Within minutes news was brought to The Mayor that Dr. Martin Luther King Jr. had been shot to death in Memphis.

It is not enough to say that many Chicagoans were sick with grief when they learned of the assassination of the man who had won the Nobel Peace Prize. It also must be said that many Chicagoans were sick with elation. They had said, over and over, "Somebody ought to shoot the black son-of-a-bitch." The shooting had been done, and this would be a night of celebration as well as a night of mourning.

The Mayor who so desperately wanted racial peace knew, as he hurried away from the Drake, that the cause of peace had died on the balcony of the second-class motel in Memphis.

He is a sentimental man, this mayor, and he was rent by the memory that he was the only white politician in America to score a victory over the man who had espoused nonviolence. After his triumph at Selma, Dr. King had chosen Chicago as his first stop on his northern crusade. He would go to Chicago, he said, the "go" sounding like a train whistle of yesteryear trying to find an escape through the curtain of the night. "I will go to Chicago." He would go there and expose the hypocrisies of the "most segregated city in the North."

Chicagoans were not sure that his coming was the thing to do. White Chicagoans were offended. They believed that this city, of all cities, had done so much for the Negroes. "That Daley gives the niggers everything they ask for." Black Chicagoans were apprehensive. They feared that Dr. King would build the pressure past the bursting point.

He would go to Chicago. He would seek out his objectives and he would march, his disciples, black and white, fanning out behind him. He would fill the streets. He and they would march together. They would come from every section of the country, to sing "We Shall Overcome," as they always came when he sounded the call.

He came. He and they marched. He spent three days in Chicago in July of 1965. There was a reason to march. According to some blacks, the superintendent of Chicago's public-school system, Benjamin C. Willis, was a racist, and Willis was Daley's man. With the encouragement of The Mayor, Ben Willis became the greatest builder of schools and ersatz schools in the history of Chicago. When a school district in the Black Belt had become so jammed with children that the addition of a few hundred more would burst walls and send roofs flying on the wind, Willis was a whirlwind of action. He gave that district new buildings, as fast as possible, and he gave that district fixed "mobiles" overnight. The mobiles became part of the landscape, and they also acquired a name. They were "Willis Wagons." What the superintendent did not do, black citizens cried, was locate empty schoolrooms in white communities and fill those rooms with Negro children.

Under Willis the schools were segregated. In 1963, 81.6 percent of the city's elementary schools had enrollments that were all white or all black. The percentage had risen to 82.3 percent by 1965.

The superintendent's most bitter enemies charged that he was a dictator. Even his most devoted admirers conceded that. He would run the schools and in running them he treated the eleven members of the Board of Education as stupid lackeys. In a few cases his evaluation was correct.

Willis did not stand alone. In his way he was as shrewd politically as the most bigoted alderman who sat in the City Council. The great majority of white Chicagoans endorsed his results and understood his basic philosophy. Those white Chicagoans were with him as long as he kept black children out of "their" schools.

Ultimately, Willis' arrogance became too much for three of Chicago's four daily newspapers. The reporters who covered the Board of Education for those newspapers had been telling their editors for years of the abuse they had taken from this autocrat. The protests finally penetrated, and the three newspapers turned on the superintendent.

The members of the Board of Education took an unofficial poll on Willis' future in May of 1965. Seven of the eleven members voted their opinion that Willis' contract should not be extended beyond its expiration date, August 31. Ten days later the Board met to vote officially. Three members switched their votes, and the superintendent was retained. As a compromise, the full Board extracted from Willis a promise that he would retire on his sixty-fifth birthday in December of 1966.

Civil-rights groups cried "betrayal." Albert Raby, a slim, messianic Negro schoolteacher who was a leader of the protesters, said, "We felt that the slap in the face we got with the reappointment of Willis came directly from the mayor."

The three Board members who had switched were thought to be close to The Mayor. One was Mrs. W. Lydon Wild, a family friend, who would be a cohostess for tea parties before the weddings of Daley's two eldest daughters. Mrs. Wild and the others said that they changed their vote after Willis agreed to be more cooperative in the immediate future and retire on schedule. Face was saved, but the reputation of the city was not.

Into this divided camp Dr. King came walking, his black-prizefighter face masked by the look that some accepted as visionary and that others thought to be fanatical. Every man and woman who looked into that face was affected by it, but the effect was transcribed on the screen of the mind not by the power of the transmitter but by the attitude of the receiver.

For Martin Luther King, 1965 had been a continuation of the victories that had begun with the Nobel Peace Prize for

1964. He had gone to Selma, Alabama, in January to open the
drive to register Negro voters and during that month he had
returned to his city, Atlanta, to be honored at a dinner attended by 1,500, half of them black. Atlanta Mayor Ivan
Allen Jr. had said, "Through the years, as history is wrought,
some men are destined to be leaders of humanity and to
shape the future course of the world. Dr. King is such a
man."

Later he went to Washington to ask for a meeting with
President Lyndon B. Johnson. Dr. King was seen first by
Hubert Humphrey, the Vice-President, and by Nicholas deB.
Katzenbach, the Attorney General. He pleaded for a law that
would permit the registration of Negro voters by agents of
the federal government. In March he led white and Negro
demonstrators, their numbers swelling from three thousand
on the first day to twenty-five thousand on the fifth day, from
Selma to the Alabama capitol building in Montgomery. During the most bitter hours of the Selma confrontation, President Johnson spoke to a special evening session of both
houses of Congress and asked for an immediate end to all
"illegal barriers" that kept blacks from voting. The President
said, "Our mission is at once the oldest and the most basic of
this country—to right wrong, to do justice, to serve men."

Before the bill was signed into law, Dr. King came to Chicago, seeking another triumph. For three days there were
signs of a great victory, but after he had gone, some of his
followers and many of his detractors reached a similar conclusion. The victory had been a shimmering, illusionary
thing. Chicago, a tough and cynical city, had absorbed him.

There was an analysis in the August 11, 1965, issue of the
influential Protestant weekly *Christian Century*, which is
published in Chicago. The *Christian Century* reported, "In a
three-day whirlwind visit, King accomplished in the Midwest's greatest metropolis what local civil-rights leaders have
not been able to achieve in weeks of demonstrations against
public-schools superintendent Benjamin C. Willis—the

biggest civil-rights protest in Chicago history."

The bigness was not denied by partisans on either side of the bitterly contested issue. Chicagoans admire big things, no matter what side they happen to be on. The *Christian Century* emphasized the huge rallies addressed by Dr. King, "including one attended by more than ten thousand people— mostly white—on the village green of Winnetka, a wealthy, racially exclusive North Shore suburb."

Chicagoans, abhorring everything suburban as they do, thought that Winnetka was the ideal place for such a rally. It was far enough away, on the home grounds of Winnetkans who knew nothing about Chicago's racial dilemma and cared even less. "Let Winnetka keep him," Chicagoans said.

"At the climax of his Chicago campaign," *Christian Century* continued, "King led a crowd of Negro and white demonstrators, their numbers estimated from 15,000 to 30,000 depending upon the viewpoint of the demonstrators, in a march on City Hall."

The march to City Hall was impressive, and it left a good feeling in the souls and the hearts of those who had participated. Its effectiveness, however, was questioned by *Christian Century*. "King may be up against an obstacle in Chicago more frustrating than the violent opposition the Southern Christian Leadership Conference has encountered in Montgomery and Selma," the magazine suggested. "Big, cosmopolitan, preoccupied Chicago apparently received, absorbed and dissipated King's coming as though it were a temporary entertainment—just another State Street parade—or a passing irritant. Neither city officials, nor police, nor disgruntled white spectators, nor the civil-rightists provided an incident that could have become the fulcrum of effective action. The day after King left Chicago, the daily march against Superintendent Willis was back down to its 100 to 200 demonstrators. The 15,000 or more Negroes and whites who marched with King represented, as he said, many more sympathizers than were able to march on a particular day.

But even when allowance is made for this possibility, we have to conclude that metropolitan Chicago—including its nearly one million Negroes—smothered King with apathy. Why?"

The apathy was there, and it convinced white Chicagoans who refused to accept Dr. King's philosophy that "the Negroes aren't buying him, either."

The *Christian Century* concluded with this thought: "We suspect that a wise man left this city wiser still and that he will return with renewed power and better strategies. We welcome that return."

The city had met the test and passed it. Dr. King had not comprehended the mass mind of Chicago. There had been no violent reaction from Chicagoans. The professionalism of the Police Department was extolled. The Mayor had reason to be proud of his city and its people. He had not been there when Dr. King led the crowd to City Hall. The Mayor had been in Detroit attending a conference of mayors.

That meeting in Detroit also was the reason why The Mayor had turned down Dr. King's request for a man-to-man meeting. Some civil-rights leaders expressed the belief that The Mayor had made a strategic error. "He missed his chance," one said. "It would have been a great coup, and snuffed out our movement, if Daley and King had issued some sort of joint statement."

This had the sound of wishful thinking in July of 1965. The Mayor had his coup. He could call it, if he chose, non-violence.

The Mayor who was not there issued a statement, his statement. He said of Dr. King, "The presentation of his position against poverty and discrimination for which he was deservedly awarded the Nobel prize is a position that all right-thinking Americans should support."

The Mayor carefully avoided anything that would sound like a criticism of King. The Mayor also avoided the issue, which was the policies of Benjamin Willis.

5

Man vs. Pillow

His power renewed and his strategies revised, Martin Luther King Jr. returned to Chicago on January 31, 1966. This would be the first all-out offensive by the Southern Christian Leadership Conference in a city of the North. This would not be a three-day effort. This would be day after day after day. The theme was "End Slums." The cause was one that no rational Chicagoan could oppose.

This time The Mayor reacted with strategies of his own. Richard J. Daley never has pretended to be other than a politician, but in his view politics is a noble profession, a profession that occasionally can be art. He worked his political knowledge upon Dr. King, who had been competing in the minor leagues during all the seasons that preceded Chicago. In Chicago he came face to face with the man who had governed the nation's second-largest city for eleven years and governed it remarkably well.

It has been written that Dr. King realized that he was "fighting a pillow" after he had gone a few rounds with The Mayor. Each time the evangelist from the South unleashed what he thought would be a shattering verbal blow, The Mayor absorbed the criticism and moved forward, a friendly smile wreathing the jowls and the chins of the face that is a caricature of itself. There would be no Bull Connor or Jim Clark in Chicago. This was not a city that needed the repressive tactics of a Southern sheriff. Here kindness and conciliation would be the controls.

Dr. King was welcomed to Chicago in January of 1966; all the departments of the city were anxious to cooperate with him, The Mayor said.

King did not wait for that cooperation. In February his lieutenants took over a falling-down, six-apartment building in Lawndale, the West Side ghetto. Tenants were told to pay rents to King, who would use the income to renovate the building and turn over surplus funds, if any, to the slum landlord. Almost sorrowfully The Mayor explained that the landlord had been charged with violations of the building code and added that there are "legal ways and illegal ways" to eliminate slum conditions. Dr. King said his takeover was "supralegal trusteeship," but Judge James Parsons, the first Negro to be appointed to a federal district court within the continental United States, had another term for it. Parsons called it "theft."

Dr. King's organization spent $1,000 to improve the building, but no rents were paid to the S.C.L.C., and an injunction prohibited members of the organization from entering the six apartments.

During the late winter, the spring and the early summer The Mayor skillfully anticipated the minister's demands. Building-code violations? The Building Department would insist on corrections. Slumlords? The Legal Department would prosecute. Garbage collections? The Sanitation Department would wash down the alleys until they glistened.

When Dr. King said, "We shall overcome," The Mayor said, "Your goals are our goals." When Dr. King said, "I shall march," The Mayor answered, "Let us move forward together to make this an even greater city."

There was something new on the horizon of race relations —the black nationalism advocated by Stokely Carmichael, chairman of the Student Nonviolent Coordinating Committee. King had been one of the organizers of S.N.C.C. in 1960, but he turned away from the new policy of Carmichael. King was thirty-seven years old in 1966, and he too was experiencing the isolation of all who were on the far side of the Generation Gap.

During June Dr. King found it impossible to continue his single-purpose concentration on Chicago. James Meredith, a man who marched alone, had been shotgunned in Mississippi. King had to join that protest too, and he hustled back and forth from Chicago to the line of march in the South. There were indications in Mississippi that Dr. King was losing his tenuous hold on the emotions of black Americans. When he asked for an end to the cries for "black power," Lincoln Lynch, an official of the Congress of Racial Equality, had responded tartly. Lynch saw in King's pacifist philosophy a "basic misunderstanding" of what Negroes wanted. "We need black people standing on their two feet and all the shouts of 'Freedom now' are meaningless and empty phrases until we accomplish this," Lynch said.

These cracks in the armor of the King may have alarmed the functionaries of the S.C.L.C. They should have disturbed the mayor of the city to which Dr. King returned after his periodic appearances in Mississippi. The Mayor may have been a contributor to the decline in the minister's power. "Mayor Daley has gone into partnership with me," Dr. King complained to his associates, and the black-prizefighter face wore a look of puzzlement. The Mayor smiled his Buddha smile. The Negro masses of Chicago were not responding to Dr. King. They didn't seem to need him. They had Mayor Daley, and Mayor Daley had programs.

There were hints that programs would not be enough. On June 24 the Chicago *Daily News* published a picture of a grammar-school class that had graduated long ago and asked readers to identify a chubby little boy in the first row. Naming the boy was not difficult. He was Richard J. Daley, with the other children in the 1916 graduating class of Nativity of Our Lord School. A news story below the picture was headlined, "6 Arrested in Park After Racial Jeers."

What Chicago needed then, far more than cool heads, was a series of thundershowers that would drive the haters off the beaches and streets. The storms were not forthcoming. The city has no program for that.

On Sunday afternoon, July 10, Martin Luther King Jr. attracted a crowd of forty thousand to Chicago's vast, old stadium on the lake front. The numbers sounded impressive but they must have been a disappointment to the S.C.L.C. and a pleasing revelation to The Mayor and his aides. If King had been getting through to the blacks of Chicago and to their white allies in the struggle for an end to slums and for open housing, a crowd of a hundred thousand in Soldier Field would not have been startling.

Those who were expert at the organization of rallies realized that the men around Dr. King did not understand the logistics of a successful rally. Too many thousands who would have been there, who should have been there, were not there. King was a successful dramatic actor, but he was a failure as a producer. But on that afternoon of empty seats, outside forces extricated the black leader, and the pillow began to lose its resiliency.

For the first time the blows began to reach The Mayor. The most damaging came from The Mayor's beloved Roman Catholic Church. To the Soldier Field rally John Cardinal Cody sent a document that told Dr. King, "Your struggle and your sufferings will be mine until the last vestige of discrimination and injustice is blotted out here in Chicago and throughout America." The statement was read by Auxiliary Bishop Aloysius Wycislo.

The Catholic Church was not alone at the rally. Reform Rabbi Robert J. Marx, of the Union of American Hebrew Congregations, Chicago Federation, was on the platform, as was Dr. Edgar H. S. Chandler, executive director of the Church Federation of Greater Chicago.

The Catholic Church had to be present in the name of

Christ, if for no other reason, but the finality of the Cody statement was somewhat unexpected. To oppose Dr. King now would be to oppose the Cardinal Archbishop of Chicago —to oppose, in fact, the Catholic Church that meant so much to Richard J. Daley. The Mayor would live with that statement and try to live by it, but many Catholic Chicagoans were quite willing to oppose their Cardinal and their Church. Those Catholics now had two ministers to hate, King and Cody. They were ambivalent about The Mayor. They were watching him to see what would happen next.

The vigil was brief. On Tuesday, July 12, while Chicagoans were enduring a record heat wave, a riot began, as so many others have, with a seemingly unimportant gesture. Fire hydrants, which had been turned on to provide cooling showers for many children and a few adults, were turned off by firemen, who were concerned about the lowering of water pressure in a Lawndale area that is a potential bonfire. The people turned on the hydrants again. The firemen turned them off. Tempers were ignited by the near-100-degree heat. Police who had come to restore order were fired upon at the intersection of Pulaski Road (4000 West) and Roosevelt Road (1200 South).

That was the beginning of three days of shooting and looting. Governor Otto Kerner ordered 4,200 National Guardsmen into the riot area on Thursday. The toll was two dead and sixteen wounded when the Guard finally put down the riot. During these three days of terror, Martin Luther King Jr. served Chicago as though the city were his birthplace. He canceled a speech that he was scheduled to make at the World Council of Churches in Geneva and devoted his energies to Lawndale.

Many white Chicagoans did not appreciate Dr. King's efforts on those three days. "He ought to be there," they cried. "It's all his fault. He got them all worked up. Now he can see what he's done. Why don't he go back where he came from and leave us in peace?"

They blamed him for the deaths, the wounds, the fires and the thefts. In so doing they were blaming him for the hydrants, on or off, and they were blaming him for the weather. It was absurd, but that's precisely how it was in Chicago during the second week of July, 1966.

After the riot The Mayor and Dr. King had a meeting, and out of it came another program. Sprinklers would be attached to some fire hydrants so the plugs could be opened by firemen on excessively hot days. The Mayor also said he would ask for federal funds to build swimming pools in slum areas. And there was the traditional appointment of a citizens' committee, this one to suggest ways of easing tensions in the riot areas.

Chicago was braced for the worst, and whether the events of August were worse than the July riot depended on a Chicagoan's personal scale of values. Two persons had died in Lawndale, but was blacks being killed by other blacks or by the police as serious as blacks invading a white community? The answer came tragically clear from the communities of Gage Park and Marquette Park on the South Side and from Cragin on the Northwest Side. The man of peace had the temerity to carry his marches for open housing into neighborhoods that were exclusively white and predominantly Roman Catholic. Dr. King was felled by a rock. Catholic priests and nuns who walked with him were cursed and spat upon. The kooks of the American Nazi Party were there, egging on the neighborhood youths, many of them educated in Catholic schools. King discovered that walking into the white communities of Chicago was somewhat more challenging than leading a procession on State Street and almost as dangerous as a hike to Montgomery.

Again the Chicago police were masterful and professional. During the Marquette Park confrontation, 960 policemen skillfully extricated some 600 marchers who were in danger of being swallowed, literally perhaps, by 4,000 good Christians from the community. The performance of the Chicago police in these emergencies was a revelation. This big-city department, which had at least its share of haters, had developed a high degree of skill in riot control. Observers of the Marquette Park feat came away convinced that the Chicago Police Department might have rescued the Light Brigade from the Valley of Death.

After it was over Dr. King said, "I think the people of Mississippi ought to come to Chicago to learn how to hate."

His words would not have been lost on a burly member of the Police Department, who came back to his station in a shirt almost dyed by bloodstains. Picking out the spots with a thick index finger, he told a superior officer, "This is the blood of a Polack. And this is the blood of a Lugan. And this one is a Dago. And that's a nigger."

He hated, but his hatred was a thing of equality that enabled him to do his duty.

The summer of 1966 was the high point of Martin Luther King's crusade. He came back from time to time—The Mayor denounced King for attempting to influence the elections of November, 1966, by returning to Chicago in late October—but the vigor seemed to be seeping from the leader of the S.C.L.C.

And now he was gone.

6

||||||||||||||||||||||||||||||||||||||

The Fires of Friday

> *. . . for false witnesses have risen up*
> *against me, and such as breathe out*
> *violence.*
> —*Communion Psalm of the Mass*
> *for Friday in Passion Week*

THE Lawndale riot of 1966 was the second in the community
within a year. At approximately 9 P.M. on August 12, 1965, a
Fire Department hook-and-ladder truck had pulled out of a
fire station at 4000 West Wilcox Street. The driver did not
know that he had left without his tillerman, the fireman who
steers the rear section of the long vehicle. The rear of the
unit fishtailed out of control, struck a traffic-sign pole and
uprooted it. Dessie Mae Williams, of 4047 West Jackson
Boulevard, was struck by the pole. The twenty-three-year-
old Miss Williams, who had been waiting for a bus, was
killed instantly.

Rioting began soon after word of Miss Williams' death and
the circumstances of the accident had spread through the
community. The disorders erupted on Friday night, and did
not subside until Saturday. The flames of bitterness were fed
by carefully worded leaflets. Those who wrote the text were
not diffident about inciting to riot, but they obviously did not
wish to face libel litigation in the process. The leaflet read:
"Allegedly Drunken White Fireman Kills Black Woman!!"

49

The all-white crew at the firehouse was replaced on Friday by an all-Negro unit under the command of a white officer. Eighty persons were injured and 169 were arrested before the violence ran its course. The Reverend Shelvin Hall, pastor of Friendship Baptist Church, served the city along with other West Side ministers by distributing ten thousand pamphlets that urged an end to the disorders.

The Mayor was magnificent during and after this crisis. He ordered a command post set up in his home so he could be on top of the situation every moment. Later he praised the performance of the Police Department during the riot and hailed his superintendent of police, Orlando Wilson, as "an outstanding administrator."

Reasonable explanations could be offered and accepted for the city administration's being caught off guard by the Lawndale riots of 1965 and '66. No intelligence force can be expected to predict trouble at a specific fire hydrant or to know precisely when a hook-and-ladder will come out of its house a man short. The best that can be expected of the city's security forces is that they be on a "general alert" basis and ready to move.

The city had to be prepared for Friday, April 5, 1968. Everybody had to be aware that trouble was imminent, trouble such as Chicago had not seen in many years. The Mayor and his administration had excellent intelligence sources in the black communities through the precinct captains of the Democratic party and policemen who worked in the Negro districts or lived in them. The feelings that had been building Thursday night had been transmitted to City Hall.

The initial reaction to the slaying of Dr. King was a sickening feeling, the same wrench-in-the-pit-of-the-stomach that followed the realization that John F. Kennedy had not survived his wounds. The difference was that the numbness of the Kennedy time never quite wore off. Just as we were beginning to react again, Jack Ruby wiped out Lee Harvey Oswald before our eyes and the numbness came back. This time there was no Jack Ruby, no Lee Harvey Oswald to keep us anesthetized. This time there was the man lying in his blood on the balcony. The numbness was dissipated quickly in the ghetto, and as it lifted outrage moved into the void that Martin Luther King had left on the South Side, in Lawndale and in the smaller Negro communities on the Near North Side and the Far Southwest Side.

"He tried to do right and they killed him," the blacks said. "He told us to be nonviolent and they shot him down in cold blood. He told us to love our brother and they made him die for it."

This time, for a change, "they" meant the white citizens of America. They who often had indicted the entire black race for the crimes of a few were accused of complicity in the assassination of the man who preached love. Thoughtful Chicagoans feared that the outrage of the ghetto would be turned upon the white community Friday morning.

The outrage of the ghetto was not the only emotion felt in Chicago as Thursday moved toward Friday. That was less than half the story. There was exultation from the twisted who sincerely believed that the world was better off without Martin Luther King Jr. The white supremacists and the bigots and the "I like Negroes but . . ." group were elated.

Pour all those emotions into the caldron that is Chicago, stir, let simmer overnight, and stand by for the explosion.

The Mayor sent word that the American flag was to be flown at half-staff above every municipal building. Even this traditional gesture would be resented by many Chicagoans, but to hell with many Chicagoans. The Mayor would not say that in so many words, but that was how he felt about them. He also ordered a memorial service in City Council chambers.

Martin Luther King was "a dedicated and courageous American who commanded the respect of the people of the world," The Mayor told the crowd at the Council service, and his words were recorded by radio and television so that the rest of the city would know how he felt. "That the life of this man should be brought to a shocking end by brutal violence grieves all right-thinking citizens everywhere. Violence accomplishes nothing."

Richard J. Daley then made a request that would be ignored by some. "All of us," he said, "must soften the grief of Dr. King's family and associates by demonstrating that his life was not in vain."

The Reverend Jesse Jackson, all of twenty-six years old then, had something quite different to say to the aldermen. Jesse Jackson, former football player, who had met Martin Luther King in 1963, while the younger man was president of the student body at North Carolina Agricultural and Technical College, was director of the Southern Christian Leadership Conference's Operation Breadbasket. Jesse had been there when his leader was slain. Jackson spoke not of tomorrow and its fulfillment of King's dream, or of today and its anguish, but of yesterday and its indignities. "The blood is on the chest and hands of those that would not have welcomed him here yesterday."

Shut up, white members of the Council said to themselves, not looking at their hands. Too much, Jesse, black members of the Council said to themselves, not looking at their chests. While they listened and muttered, the blood of others burst the dams of nonviolence on the West Side and the South Side.

Students at John Marshall High School, 3250 West Adams Street, had come to school carrying fliers with this message: "Dr. Martin Luther King has been assassinated. Show your respect by staying out of school."

Negroes began to assemble in Garfield Park, a huge city park at Washington Boulevard and Central Park Avenue. Most blacks who came there were high-school students or elementary-school pupils. A militant speaker attempted to combine violence, ethics and respect in two brief sentences of command. "Break out windows if you want to, but don't loot," he told the youngsters. "Looting discredits the avenging of King's death."

The schoolchildren moved into Madison Street and within minutes became a mob. They smashed windows and they came through the broken panes to snatch merchandise—appliances, food and liquor. The first wave of looters was a small army of children, high-school age and younger. The policemen who were ordered to the scene were helpless. There were too many youngsters, too few police. The police could not have been effective during the first stages of the insurrection unless they were willing to gun down children in cold blood, adult witnesses insisted. The police obviously never considered such brutal action.

Anguish was the motivation that sent the black schoolchildren to Garfield Park. They went to mourn the dead hero many of them had not understood while he lived. But as they rampaged along Madison Street, hatred was their motivation. Hatred for white shopkeepers, for white landlords, for white cops, for anything and anybody white. They hated all who were glad that Dr. King was dead, and they perpetuated his doctrine of nonviolence by snatching, by looting, by punching, by screaming. And then they attempted to burn out their own community.

Chief Fire Alarm Operator David Sullivan arrived in his office on the sixth floor of City Hall at 8:30 Friday morning. His day was busy but uneventful until 3:49 P.M., when an alarm reported a fire in a furniture store at 2235 West Madison Street. This was the first report from the riot area. Within a minute an alarm was received for a fire at 2335 West Madison, a block away from the furniture store.

Fireman Robert A. Freeman of Engine 44, one of the companies that went to the fire at 2335 West Madison, described the incredible action in an article he wrote for the *Chicago Fire Fighter* magazine:

While operations progressed in getting lines stretched and ladders raised, firemen were hampered by droves of looters and by flying missiles. Several other stores in the 2300 block of Madison Street were discovered to be on fire. . . . By orders of the Second Division Marshal, a 2-11 alarm was struck . . . at 4:04 P.M. bringing Engines 57, 95, 103 and 114; Trucks 5 and 26; Salvage Squad 2; Snorkel Squad 2; Snorkel 7; Ambulance 2; the Fifth Battalion, and corresponding Second Deputy Fire Marshals.

More fires were being discovered west along Madison, at Western (2400 west) and beyond. . . . The area was becoming very dark now with tremendous columns of smoke blotting out the sun. . . . Other fires were being covered as best they could: 16th and Lawndale; Roosevelt (1200 south) from California to Independence; Fifth Avenue from Jackson to Central Park, and in the Madison Street area from Albany to Homan.

Fireman Freeman is describing a fire area approximately a mile and a half square—this was during the first twenty minutes of action—and he continues:

Almost the entire 2300 block of Madison was now envolved [enveloped], with everything possible being done to hold in check this fire which seemed to ignite everything in its path. A notification was made . . . that Truck 34 was on the way to quarters of Truck 26, just two miles west of the original fire. Truck 34 had traveled almost 20 miles across the city . . . with four Eastman Multi-Versal portable deluge guns. . . .

Engine 96 reported available at Western and Madison and was told to "pick out a fire and go to work. Let us know which one you're working on." . . . Then the terrible news that everyone had expected all the time. . . .

Battalion 28 reported that the engineer of Fog Pressure 1 had been shot in the leg and was being removed under police guard to a hospital. Engine 123 reported being stoned at Keeler and 16th. . . .

Chief Fire Alarm Operator Sullivan continued on duty for twenty-three hours. "During the first day we logged only 599 fires," Sullivan said. Only? "What I mean by that is we had so many alarms coming in here, we just couldn't log them all."

During the first hour of chaos, it was not possible for Sullivan and his assistants to handle all the alarms that were dinging into the office. "You can't tell where the fires are," Sullivan told news reporters. "They're walking west and burning as they go."

Into the artificial night under the canopy of smoke came half the men and half the equipment of the Chicago Fire Department during the first hour, but now the flames were marching west on Madison Street, following the crazy torch parade of the rioters.

At 2 P.M., almost two hours before the first fire alarm, The Mayor was phoned by James B. Conlisk, superintendent of police. Conlisk urged that the Illinois National Guard be called. The numbers of children and high-school students in Garfield Park and Police Department experience in previous West Side disturbances were the ostensible reasons for Conlisk's early reaction. An hour later The Mayor called Lieutenant Governor Samuel Shapiro and asked that the National Guard be sent to Lawndale.

Fear rose as high as the jagged peaks of gray smoke, which could be seen by tens of thousands of whites at work in the Loop. Some white-collar workers had left the Loop even before the smoke appeared, driven by rumors that Negroes were looting stores and attacking whites in the downtown district. The rumors were distortions, but anything was possible on this day. Suburbanites were so very aware that black extremists who were willing to die could close off exit routes from the Loop simply by setting up machine-gun positions on bridges over four major expressways. The police would wipe out those roadblocks ultimately, but while the extremists held the bridges they could kill thousands of whites and pile up wrecked cars by the hundreds.

The Mayor spoke to the citizens of Chicago at 4:20 P.M. He did not attempt to minimize the situation. He did not tell the public that everything was going to be all right. His manner clearly revealed that nothing was right at this moment. He did his best to convey calmness, but those who were watching him on television screens saw controlled tension.

"Stand up tonight and protect the city," he implored in the whispery-prayerful tones he uses in times of emergency. "I ask this very sincerely, very personally. Let's show to the U. S. and the world what the citizens of Chicago are made of."

The Mayor also informed the public that the National Guard was en route to Lawndale. His little talk, meant to calm, convinced too many Chicagoans that The Mayor thought there was danger of the entire city going up in flames. That had not happened in almost a century and was unlikely to happen again, but the strong east wind that was carrying fire from building to building on Madison, Monroe, Roosevelt and Sixteenth imperiled much of Lawndale and the suburbs to the west.

In New York a tough little priest, who had worked for eleven years at St. Agatha Church in Lawndale, watched the fires of Friday on a television news show. To himself Father Dan Mallette said, "They wouldn't care if the whole damn West Side burned down."

"They" were not the arsonists but The Mayor, his department heads, the aldermen, and the business leaders of Chicago.

7

He Couldn't Run

PONOWELL HOLLOWAY, who couldn't run fast, was the first to die. Ponowell, a sixteen-year-old sophomore at John Marshall High School, had a damaged foot and a plate in his head. He had been hit by a train when he was a child. Police said that young Holloway had been shot to death while he was looting a store.

Nine persons were to be killed before Passion Week ended, all of them Negroes. No policeman was shot. No National Guardsman was shot. One fireman was shot.

Four of the nine victims were shot to death in the 4100 block of West Madison. Strangely, none of the other five was killed in the vast riot area of the West Side. They died elsewhere in the city—three by gunfire; one in a fire; one was cut on the leg by broken glass and bled to death.

There were riotous conditions in scattered sections of the ghettos on the South Side and the Near North Side. If the South Side had erupted, the police would have had virtually no chance to control violence on two fronts. Much of the city might have been destroyed before the National Guard finally rolled into the streets at eleven o'clock Friday night. Fortunately, the established black communities on the South Side remained quiet. Major credit had to be given to two large youth gangs usually associated with violence, the Blackstone Rangers and the East Side Disciples. Middle-aged and middle-income blacks on the South Side didn't want their buildings to go as Madison Street was going, but they would have been powerless if the Rangers and Disciples had chosen to burn.

The Mayor did not go home to dinner Friday night. He left his office only once during the long afternoon and night. He walked through the north exit of City Hall and crossed Randolph Street to the Sherman House, a hotel. He ate hurriedly. He was back in his office twenty-five minutes later.

As they watched the horror show, Chicagoans and suburbanites wondered whether the firemen could contain the conflagration, whether the police could control the riot, whether order could be restored to the city. Would the riot move downtown in the early hours of Saturday and surge from there into the white communities?

Out of the flames there came the tearing cry, "The King is dead! Long live the King!"

It had been a ghastly day for Chicago.

8

Why Did They Do This?

Have pity on me, O Lord, for I am in distress . . .
—Introit Psalm of the Mass for Saturday in Passion Week

EARLY Saturday morning, The Mayor toured the riot area, guarded by policemen who followed in an unmarked squad car. The wind had subsided and the flames had become controllable. The Mayor talked with policemen, firemen and sanitation workers. The sanitation men had moved in quickly to clear the streets of wreckage. In Chicago cleanliness is next to martial law.

Many legends have come out of the unbelievable hours in Chicago after the slaying of Dr. King. One of the most persistent is that during this Saturday morning inspection of the carnage, The Mayor turned to somebody and said, "Why did they do this to me?"

Not why had it been done to Chicago but "to me." As this sentence echoed through the city, three interpretations of it were heard. Those who opposed The Mayor were sure that he had revealed, in a moment when anguish had him off guard, how he felt about Chicago. He thought it belonged to him, they said. Blacks insisted that the unspoken half of the sentence was essential to an understanding of Daley's race philosophy. "Why did they [Negroes] do this to me after all I have done for them?" is what The Mayor intended to convey, according to the black interpretation. And the question was sufficient proof that The Mayor had been deceived about the ghetto dwellers' reaction to him, the blacks argued. Those who admired The Mayor said that the question came out of his heartbreak, that he sincerely believed that he had been personally injured and offended.

Whether or not The Mayor put his reaction in precisely those words, he surely experienced the emotion depicted by them. To feel otherwise would have been less than human. This man had been involved totally with Chicago for thirteen years. Forgotten in the horror of yesterday, April 5, was that it was the thirteenth anniversary of Richard J. Daley's election to his first term as mayor. He did not believe that Chicago belonged to him, but he believed, with typical religious fervor, that he belonged to Chicago. There was no question about his identifying with the city. To do harm to Chicago was to injure him.

It was human, too, for him to ask questions of himself and of his precious programs as he stared at seemingly endless rows of city blocks that had been virtually razed by fire.

Federal troops, ordered to Chicago by President Johnson, were flying to the city from Fort Hood, Texas, and Fort Carson, Colorado. Brigadier General Richard Dunn's National Guardsmen were federalized and all units would be under the command of Lieutenant General George R. Mather, United States Army.

Sniper fire from upper floors of Chicago Housing Authority buildings was reported Saturday morning. The Loop, usually jammed with shoppers on Saturday, had a Sunday look about it. Persons going to work in the Loop on Saturday could have walked in the streets if they wished. There was very little traffic. Chicagoans were frightened. Those who had to drive through Negro communities turned on headlights during daylight hours as a gesture of respect to the memory of Martin Luther King, whether the respect was sincerely felt or not. The last time Chicagoans had done this was during the days of mourning for John F. Kennedy. Then it had been symbolic. Now, for many, it was a pass through enemy lines.

Saturday afternoon Mayor Daley ordered a curfew, from 7 P.M. to 6 A.M., for all under twenty-one years old. After he had announced the curfew The Mayor was asked about his attitude toward shooting looters. "Well, it's a pretty serious thing to be talking about shooting looters," he answered slowly, "but I am hopeful there will be sterner action taken by the military and the Police Department today and tonight."

Sterner action was not necessary Saturday night. There was more trouble on the West Side, but it was reflexive rather than the beginning of a new riot. The two transparent reasons for the retreat from insanity were the presence of heavily armed, uniformed troops and the imposition of the curfew. Besides, the youngsters had had enough of breaking, looting and burning.

Residents of all-white communities on the fringes of the city were startled Saturday night when they realized that Army convoys were traveling on residential streets. That had not happened during World War II, when millions of Americans were moving from camp to camp. Chicago was a city of partial curfew. It also was a battleground.

Four firemen were injured Saturday night. Their injuries were minor.

9

Palm Sunday

. . . reach up, you ancient portals,
that the king of glory may come in!
—Psalm for the distribution
of palms on Palm Sunday

AFTER he attended Mass Sunday morning The Mayor flew over the riot scene in a helicopter. He was accompanied by Fire Commissioner Robert Quinn, whose men had done such a heroic job. After crisscrossing the West Side for forty-five minutes, the helicopter fluttered to a landing. "It was a shocking and tragic picture of the city," The Mayor said. "I never believed that this would happen here. I hope it will not happen again."

The final assessment of what had happened never would be made, because the major damage to Chicago was something beyond the realm of arithmetic. Figures would trickle in on the rest of it, and the public would be informed that there had been 12,000 Army troops and 7,000 National Guardsmen; that 11,500 policemen had been available around the clock and that half the men of the force had been assigned to riot duty; that 2,931 arrests had been made; that 162 buildings had been destroyed by fire; that 268 buildings and homes had been looted; that the property loss was $13 million; that 500 persons had been hurt.

And—oh, yes—that nine Negroes had been killed.

The damage that could not be calculated on a pad with ballpoint pen or run through the clanking brain of a computer had been done to race relations in the city. Even those few Chicagoans who had been struggling against the polarization of the races that had been stressed in the Kerner Report moved away from one another after the events of Passion Week.

Whites who had thought it was time to prove that integration could work were repelled by the senseless violence. "If they will destroy the places where they live, what might they do to me?" was the unasked question.

Blacks had a question, equally difficult to answer. "If they won't accept a Martin Luther King as a human being, why should I expect them to accept me?"

The white haters said, "See, they're nothin' but animals. Just like I been tellin' you."

The black haters said, "We better kill them before they kill us."

Some blacks insisted that Richard J. Daley be held responsible for the riots. Some whites demanded that the blame be fixed, like a posthumous medal of dishonor, upon Martin Luther King Jr.

Where he had sown love, there was hate. Few had listened to him in life; fewer still could hear him from beyond the balcony in Memphis.

General Dunn of the National Guard said his men had fired weapons on only one occasion during their tour of duty in the riot area.

White officials who toured the area in the wake of The Mayor were puzzled by their discovery that not one pane of glass had been broken in the Faraday Elementary School, 3250 West Monroe Street, a half block from gutted buildings on Madison Street. Black officials understood.

10

The Odors

Back to a ghetto much more familiar to him than Lawndale is, The Mayor would have continued the westward processional on Thirty-fifth Street. With the crowd behind him, he would have passed a tavern, a short-order restaurant, another bar, a cleaner's shop, all between Giles Avenue and the next street over. That street is Prairie Avenue, and there was a day in Chicago's history when it was the most glamorous address in Chicago. The rich men who owned the packinghouses lived there before they built even more ornate homes in the "wilds" of Lake Shore Drive or way up on the North Shore, beyond the city limits.

In his book *The Gold Coast and the Slum,* Harvey W. Zorbaugh, one of the first of the urbanologists, observed:

> The outskirts of the city have always been about forty-five minutes from the heart of the Loop. In the days of the horse-drawn cars they were not beyond Twenty-second Street on the South Side. With the coming of the cable car they were extended to the vicinity of Thirty-sixth Street. The electric car—surface and elevated—again extended the city's outskirts, this time well past Seventieth Street. How far "rapid transit" will take them, no one can predict.

Zorbaugh's book, which was subtitled, *A Sociological Study of Chicago's Near North Side,* had been published in

1929, but his knowledge of the thought process of the Chicago commuter was valid almost forty years later. Whether he traveled by horse, by cable car, by streetcar, or on expressways built for high speed, the man who worked in the Loop did not want to be more than forty-five minutes from home. Now Prairie Avenue of yesteryear's wealthy was part of the Inner City and Thirty-fifth Street was no more than ten minutes from the Loop. The most remote corners of Chicago were within Zorbaugh's forty-five-minute range—barring a vapor lock or two on an expressway—as were many of the suburbs. Perhaps the basic reason for the problems of the city was the fact that the transportation experts had outstripped the sociologists.

Between Prairie and Indiana Avenues The Mayor would have marched past Fannie's Fish House and then come upon Perry's Bar-B-Q at Indiana. Fish houses, bar-b-q's, taverns, short-order restaurants and cleaners' shops seem to be the bulwarks of a business street in a black community, and they are another reason white Chicagoans give for making preparations to flee a "changing neighborhood." When West Seventy-ninth Street, out beyond Zorbaugh's electric-car limits, was changing, the Irish objected strenuously on learning that a service-station site would be cleared to make way for a Fast-Food franchise that would feature fried chicken.

"They'll probably build right over the old grease pit," an old settler said, "and that will give 'em all the deep fry they'll need for years."

When the store was built, it turned out to be a member of a nationally advertised chain that has thousands of franchises in white neighborhoods. Somehow, though, the odor of "Colonel Sanders Kentucky Fried Chicken" isn't as aromatic to whites when they are breathing in a community that has been taken over by blacks.

Some who would have been walking with The Mayor on Thirty-fifth Street have insisted that he does not have biracial nostrils, either. They have argued that the smells of the ghetto offend him as they do his white constituents. One who sees The Mayor that way is Warner Saunders, towering, bearded former athlete, who is executive director of the Better Boys Foundation.

Saunders knows the ghettos of Chicago as well as he knows the backs of his big, black, basketball-player's hands. He was brought up on Forty-seventh Street in the Black Belt and he has worked for eleven years, as teacher, sociologist and juvenile-delinquency-preventive agent, in Lawndale.

"Daley's biggest problem is white paternalism," Saunders has said. "It is tremendously difficult for him to escape that paternalism, based on his background, his ethnocentrism, his return every night to the womb, so to speak, to be restored.

"I've been in Daley's office in City Hall twice. When you walk into that office, something happens to you. You go in with things to say, suggestions to offer, complaints to put on the record. And then you realize that he is doing all the talking. He makes all the decisions that you supposedly were called in to discuss. He kind of neutralizes you, makes what you say seem foolish. He has that air of knowing more about the situation than you do.

"Trouble was expected on the West Side last June," Saunders said. "There would have been trouble, but, fortunately enough, it rained. He wanted to know why there might be trouble and I told him that things weren't working out on the West Side. Then he said to me, 'How about all those city programs? Aren't they working?' I said, 'No, they aren't working.' 'Why aren't they working?' he wanted to know. 'Because the people who are going to raise hell aren't in the programs,' I told him.

"The last time I went into the Mayor's office with a group, he began chiding us and I left."

On the southwest corner of Thirty-fifth and Indiana is Poor Woods Food & Liquors. Across the street and up the block is the Second Ward Regular Democratic Headquarters

at 3435 South Indiana. This is one of the many power bases
of octogenarian William Dawson, United States Representative from the First District of Illinois. To many white voters
William Dawson is a mythical figure. They think of him as
someone who ruled the Black Belt in the days when Hinky
Dink Kenna and Bathhouse John Coughlin were the political
patron saints of every bum, whore, gambler, slugger and con
man in the First Ward. Old as he is, Dawson was merely a
boy when Kenna and Coughlin were driving reformers to
early graves, but Bill remembers where everybody was buried and why. Chicagoans almost never see him on television,
hear him on radio, or read of him introducing important legislation in Congress. When he reappears on the scene, a few
weeks before an important election, white voters say, "Is he
still alive?"

To paraphrase the immortal words of Casey Stengel, most
people Dawson's age are dead but the blacks of the South
Side know that he is alive and well and running his sector of
Chicago from Washington. Before Franklin Delano Roose-
velt captured the hearts and the votes of black Americans,
Bill Dawson had been a Republican. He came over to the
Democrats in 1939, a few years behind many of his black
constituents, but Bill's tardiness did not weaken his control.
The Second and the Third Wards belonged to him, as did the
ward committeemen and the aldermen.

Dawson had been a member of the slatemaking committee
that decided, late in 1954, that Cook County Clerk Richard
J. Daley should be the Democratic party's candidate for
mayor in 1955.

Much political history has been made in that Second Ward
office. When Harry S Truman won Illinois by 33,612 in the
Presidential election of 1948, this ward and the ten other
wards in which Negroes then lived gave Truman 76 percent
of their vote. In 1963 the Second Ward was a major contributor to Daley's reelection in an all-out battle against Republi-

can candidate Benjamin Adamowski, a former Democrat. Adamowski carried thirty-one of the fifty wards. The Mayor was given only 49 percent of the white vote, but the Negro wards delivered 82 percent to him.

Bill Dawson is a patriarch now and removed from the day-to-day political battles, but The Mayor hardly could have walked up Thirty-fifth Street, with that huge crowd behind him, and not have stopped to say hello to the boys in the Second Ward office. It would have been expected of him, but more important than that, he would have wanted to do it. He would have wanted these people to know that the Second Ward was important to the Democratic party of Cook County and important to him.

This Second Ward office and Bill Dawson represent half of the flawless formula for getting elected in Chicago, a formula that was worked out in 1914 by Fred Lundin, the manipulator behind William Hale Thompson. The formula was simple: Control the Negro vote and dazzle the white electorate with building projects. It had worked for Big Bill Thompson, the only Republican to be mayor of Chicago in more than a half century, and it worked equally well for Richard J. Daley.

Until recently both halves of the formula worked without anyone so much as pressing a button. They operated on the endless-belt principle. Property taxes and grants from Washington and Springfield, the state capital, provided the cash to keep the expressways and other public-works projects abuilding and private enterprise concentrated on revisions of the Loop skyline. In the Negro wards the votes provided the patronage, and the patronage provided the jobs, and the jobs provided the votes.

With that formula functional, a party could not lose a city election unless all its members were stupid. About 1968, though, strange sounds were heard in the party machinery in the Negro wards, sounds that warned of a potential breakdown. There was a restiveness, a rebelliousness. Young blacks were questioning the paternalism of Bill Dawson, just as Warner Saunders put a long finger on the paternalism of The Mayor. Young voters in the ghetto didn't want a "Papa Doc" to tell them what to do. They were asking "in," and when their requests were ignored, they tried to muscle in. Even the two massive youth gangs, the Blackstone Rangers and the East Side Disciples, were moving in on the political arena.

"Institutions stabilize a community," Warner Saunders said, "and the most stable institution here is the political machine. And it is against the people."

Saunders was talking about the West Side, but many who would have been marching with The Mayor would have agreed that Saunders' words applied to the South Side as well.

⅏⅏⅏⅏⅏⅏⅏⅏⅏⅏⅏⅏⅏⅏⅏⅏⅏⅏⅏⅏⅏⅏⅏⅏⅏⅏⅏

From the Hip

THOSE who were with The Mayor on Monday and Tuesday of Holy Week, 1968, were disturbed by the change in him. He seemed in a state of shock. Had his fighting spirit been broken or was it nothing more than age finally beginning to show? From Thursday night through Sunday night, he had been under pressure such as few Chicago officials had been asked to endure.

"No city has as many programs as Chicago," The Mayor said again. He sounded like a man wringing out his heart in public.

Dr. Martin Luther King Jr. was buried in Atlanta on Tuesday, and Chicago was quiet. Was it too much to suppose that the haters were beginning to understand that Martin Luther King had spoken truly to the people of America?

Crane Technical High School in the riot area was fire-bombed Wednesday, but three minor fires within the school were quickly put out. It was obvious that the horror had ended. The Mayor lifted the curfew. Lieutenant Governor Shapiro informed President Johnson that the federal troops could be withdrawn from the city.

Even before the curfew was lifted, City Hall and its multiplicity of departments had moved into Madison Street and the other streets that had been the battleground not so many hours earlier. Bulldozers waddled into Lawndale Monday to knock down burned-out buildings. Behind the bulldozers came the earth graders to bury and to smooth and to turn a riot scene into nothing more than a succession of virtually immaculate vacant lots. "It's astonishing what the city can do when it wants to look good," Father Dan Mallette said, laughing sardonically. "I look at this obsession for neatness and then I think about how long we had to wait when we asked them to send out a crew to clear a vacant lot for a ball diamond."

After The Mayor told the assembled reporters that he would lift the curfew, he was asked the leading question. Was he concerned about the possibility of disturbances at the Democratic National Convention in August? According to rumors, the hippies were coming to Chicago for the Convention, and they would be reinforced by a new rack of odd-balls known as the Yippies, in numbers 100,000 strong. Like a man who no longer cared to anticipate the crises that the future might bring, The Mayor said he hoped there would be no problems during the Convention. Moments later his zestful pride in all things Chicago returned to him as he reviewed the days and the nights of the tragedy that was Lawndale.

"I thought the Police and Fire Departments did an outstanding job," he said. "It's easy to criticize, but I think they did an outstanding job."

He is getting it back, perceptive reporters said to themselves, he's finding the touch again. The Mayor was perfect for that fleeting moment. He was emphasizing the good and he was minimizing the bad. He had grabbed the best public-relations baton available to him, and he was ready to run with it.

The performance of the firemen had been superhuman. There was no other word to describe it. This was fire fighting under guerrilla-warfare conditions. For the first time in their careers, and they hoped the last, the men of a truck or an engine had no other orders than "find yourself a fire." There were so many fires and there was so much equipment jammed into a city block, the traditional chain of command could not function. This was "man against fire," and the individuals of the Chicago Fire Department responded magnificently. Often under siege of rocks and bottles and never certain that they were out of range of sniper fire, the firemen brought glory to their department. They could be credited, without exaggeration, with saving much of the West Side and the suburbs across the city limits.

There had been accusations against the police, as there always must be. Some policemen had gone into business with the looters, according to witnesses, but these charges never were made in court. There probably were men on duty Friday and Saturday whose conduct violated the rules of decency, as well as departmental rules, but the great majority of policemen rose to the occasion. A handful held the line against the mob early Friday afternoon. After the fires had begun to ravage the area, the policemen protected the firemen and attempted to check the looting. It should be remembered that the police were the only line of protection until the National Guard rolled into the streets at 11 P.M. Friday.

The greatest and most unforgettable characteristic of most of the patrolmen and officers was humanity. Had they gone berserk, the gutters of West Madison Street might have run red with the blood of children. The police did not attempt to put down the riot by gunfire. Forty-three persons had been killed in Detroit's ghetto in July of 1967. Nine died in Chicago in April of 1968. Nine was enough. Nine was too many. But nine was not forty-three.

All the elements of heroism and drama were there. Nothing more was needed than a staff of historians assigned to the Fire Department and the Police Department and a few days to prepare the stories. Black firemen and white firemen. White policemen and black policemen. Little children thanking the firemen and the policemen for saving their homes, their lives. Experienced reporters could see the campaign of heroism drumming the hate from the minds of Chicagoans.

And then The Mayor, The Mayor who could take the pulse of his city instinctively, dropped the baton. The clatter was heard around the world.

On Monday, April 15, the man who had said that it was easy to criticize, criticized. The Mayor said that he had ordered the police to "shoot to kill" all arsonists; to "shoot to maim or cripple" looters, and to use Mace, a chemical deterrent, against children involved in arson or looting.

City Hall reporters were astonished. They had not expected this from this man. If he had been nothing else during his thirteen years as mayor, this man had been compassionate. And now this . . . So there would be no misinterpretation of what he meant to convey, The Mayor added that he had issued similar orders before the riot. "I assumed they [the orders] would be followed, but they were not," The Mayor said. He told the press that he had called in James B. Conlisk, superintendent of police, that morning and reissued the same orders.

The words came tumbling after one another. The Mayor was like a man who had decided, with finality, to tell off his best friend. He went on to say things about the schools that even his most bitter opponents had not mentioned. The agitators of both races had been shrewd enough to let that subject lie. "The conditions of April 5 in the schools were indescribable," he said. "The beating of girls, the slashing of teachers and the general turmoil and the payoffs and the extortions. We have to face up to this situation with discipline. Principals tell us what's happening and they are told to forget it."

The city had been swept by rumors of violence at various schools, in the riot area and out of it. That there had been turmoil nobody doubted. But to lump it all together now—

what could be his purpose? What was he thinking about?

Payoffs and extortions had been part of juvenile racketeering in slum schools for years. Why had not The Mayor been disturbed by it long ago, black adults asked. Why was he bringing it up now?

The beating of girls had not happened in the ghetto schools, so The Mayor must be talking about integrated schools in which white and black students clashed on the Friday after Martin Luther King's assassination. If a high-school boy from one of the white-supremacy belts on the outskirts of the city said, "We'll be better off without King," was his black classmate expected to take it? Or if a black bully decided to observe a day of mourning by swaggering and threatening, was his white classmate expected to do nothing? But were the white-supremacy boy or the black bully responsible for their attitudes? Weren't they merely reflecting the ignorance and the smallness of their elders?

The Mayor is telling the truth, white rights advocates shouted. The Mayor is making a racial issue of it, black nationalists stormed. The Mayor is just letting off steam, his friends said.

And Martin Luther King Jr. may have been writhing in his grave.

The beating of girls and the slashing of teachers had not been confirmed, but the man most responsible for keeping rumors from spreading was indulging in rumor mongering. The reports of beatings and slashings would never be detailed. They never would be confirmed, either, except for isolated incidents. Years later Chicagoans would continue to believe in the reports, because they heard of them from The Mayor.

Even while The Mayor was talking, rumors of another kind began to filter through City Hall. Daley and Conlisk had had a confrontation during a meeting of The Mayor's cabinet the previous Friday, according to these rumors. Fire

Commissioner Robert Quinn, who had Daley's ear during the helicopter flight over the riot area, as he does much of the time, supposedly had blasted Conlisk's police for failure to protect Quinn's firemen. Quinn would deny any involvement in the Daley-Conlisk dispute.

Adverse reactions to the "shoot-to-kill" order were instantaneous. The great majority of those who reacted expressed indignation. The public outcry may have been the reason why The Mayor began to have third thoughts. Or perhaps he moved away from his position because he finally realized the enormity of what he had said. He spoke at a dinner of the Western Railway Club Tuesday night, and after his talk a reporter asked about the "shoot-to-kill" statement.

His order had "been completely misunderstood," The Mayor insisted. "Everyone has blown this thing out of proportion," he complained. He emphasized that he had referred only to "obvious arsonists."

Daley was committing the strategic blunder that most newspapermen and telecasters thought was beneath him. He was charging "misquote" in an electronic era when every word spoken by an important public figure is recorded. The text of his speech made a mockery of his correction of himself. This is a partial transcript of what he had said:

I have conferred with the superintendent of police this morning and I gave him the following instructions, which I thought were instructions on the night of the Fifth that were not carried out:

I said to him very emphatically and very definitely that an order be issued by him immediately and under his signature to shoot to kill any arsonist or anyone with a Molotov cocktail in his hand in Chicago because they're potential murderers, and to issue a police order to shoot to maim or cripple anyone looting any stores in our city. Above all, the crime of arson is to me the most hideous and worst crime of any and should be dealt with in this fashion.

I was disappointed to know that every policeman out on the beat was supposed to use his own decision and this decision was his [Conlisk's]. In my opinion, policemen should have had instructions to shoot arsonists and looters—arsonists to kill and looters to maim and detain. . . .

I assumed the instructions were given, but the instructions to the policemen were to use their own judgment. I assumed any superintendent would issue instructions to shoot arsonists on sight and to maim the looters, but I found out this morning this wasn't so and therefore gave him [Conlisk] specific instructions.

Let's get one thing straight: A county official said there were no city officials out there. They closed the Lawndale Public Aid Station down at 1 P.M. and it was burned down. City officials stayed there far into the night. . . .

12

Second Thought

THOSE who abhorred the "shoot-to-kill" philosophy, whether it was espoused by a loutish Southern sheriff or by a gentlemanly Northern mayor, were not placated by Richard J. Daley's interpretation of his statement. In the first place, he had not made a distinction between "obvious arsonists" and, let us say, covert arsonists. In the second place, even those who reflexively denounced every action of the Police Department were certain that a policeman, who believed that his star was at all meaningful, would shoot a man or woman who was seen carrying a can of gasoline into a store where a small fire was burning.

Daley's version of "what I really said" infuriated the weary police. Many of the men who had been on riot duty had expected a commendation. Instead they were being second-guessed, criticized and all but indicted by the man who is, in effect, their commander in chief. The officer who said, "If he thinks I'm going to shoot a little kid for grabbing a television set, he's got to look for another boy," summed up the sentiment of most members of the department.

The undermining of the Police Department, unintended though it might have been, was especially insidious because so many Chicagoans wanted to believe The Mayor. They read between the lines of what he had said and said to one another, "Something happened to police discipline during the riot. I wonder what it was?"

Less emotional observers were drawn into the speculation,

too. They wondered if the professional standard of the police had deteriorated under the terrible pressure of Lawndale. If this were true, they argued, The Mayor owed a full explanation to the citizens and an exposé of the department was mandatory.

In every version the policeman was the loser and he had taken more heat than he needed. Next time, if there should be a next time, The Mayor might be given more shooting than he needed.

By Wednesday The Mayor had banked the fire of his temper. He could not bring himself to say that he had been terribly wrong, but he did say something other than what he had said on Monday. This is the text of the statement he made Wednesday during a meeting of the City Council:

> Throughout the nation on May 1 there will be the observance of Law Day. This is the eleventh annual observance, but at no time can this occasion have greater significance to every citizen.
>
> It is the established policy of the Chicago Police Department—fully supported by the administration—that only minimum force necessary be used by policemen in carrying out their duties. But this established policy was never intended to support permissive violence, destruction, and a complete denial of that respect for law which is vital to our democratic way of life.
>
> Certainly an officer should do everything in his power to make an arrest to prevent a crime—by utilizing minimum force necessary. But I cannot believe that any citizen would hold that policemen should permit an arsonist to carry out his dangerous, murderous mission when minimum force necessary cannot prevent or deter him. There are few crimes that hold the potential of loss of life, or threat to the entire community as does arson.
>
> Nor do I believe that any citizen supports the theory that in times of riot and chaos any person has the right

to willfully and maliciously throw a brick through a store window for the purpose of burglary, encourage mob behavior and urge persons to become burglars and thieves and thus exposing themselves to serious injury from possible police action. Again, that such a person should be restrained if possible by minimum force necessary—but he cannot be given permissive rights for his criminal action.

Much has been written and said—and I have been both highly praised and criticized—about the role of the police during a dangerous and inflammable riot.

I believe the basic responsibility of the Police Department is to protect the hundreds of thousands of citizens of the community—from loss of life, destruction and mayhem.

There can be no possible justification of a deliberate criminal act which results in helpless and homeless victims. All the people on the West Side had one universal demand—protect us from the arsonists, from the looter, from the mob and its leaders.

Men poised with Molotov cocktails, incendiaries, or fire bombs of any kind are the same as the assassins who pulled the triggers on the guns that killed the Reverend Martin Luther King Jr. and the late President John F. Kennedy.

We cannot resign ourselves to the proposition that civil protest must lead to death and devastation—to the abandonment of the law that is fundamental for the preservation of the rights of all people and their freedom.

I have directed the superintendent of police and fire commissioner to arrange for the compensation of the firemen and police who worked during the recent emergency.

The Mayor's emphasis upon "minimum force necessary" in

his Wednesday statement was proof that his temper and his despair had inspired his shoot-to-kill order to Superintendent Conlisk. As a lawyer, The Mayor should have known that Conlisk could not issue such an order. The statutes of the State of Illinois, to protect the citizenry from potential police repression, impose stringent restrictions upon the use of deadly force by police. As a lawyer, The Mayor knew the statutes, but he had not been thinking as a lawyer when he upbraided Conlisk on Monday morning.

Hans Mattick, associate director of the Center for Studies in Criminal Justice at the University of Chicago, said that The Mayor's shoot-to-kill order was "a poor contribution at a time when they're asking everybody to register guns." Prophetically, Mattick said that issuance of the order "has put people on notice that he [The Mayor] condones very drastic action and that is likely to escalate any future conflict."

But on the same day that Mattick made his comments Joseph Lefevour, president of the Fraternal Order of Police, sent The Mayor a telegram. Acting on behalf of his organization, Lefevour expressed "our deepest respect and admiration."

Many of the policemen who had been on duty in Lawndale wondered whose side the Fraternal Order of Police was on.

The Chicago *Tribune* attempted to stiffen Daley's resolve, to keep him on the side of righteous right. The *Tribune* quoted Senator Cliff Hansen of Wyoming, who praised The Mayor and the *Tribune* for "the firm stand they have taken against rioting."

By heritage and tradition an implacable foe of all that the *Tribune* stands for in national politics, The Mayor has come to accept the newspaper's endorsement of his works as proof that he had made untenable its earlier position of opposition to him, but the enthusiastic support of an arch-Republican journal and a Republican senator must have made him a bit uncomfortable.

The Mayor had more support than the editorial voice from the Tribune Tower on Michigan Avenue. Colonel Jack Reilly, special-events director for the city, announced that ten thousand letters and one thousand telegrams had been received by The Mayor after he issued his "shoot-to-kill" manifesto, and what really mattered, as Reilly emphasized with pride in his chief, was a 15-to-1 ratio in favor of "shoot to kill." Reilly did not have a breakdown available, so the world will never know how many letters came from correspondence-conscious groups such as the Minutemen, the American Nazi Party and the National Rifle Association. Nor was Reilly's moment in the spotlight meant to imply that the riot had been one of Chicago's special events.

Had the police only known that their reluctance to "shoot to kill" would be rejected by the electorate 15 to 1, they might have reacted differently, and The Mayor could have spent the rest of his days explaining that away. Chicago had had something like that many years before. It is remembered as the Haymarket Riot.

All in all, there was an abysmal lack of the kind of humanity that had been generated spontaneously and naturally by the policemen and firemen in circumstances that bordered on the impossible.

Even while The Mayor was changing his mind on Law Day, his shoot-to-kill statement was criticized by Ramsey Clark, United States Attorney General; by John V. Lindsay, mayor of New York, and by the conservative City Club of Chicago.

Those who looked to The Mayor for authentic leadership, those honest admirers who did not fawn upon him with "Yes, your Honor," and "You're right, your Honor," in response to everything he said or did, were most aware that the basic wrong in the shoot-to-kill shocker was that it had been totally unnecessary. At a time when Chicago and its reputation were lying in the shambles of Madison Street, the city needed cool heads and closed mouths.

Nobody of stature had been critical to that point, with the exception of some black leaders who lived in the riot area. Nobody from outside had charged the police or the National Guard with dereliction. Of the three Democratic Presidential candidates, Senator Eugene McCarthy had made the only comment. McCarthy praised the police and the National Guard. Vice-President Hubert Humphrey had said, "No comment." Senator Robert Kennedy had ducked the issue.

Those who sincerely admired The Mayor had expected better of him.

In a city that always had hated much more intensely than it had loved, almost everybody seemed to hate him now. There had not been such near-unanimity in the 131-year history of the city. The two races that comprised the greater part of the city's population hated him with an impartiality that was separate but equal. Whites hated him because "he is too much for the niggers." Blacks hated him because he did not do enough for them. National groups hated him with a fervor that in the past had been aroused by other national groups. The Irish hated him because he was one of their own. The Poles hated him because he so often had beaten down one of their own. The Italians, Lithuanians, Germans, Swedes, Puerto Ricans, Chinese and Syrians hated him for reasons of their own—for the driveway permits that were denied; for the parking tickets that were issued; for the STOP sign that wasn't authorized; for the taxes that were imposed; for all the problems and aggravations of big-city life.

Looters hated him because he had decreed death, retroactively, for them. The police hated him because he had not supported them. Only the liberals did not hate him. Chicago's liberals do not have sufficient energy to generate strong emotion.

The Mayor had never sought love. It had been believed that he did not want love. There was an apartness about him that some thought to be unusual in a man of Irish heritage, but those who were Irish understood this remoteness. The late Emmett Hartnett, one of the few men who were considered confidants of Daley's, told a reporter, "Nobody is close to The Mayor except his wife."

He had not sought love, but this landslide of hate was not the return he had expected from the city to which he had given so much. He had been proud of his ability—or perhaps *instinct* is the better word—to anticipate the desires of the people. He had miscalculated the temper of the citizenry only a few times during his thirteen years of service, but those errors had been minor, when compared to this. They had been political misinterpretations. This was disaster.

If his remoteness had not deluded him and if his advisers had not misinformed him, these would have been his hours of greatest triumph. During Friday and Saturday of Passion Week and on Palm Sunday, the people had clasped him to their hearts for the first time—the distant, decent people who had wept at the bier of John Fitzgerald Kennedy and had been shattered by the death of Martin Luther King. For the first time they had seen The Mayor as human. He had been as shaken by the events as any of them. The professional politician and the professional Irishman had been replaced by a human who admitted by words and actions that he did not know the answers, that he had no program for tragedy. He had been magnificent in his abjectness.

The decent people took him for their own, and for eight days they empathized with him. Then, after all those hours he had been given for reflection, he became assured again. He became the politician again. He said "shoot to kill"—and he lost them.

The disaster had been visited upon him by the ghost of the man who had been the symbol of The Mayor's most publicized psychological victory. The man who had come to Chicago preaching love had won from beyond the grave. It was a victory Martin Luther King Jr. would not have wanted.

13

ꟷꟷꟷꟷꟷꟷꟷꟷꟷꟷꟷꟷꟷꟷ

The Institute

THERE are reminders everywhere in Bronzeville of Joe Louis,
the immortal heavyweight boxing champion, who was a resident of Detroit but belonged to Chicago. Here is another
that The Mayor and his crowd would have passed as they
paraded on Thirty-fifth Street between Indiana and Michigan Avenues. It's the Joe Louis Theater, very much the
worse for wear now and a rather unhappy reminder of the
days when Joe Louis and Bronzeville were younger.

On the south side of the street, across from the theater, is
the African Village, an apparel shop. When Joe Louis ruled
the prize ring, a resident of the Black Belt would have been
insulted by a reference to anything African.

Just ahead, on the northwest corner of Thirty-fifth and
Michigan, is a building that never fails to make the heart of
The Mayor leap. That's the gymnasium of DeLaSalle Institute, the high school that Richard J. Daley attended for two
years. The Mayor loves sports—that's always been one of his
strongest links with the black communities—and he has seen
hundreds of memorable basketball games in this gymnasium.

Two Notre Dame All-Americans, Ed (Moose) Krause and
Eddie Riska, played for DeLaSalle in this gymnasium, as did
many of The Mayor's protégés in the city government. The
cornerstone tells that the building was begun in 1929, almost
forty years ago, but The Mayor always thinks of it as "the
new gym."

For many years DeLaSalle had been a white island here in

Bronzeville. Now the Institute was integrated, as were all the Catholic high schools in the city, but in recent years the changes in environment had gone far beyond integration. Across the street from the DeLaSalle gymnasium, at 71 East Thirty-fifth Street, is the Willing Worker Spiritual Church, one of many store-front churches in the Belt.

The ancient limestone pile that is the main building of De-LaSalle Institute towers above the corner of Wabash Avenue and Thirty-fifth Street. "Where is the cornerstone?" a reporter might ask. The Mayor would explain that instead of a cornerstone there is a dedication stone, very small, below the cement sill of a first-floor window. The inscription reads: "Religion, Morality, Knowledge A.D. 1889 Signum Fidei."

This building is almost eighty years old—if it were a public school or a Loop office building, it probably would have been razed long ago—but The Mayor remembers when it seemed new to him. In a time when a college education was beyond the dreams of a workingman's son, Dickie Daley had enrolled in the two-year business course taught by the Christian Brothers in their odd little white collars that looked like wings reversed.

In the middle Fifties, when almost everything surrounding the school had been slum property, the Christian Brothers might have chosen to close this building and move DeLa-Salle to a spacious plot of ground in one of the all-white communities on the fringes of the city or to a meadow in a suburb. The Christian Brothers decided, instead, to demonstrate their faith in God, in Chicago and in their loyal alumnus at City Hall by continuing to operate right there at Thirty-fifth Street. The transformation was a miracle that testified to the efficacy of prayer and the efficiency of The Mayor. Terrible old tenements were torn away, principally to provide space for expansion of the nearby campus of Illinois Institute of Technology, but DeLaSalle benefited, too. The vista north from the high school, once jammed with ramshackle buildings, is bright and open. Beyond the open spaces are the

buildings of Illinois Institute of Technology, and their prox-
imity made DeLaSalle part of a striking education complex.
Wabash Avenue, which had been a thoroughfare from Sixty-
third Street into the south end of the Loop, was closed at
Thirty-fifth Street to provide safe progress for the students of
the two institutes. The Mayor had done a lot for his old
school; it had done a lot for him.

The Brothers stayed, and DeLaSalle's break with its past
was dramatized not so many years ago when the school's outstanding basketball player was a black youngster whose first
name is Luther. The Negro students came from Bronzeville
and from the newer black neighborhoods south of the old
Belt. The white boys came from the other side of the Rock
Island tracks, from Bridgeport and from Back of the Yards,
two communities that had sent many students here during
the two years Dickie Daley had worked at the course for future bookkeepers, clerks, stenographers and bank tellers.

Those sons of Irish pig-stickers and Lithuanian manure-
shovelers had taken the business course at the Institute because the father of each had said, in his own way, "Kid, I
don't want you to have to work in the Yards the way I've
been working. You're going to go to school and make something of yourself."

The fathers knew from bitter experience that the route
toward the top rarely started in the hog house, the cattle
pens or the tannery. They believed that the most direct approach to the top began near the top, in the offices of the men
who wore white collars. Boys were driven into education by
the grim knowledge of what their fathers were going
through. Education for them was the escape hatch that led
out of the Stock Yards, just as it took other youths out of the
coal mines of Pennsylvania and out of the steel mills of South
Chicago, East Chicago and Gary.

For Dickie Daley the motivation was somewhat different.
His father, Michael, a sheet-metal worker, had not been
ground down to a point of constant fatigue as had many men

of their neighborhood. Neither were the parents of Dickie Daley haunted by the specter of poverty as were so many Irish-Catholic families of Bridgeport. Young Dick was a rarity in Nativity of Our Lord parish—an "only child."

Dickie might have followed his father and his uncle, Al Daley, into the Sheet Metal Workers Union when the youngster was old enough to get his working papers, but Lillian Dunne Daley had other plans for her son. Lillian Daley had worked for the right of women to vote, and one of The Mayor's most vivid memories is of being taken by his mother to watch a victory parade of suffragettes. That was in 1913, when he was eleven years old.

Those parents who dreamed of instant advancement to the executive suite persuaded their sons to become secretaries. Most executives in the packing plants and in Sam Insull's public utilities employed male secretaries to take dictation, type letters and file invoices. Every neighborhood had its story of the "lad" who was being groomed by the president of the concern, himself, to take over when the president retired, or better still, who had inherited the president's vast wealth when the dear old fellow shuffled on. An inordinate number of presidents in those days were orphans and bachelors. Dickie Daley had done even better than the stories. He had worked as a secretary and, in time, he took over the entire city.

Most DeLaSalle men had done well in business, in banking and in politics. The Brothers trained their boys to be ready. The Mayor's immediate predecessor, the late Martin Kennelly, also had been educated at DeLaSalle.

On the south side of the street, across from the high school, there is a Colonel Sanders Kentucky Fried Chicken store on one corner and a McDonald's hamburger stand on the other. One wonders whether the aromas that mingle at Thirty-fifth and Wabash smell the same to the black and the white students at DeLaSalle.

14

Skyscrapers and High-Rises

WEST of DeLaSalle there is a continuation of the open spaces. There is a modernized station on the elevated line that serves the community, the schools and White Sox Park. The Mayor dreams of the day when all the stations on the "L" will look like this one. Then comes the broad sweep of State Street, the same street that is mentioned in the song that most native Chicagoans detest. A "toddlin' town" Chicago isn't.

Across State on the north side of Thirty-fifth is the striking Research Institute Building of I.I.T. Ted Erickson, Chicago's conqueror of the English Channel, works there and trains in the pool of the new fieldhouse, just a short walk to the north.

The redevelopment of this area, north to Thirty-third Street and west to the elevated tracks of the Chicago, Rock Island and Pacific Railroad, has provided The Mayor with immense satisfaction. There were slum buildings here, too, but Illinois Institute of Technology had cleared them with the help of the city. This slum-clearance project had been resisted by the black residents of the area, but in the end they had capitulated and moved on. Who was to say that they, as well as the city, were not better for it?

The Mayor is sentimental about Illinois Tech. When he was a young man, the school was known as Armour Institute, and contemporaries who had chosen engineering as their way to success had attended night school there, while he had taken night courses at DePaul University and later at DePaul Law School.

Some critics persistently say that the slums that had surrounded Illinois Tech had merely been moved, instead of eradicated, but as The Mayor sometimes says, it is easy to criticize. At this point, though, in his revealing walk along Thirty-fifth Street, he would have been joined by hundreds who could offer criticism from personal experience.

They could have come from over there, from the high-rises. That is Stateway Gardens, one of forty-eight projects operated and managed by the Chicago Housing Authority. South of Stateway Gardens is its "mother" project, the Robert E. Taylor Homes, the most gigantic complex of public housing in the world. Chicagoans usually are enchanted with things gigantic, but Taylor Homes and, to a lesser extent, Stateway Gardens have become hated monuments to all that has been going on in Chicago. The projects are hated especially by those who live in them.

In 1950, when the nation was recovering from one war and plunging into another, every major city wanted public housing. On July 8, 1949, Congress had passed a new housing bill, and on that same day, the Chicago Housing Authority put before Mayor Martin Kennelly its proposal to build 40,000 units within the city during the next six years. Those 40,000 units would have housed a population greater than that of Rockford, Illinois's second-largest city, which had 92,503 in the 1950 census.

The C.H.A. had been run since 1937 by Elizabeth Wood, a feisty graduate of the University of Michigan and a former teacher at Vassar. She may have been the only woman in Chicago history who was feared by members of the City Council. Elizabeth Wood—no man ever would have thought of calling her Betty—was by background an aristocrat and by nature an autocrat. She ran the Housing Authority with an iron hand in white glove and during the long reign of big

Ed Kelly as mayor, Miss Wood and her agency were autonomous. The word had gone out from Kelly to the aldermen, "Hands off the C.H.A."

Considering the time and his background, Kelly's attitude toward the Housing Authority was so enlightened as to seem unreal when caught in the rear-view mirror of 1968. It is an attitude easily explained by Colonel Jacob (Jack) Arvey, who ran the city and county government in partnership with Kelly for so many years. The Jewish half of the Kelly-Arvey Machine said, "Franklin Delano Roosevelt made a liberal out of Ed Kelly, an inflamed liberal."

Late in 1946 Arvey and the other decision makers within the Cook County Central Committee of the Democratic party concluded that Kelly could not be reelected, a conclusion based more on fear than on fact. What Arvey and the others failed to comprehend was that Kelly's popularity with the younger voters never had been higher. The reason for this was the tremendous good will engendered by the Chicago Servicemen's Centers, which had become the pet project of Mayor Kelly and his wife, Margaret, a World War I nurse. Chicago had been a great favorite as a pass and liberty city among the millions of soldiers, sailors and marines who visited during the long war, and Chicago's own war veterans, a huge voting bloc, credited Kelly with bringing this honor to their home town.

Kelly reluctantly stepped aside—"It was a case of the dictator questioning his own power," said Benjamin Adamowski, who twice opposed Richard Daley in contests for mayor. "Kelly was an easy guy to frighten"—and the new mayor of Chicago was benevolent, white-haired Martin Kennelly. With the departure of Kelly, the C.H.A. lost its patron and protector.

By legal interpretation, Chicago has a "weak mayor" system of government. Ed Kelly made a mockery of that. His mayoral philosophy was, "You either run the organization or it runs you." In partnership with, first, Patrick Nash, and later, Jack Arvey, Big Ed ran the City Council. Kennelly's concept was entirely different. He believed that the aldermen should run the city, and when those fifty public servants realized that Kennelly was surrendering his power to them, they grabbed it and ran away with it.

When the C.H.A. was created by an act of the Illinois legislature, it was an independent agency. The City Council had no legal control over its policies and decisions. Miss Wood, chosen for the top spot by C.H.A. commissioners after consultations with national experts in the housing field, was administering ten thousand units in 1949 with the help of a staff of six hundred. She had plenty of jobs to fill, and the patronage boys bitterly resented that they controlled none of them. Elizabeth was a very tough lady.

To curtail Miss Wood's power, a bill was pushed through the legislature that made the City Council a "board of review" for the C.H.A. This bill, passed in 1948, made it mandatory that the sites selected by the Housing Authority be approved by vote of the aldermen. And in 1950 most Chicago aldermen were willing to cast a favorable vote on a housing site "provided that it's not in my ward."

After the passage of the federal housing law in 1949, Jacob Burck, editorial cartoonist of the *Sun-Times*, hit the city in the eye with a prophetic drawing that would haunt Chicago almost twenty years later. Burck portrayed a muscular Uncle Sam, a happy grin on his face and his arms filled with public-housing units. The caption read, "Where Do You Want It?"

That question was to drag down the entire program. Chicago did not have 40,000 units in 1955, as scheduled. It had no more than 12,390, with 1,859 units under construction. Thirteen years after the C.H.A.'s envisioned deadline, the city had 30,848 public-housing units. In August of 1968 Chicago had almost 10,000 fewer units than were recommended in the proposal that the Housing Authority had sent to the

City Council in July of 1949. This underscores the sadness and shamefulness of the performance, but the aldermen who were responsible for the delay had been neither remorseful nor ashamed. They assumed that they had responded to the "will of the people."

The performance on the Chicago Housing Authority sites was political expediency in its worst manifestation. It was shabby and sickening. Adamowski, who served as city corporation counsel during the early years of the Kennelly administration, recalled the most miserable performance of the mayor and the site-selecting aldermen. "We went out on a bus to the Southwest Side to look at a large proposed site," Adamowski said. "As we approached the area we noticed that a huge crowd had gathered, maybe as many as five thousand. The people had signs, and the sentiment was that they didn't want a public-housing project in that neighborhood. We drove by the first corner of the site and continued west. I noticed Martin [Kennelly] give some sort of instructions to the driver, and thought that we would drive around, to the other side, and make the crowd come to us. That would have been good strategy. Martin had to talk to that crowd and make them see that he wanted this site and why he wanted it.

"The bus driver made a left turn," Adamowski continued, "and then made another left turn. A moment later I realized we weren't going to stop at all. We just rolled right on out of the community and went back to City Hall."

The site from which Mayor Kennelly fled almost in panic, as graphically recounted by Ben Adamowski, was in McKinley Park, a large city park at Pershing Road (Thirty-ninth Street) and Western Avenue. As was too often the case, the planners of the Housing Authority had made an abysmal selection that made the case for rejection too easy. Whatever their real motive might be, opponents of the site could say, "Why should thirty acres of park land be surrendered for a housing project? The city doesn't have enough recreation space as it is." That argument was valid, even though racists might have been hiding behind the fun-and-games appeal, but once the decision had been taken by the Housing Authority, Kennelly had an obligation at least to bring the Authority's case to the people.

According to a newspaper account, the mayor saw the huge crowd waiting at the park's administration building and said, "Perhaps we'd better not stop here." Later the mayor explained that there would have been no point in stopping and getting into a discussion.

The site was to have been discussed at a meeting of the City Council's housing committee the next day, but the meeting was hastily called off after the site selectors reported what they had seen around the McKinley Park field house. Unaware that there was to be no meeting, four hundred residents of the Southwest Side area adjacent to the park had descended upon City Hall. Somebody had to talk to them, but who would be given the assignment?

The mayor? No. The chairman of the housing committee? No. The chairman of the Council's finance committee? No. The job was not entrusted to any city official, elected or appointed. The decision to abandon the McKinley Park project was announced to the joyous four hundred by the deputy comptroller of Cook County, Richard J. Daley.

Why Daley? Almost two decades later it seems strange that a county official should have been given the great political advantage of telling "the people" what they wanted to hear, but the reason probably was that Mayor Kennelly and the City Council leaders could not afford to bow to pressure in public. Another probability is that Kennelly feared he would not be believed by the protesters from Marquette Park even when he came as bearer of good news. Dick Daley was from the Eleventh Ward, just to the north and east of the ward in which Marquette Park is situated. Daley also had represented the area in the state legislature before he made his losing race for Cook County sheriff in 1946. He was known and trusted by many of the five thousand who had assembled at the field house.

That was the end of selective site programing for the C.H.A. and for its friends in the City Council. The pressure of numbers had prevailed, and the word went out into the city. "All you have to do to keep public housing out of your ward is raise a little hell. Kennelly can't take the heat." The aldermen would dictate to the Housing Authority, from that day forward, just as they had been dictating to Kennelly on everything else.

Some who examine the deliberate delay that sabotaged the C.H.A. in 1949 and '50 contend that the aldermen were merely voting the inflexible opinion of their constituents. There is truth in this, but there is a lie in it, too. Many of the aldermen and ward committeemen in the so-called "conservation areas"—the white communities on the periphery of the ghetto—were at least as biased as the people they served. Some were the furtive leaders of the bigots while giving lip service to brotherhood. Their concept of brotherhood was expressed in the catch-all phrase, "We've got to keep the Negroes in their place." When spoken of informally in a corner tavern or at a "social" club, "Negroes" might happen to become "niggers."

At a time when leadership was demanded of them, leadership they had been straining to exercise during the long years they were kept on a short leash by Mayor Kelly, the aldermen took Chicago into the quicksand. The city still would be trying to extricate itself during Richard Daley's fourth term.

The obstructionist tactics of the aldermen were the result of a stubborn refusal to read and use history and of a probable misconception of the mood of the time. Their strategy focused upon locating a maximum percentage of the public-housing units in the Black Belt. Elizabeth Wood's hope was that a reasonable percentage of the units could be built in outlying districts that were virtually all-white.

Had the aldermen looked at the past that was so familiar to so many of them and anticipated the future, they would have comprehended that theirs was a Pyrrhic victory. Historically, the Black Belt had grown door to door, a block at a time, with the whites fleeing ahead of the Negro "invasion." Given the tremendous increase in the population of the Belt in the decade since 1940, the breakout was coming and it had to follow the traditional pattern. The white aldermen who thought they were "saving" the conservation areas by roadblocking the C.H.A. would have served their constituencies much better in the long run if the aldermen had fought for Elizabeth Wood, instead of against her.

The probable misconception was a misreading of the seriousness of the housing problem. In all the wards of the city newly married veterans of World War II and their wives were living in basements, attics, stores, trailers or, most unsatisfactory of all the temporary solutions, doubled up with relatives. Had the City Council had the foresight to locate C.H.A. projects in white wards, it is reasonable to suppose that the war veterans would have put their desperate need for housing ahead of their inbred fear of blacks. Those veterans might have been willing to move into integrated projects, particularly projects that were integrated on the controlled basis ordained by Miss Wood. It was well known to the aldermen, if not to the public, that during the era when Miss Wood dictated C.H.A. policy under the protection of Mayor Kelly, she kept apartments vacant rather than upset the racial balance in a specific project.

In March of 1950, while the "don't put it in my ward" aldermen were making a travesty of site selection, the *Sun-Times* editorialized: "If they [the aldermen] understand that their decision may go far toward setting the pattern for the Chicago of 1970, they will see their task as the application of sound standards to site selection—and not the mere dumping of projects wherever political objections may seem to be weakest."

The logic of the editorial was rejected by aldermen who did not have the courage to provide leadership for the people. This was almost five years before The Mayor was elected to his first term; but in 1968, two years before the time that the *Sun-Times* editorial writer tried to make the aldermen foresee, Richard J. Daley still was carrying the cross of that long-gone expediency.

Instead of dumping the projects, the aldermen chose to pile them.

15

‖‖‖‖‖‖‖‖‖‖‖‖‖‖‖‖‖‖‖‖‖‖‖‖‖‖‖‖‖‖‖‖‖

Slum Castles in the Air

IF THE Elizabeth Wood of 1968 had been as full of fight and spite as the Elizabeth Wood of 1950, the great lady of Chicago's public housing would have found delight in the bitter ironies associated with the towers east of the Rock Island embankment. Those monuments to the shortsightedness of Elizabeth's old adversaries would have closed in upon The Mayor if he had made the Thirty-fifth Street trek after the dedication of King Drive.

The Robert E. Taylor Homes were named as a memorial for the man who had been chairman of the Chicago Housing Authority board when the aldermen were obstructing and detouring and destroying the plans and dreams of Miss Wood. Robert Taylor was a Negro, but his attitudes were more white than black. He was the successful manager of the Michigan Boulevard Garden Apartments, which had been subsidized by philanthropist Julius Rosenwald, and he was secretary of a savings and loan association. He seemed to believe sincerely that the avenue he had taken to wealth and prestige was open to all his people. In temperament and approach to his position of authority, Taylor was very much like Mayor Martin Kennelly. Had Taylor fought vigorously on the side of Miss Wood, who loved battles and battlers, they would have made life miserable for the obstructionist aldermen. In the end Taylor and Wood would have lost, of course, but their defeat almost certainly would have made Chicago a better city.

Ultimately, the City Council was given a C.H.A. board responsive to the pressure of the aldermen and that board fired Miss Wood. She departed in August of 1954. There were whispers that she was dismissed because of unsound business-management policies, but everybody knew she had been brought down because she had tried to integrate Trumbull Park Homes, a project on the far Southeast Side. "The truth is," she said, "that the differences that have arisen between the commissioners and the executive secretary have been related primarily to the issue of elimination of segregation in public housing and the opening of all public-housing projects to Negro and white persons without discrimination. The policy is rooted in the laws of the state, the resolution of the City Council, the stated policy of the Authority, reiterated four times during the last four years."

The aldermen had largely succeeded in their containment policy. Most of the C.H.A. projects that were built after 1950 went up in the established Black Belt of the South Side and the new Belt that was unraveling on the West Side. To the tactic of containment another stratagem was added, one that made the C.H.A. a political ally of the Democratic organization of Cook County. This stratagem was meant to assure that maximum use would be made of Belt land cleared of slum buildings and to guarantee that a minimum number of Negroes would infiltrate the white conservation communities.

The projects would rise straight up from the clay of Chicago and then the politicians could tell the poor, "What's good enough for the well-to-do in Lake Meadows is not too good for you." Most white Chicagoans thought the idea was splendid. When lawyers, certified public accountants, stock and bond salesmen and politicians gazed from the windows of Rock Island commuter trains that brought them to the Loop from Morgan Park, Beverly Hills and Brainerd, they saw the progress of the construction of those high-rises for the poor and were assured that "the Negroes are being kept in their place."

There was more involved than the two-faced attitude of the aldermen. Building straight up was practical and economical. Every major city was emphasizing high-rise construction, even Moscow, as was pointed out in the July, 1968, issue of *Fortune* Magazine. The Mayor had to see that issue, because he was in it, under the head: "Mayor Daley Battles a New Chicago Fire." *Fortune*'s assessments of The Mayor and his works shift with the winds of social change, and this piece in July had been somewhat critical.

High-rise public housing seemed to be the thing to do. It was almost a worldwide mania. Negroes in the Chicago ghetto were almost as enthusiastic about the high-rises as were those Rock Island commuters from Beverly Hills. A few Negroes objected. One was the father of Warner Saunders.

My father was very anti-public housing or I should say, anti-Chicago's public housing. The old Urban League, the people who ran it prior to the ascendancy of Ed Berry, the present director [as of 1968, but since retired], were opposed to the high-rise concept. Ida B. Wells was a successful project because it was built on the Rosenwald Homes concept. It was a step below Rosenwald, but it had similar prestige and snob-appeal. They built a prototype when they built Ida B. Wells. As soon as the doors opened the first day, Ida B. Wells was a community.

The Ida B. Wells project, one of the first to be built by the C.H.A. during the administration of Elizabeth Wood, is a low-rise project that centers at 454 East Pershing Road (Thirty-ninth Street) in the old Black Belt. The development was built at the south end of an area which is historically known as Douglas. The community was named for Stephen Douglas, the "Little Giant" of American politics, who defeated Abraham Lincoln in their race for the Senate in 1858 but lost to Lincoln in 1860 when they ran for President.

There is a Douglas monument at Thirty-third Street between Cottage Grove Avenue and the Illinois Central tracks. The project was named for the black woman who had been an activist in race relations long before most Negroes had heard of W. E. B. DuBois and his militancy. Ida B. Wells came to Chicago from the South in 1893, and almost immediately distributed twenty thousand pamphlets in which she accused officials of the World's Columbian Exposition of being unfair to Negroes.

Although he understands the political motivations behind the Taylor project better than most Chicagoans, Saunders is willing to give the planners the benefit of a small doubt.

They believed they were doing the right thing in building the high-rises [he said slowly], but they believed that because they never consulted the participants. That's the accusation I make against the city officials today. They don't consult the participants. When the Taylor Homes were being planned, they never asked for the opinions or used the talents of the black scholars, the black architects, the other persons who had taken the pulse of the community and knew what Taylor Homes would mean for Chicago.

Everybody is talking now about dispersal of the projects throughout the city, but if the C.H.A. had dispersed the units through the black areas then—a few buildings here, a few there—that would have been far better than what we have now. I heard my dad use those very words: "Disperse them in our neighborhoods." Dad was very big on putting a project on the site of Oak Woods Cemetery, near 67th and Cottage Grove. Hip people were talking about that and it could have been done. The city has moved other cemeteries.

The cemetery remains. Instead of the garden homes in a parklike setting that were envisioned by Saunders' father,

Chicago has the Taylor Homes, a vertical mausoleum for the hopes of the city and, more important, of those who dwell in the project.

There are twenty-eight buildings in the Taylor Homes, which extend from Pershing Road (Thirty-ninth Street) to Fifty-fourth Place, a distance of almost two miles, and fill the space from the Rock Island embankment to State Street, a block to the east. Each building has sixteen floors and each houses approximately a thousand persons. The total population of Taylor, approximately 28,000, makes the project one of the larger "cities" of Illinois.

All but a few of the 28,000 are black, and the great majority are children. The buildings must have elevators, and the lure of the elevators is the same at Taylor as in the high-rises of the wealthy on Lake Shore Drive. Children love to play with elevators. This recreational outlet means that the elevators at Taylor, inadequate at best, are frequently out of service and often unavailable when needed by adults. By commandeering elevators for their purposes, youth gangs can waylay adults who choose to make the long walk up the cavernous stairways.

The "playground" for smaller children on the upper floors is the breezeway between apartments that serves as a porch. These breezeways were designed to be open, but they have been covered with heavy wire mesh to prevent children from falling to their deaths. This safeguard is not childproof. Toddlers have fallen from the breezeways, and it has been suggested that some older children have jumped to the pavement many floors below as their way out of life in the Taylor project.

The men and women who acquiesced in this way of life for others knew very well that children would live in the soaring ghetto. The men and women did not care. Nobody cared—the politicians at City Hall least of all. What mattered to them is that the Taylor Homes, the high-rising slums, constitute a colony of voters, conveniently filed in stacks.

Such is the memorial to Robert E. Taylor. "Very few blacks on the South Side would know now who Robert Taylor was, and they didn't know then," Warner Saunders said with bitter irony. "Most probably weren't even aware that he was black."

16

‖‖‖‖‖‖‖‖‖‖‖‖‖‖‖‖‖‖‖‖‖‖‖‖‖‖‖‖‖‖‖

The John

AFTER he had led the crowd, augmented now by hundreds from Stateway and Taylor, through the viaduct that supports the Rock Island tracks, The Mayor would have been warmed by the reflections of a glorious vista. Just across the narrow strip that is LaSalle Street, Thirty-fifth Street crosses the Dan Ryan Expressway. The pavement above Chicago's depressed expressways rises to meet a traveler, as do the roads in Ireland. The slope is gentle here, and at its crest The Mayor would have paused for a few minutes to look to the north.

Less than five miles away, almost due north, is the heart of the Loop. From this vantage point it is easy to see State and Madison, the intersection that is the commercial center of Chicago. Around this center, like the charms on the city's bracelet, are more than 125 buildings that have gone up since the fourth year of The Mayor's first term. In 1958, not quite eleven years ago, none of those buildings was on Chicago's skyline.

Not more than a few days before, Chicago's *American* had printed a full-page progress report on the changes in the central business district in little more than a decade. The *American,* which had been the only Chicago newspaper to endorse Richard Daley when he ran for mayor in 1955, always has been kind to The Mayor, and he is appreciative.

"More than two and a half billion dollars in new building

has been completed, is under way, or is projected in Chicago's central area since 1958," the *American* reported in its editions for July 29, 1968. "To put it another way," the newspaper explained for statistics-oriented Chicagoans, "it stands for 35,478,000 square feet of new office, commercial and public and private institutional construction; 12,224 new apartments, and 4,691 hotel and motel rooms."

Personal and professional modesty would restrain The Mayor from taking credit for all of that, but he surely is comforted by the thought that, after he is gone, citizens will say of the new skyline, "Dick Daley did that when he was The Mayor." The privately financed buildings were not raised by him, of course, but he unquestionably provided the leadership that inspired others to invest in the dramatic construction. He will be remembered for the skyline just as the subway system under the Loop is a subterranean memorial to Mayor Ed Kelly.

There it is, an area only three miles long and less than a mile and a half wide that has been transformed dramatically because "Dick Daley knows how to get things done." That's what everybody says about him. John Dienhart, a lively, septuagenarian newspaper editor who has been mayor-watching in Chicago since the first term of William Hale Thompson, recalled Daley's simplistic but direct approach to "insurmountable" problems.

"After Dick was elected the first time I went down to see him," said Dienhart, who then was managing editor of the Hearsts' Chicago *American*.

I had traveled in Europe quite a bit and one thing that always irked me when I came home to Chicago was that our streets were dirtier than hell. I had tried to make Mayor Kennelly see that this was something that disgraced Chicago in the eyes of visitors. Martin agreed that the streets were dirty, but he always argued that mobile sweepers were impractical because they tied up traffic where they operated.

Kennelly couldn't see his way out of that puzzle, but Daley did. "I've got that solved," Dick told me. "We'll put up 'No Parking' signs on one side of a street today and move the signs to the other side tomorrow. That way traffic can continue to flow without too much interruption while the sweepers are cleaning the gutters."

It was that simple but Kennelly couldn't work it out. Another problem Daley solved quickly was the lack of funds to purchase the sweepers. The city couldn't afford to buy them when he took office, so he arranged to rent them.

Dick also told me that he was going to surround himself with young, aggressive college men instead of the usual political hacks who filled the cabinet jobs. A lot of politicians didn't think he would dare to do that, but he understood the need. "The people are crying for services," Daley told me. Now every place you look in Chicago, you see the hand of Dick Daley.

The downtown area soon would have a building sixty stories high and another a hundred stories high. With the solitary exception of the sixty-story First National Bank Building, the new office buildings downtown have no architectural style. The First National, curved in from its base, gives the illusion of flight. It is reminiscent of a gigantic rocket on a launching pad at Cape Kennedy. The other buildings are dreary manifestations of the inverted-cracker-box school of architecture and do nothing for the imagination. The city contributed to the Design for Dreariness with its thirty-one-story Civic Center, built of steel that is guaranteed to rust. The architects insisted that the rustier the building gets, the more attractive it will look, but most Chicagoans would agree that on the day the Civic Center was dedicated it

looked as though it should have been condemned. Its drab-
ness is relieved, happily, by the sculpture that was donated
to Chicago, for humorous reasons of his own, by Pablo Picasso. Tourists who come to the city forewarned that they
won't believe the Picasso return to their distant homes not
believing the Civic Center.

Far to the north of this vista is the backdrop for the new
construction, the one-hundred-story John Hancock Building.
The Hancock, corseted by huge girders, looks like a rambling
steel mill of the 1920's laid on end. This is the building that
wiped out the fortune and the future of Jerry Wolman, finan-
cier and sportsman. When the caissons of the Hancock Building cracked, Wolman's empire collapsed with the steel. Some
Chicagoans felt twinges of sorrow for Wolman, who owned
the Philadelphia Eagles (and Chicagoans are very sports-
minded), but Wolman was not from Chicago, and the citizens find it difficult to work up a lot of sympathy for out-of-
towners.

The Mayor knows that the building is referred to as "the
John," but he also is sure in his heart that the voters are
proud of this herculean addition to the city. The Mayor
would look north to those glorious towers, the steel heights
which symbolize the accomplishments of his administration.
His pennants should fly from those smog-shrouded zeniths.
Many in the crowd would look back over their shoulders to
the high-rises of Stateway Gardens and Taylor Homes, the
pinnacles that are grotesque reminders of The Mayor's fail-
ures. Atop those other towers to the south, the flag of the
City of Chicago would always fly at half-staff.

There are teen-age boys and girls in those projects who
never have been in the Loop, although all their lives have
been spent in Chicago.

17

The Hall

ALTHOUGH it can't be seen from Thirty-fifth Street and the Dan Ryan, there is another building that would have been in the mind's eye of The Mayor before he would have turned away to continue his walk to the west. That building, tucked in between the $69,000,000 Civic Center and the $25,000,000 addition to the Illinois Bell Telephone Company headquarters, is where he works—City Hall.

The Hall, as it is called by the workers out in the precincts, occupies approximately half of the building that fills an entire city block bounded by LaSalle Street on the west, Clark Street on the east, Washington Street on the south and Randolph Street on the north. Completed in 1911, the building is a great gray cement blob, eleven stories high, that looks as though it might have sprung from the same mind that designed the forts at Verdun.

The rest of the building, that part which is not City Hall, is known as the County Building. Here the officials and the department heads of the Cook County government have their offices. Observers from other places might contend that residents of city and county would be served with a greater degree of impartiality and independence if the officials of the two major governing bodies that control their lives were quartered in separate buildings, but the arrangement is a tribute to the practicality of Chicago. The politicians of that early day recognized the fact that the party that controls the city almost invariably controls the county, too, so why not house them all in one place, thereby making it easier for the party leader to keep an eye on his underlings.

There is another advantage in the sharing of space by city and county. When decisions are necessary nobody has to go outdoors into the weather. Everybody is there under one roof. This arrangement has been maintained even though the new Civic Center is across Clark Street from the main building. A city or county employe can take an elevator to the first floor, ride an escalator to a lower floor, walk through a tunnel under Clark Street, travel to the first floor of the Civic Center on another escalator, board an elevator there and be about his business. Civil servants who bring their lunch to the job never have to walk in the rain or snow except during campaign time. According to persistent legend, some employes have found sleeping space in the bowels of the City-County Building and spend their lives indoors.

During the long years of the Daley administration there has been a dwindling in the ranks of the "City Hall type" that gave the building much of its color. They were men who had jobs out in the wards, but felt that they served their constituency best by spending as many of their working hours as possible in The Hall, preferably on the first floor. The clothing they wore was as circumscribed as the uniforms of the police and firemen, who are seen in The Hall in such great numbers that a casual observer is convinced that the city fathers fear that the building will be stolen or put to the torch.

The essential item of apparel was a wide-brimmed fedora. Unwritten regulations specified that it be worn squarely on center and that the brim be upturned all around. Acceptable colors were dark brown and pearl gray. The hat was never to be removed while its wearer was on duty in The Hall. In the unlikely event that a female politician should be encountered at an entrance door or on the first floor, the wearer was to bow his head stiffly and touch the brim of the fedora like a monsignor in full regalia acknowledging a blessing.

The cut of the suit coat did not matter, but trousers had to break at the lower shin with a resounding crash. Cuffs were expected to give the illusion of touching the floor without tripping the wearer. A sports shirt buttoned at the collar was recommended. Ties were not worn except at important inaugurations, and then it was mandatory that they be wide and garish.

In this outfit the City Hall type resembled a syndicate hoodlum, who, in turn, dressed very much like a police detective. There is no body of research to determine whether this mode of dress was originated by the minor politicians, the petty gangsters, or the policemen in "soft clothes." The three groups mingled freely in The Hall and could not be distinguished, one from another, except by F.B.I. agents and experienced City Hall newspaper reporters.

In fair weather and foul, through nine months of the year, the City Hall type also wore a voluminous outercoat. Preferred colors were black and light camel hair. The function of the outercoat was not to provide warmth in a building that is heated more than adequately at taxpayers' expense, but to give a man a place for his hands when he was not talking with them. Hands were placed between the outercoat and the suit coat, against the small of the back, with the thumb of the right hand locked inside the thumb of the left hand. (Lefthanded jobholders were permitted to reverse this grip.) Elbows projected straight out from the sides, and the outercoat billowed in the back. Once he had established this basic position, a man rocked backward and forward, slowly, until he gave the impression of movement without changing the position of his feet. Viewed from the distant rear a gathering of City Hall types looked like a regatta of Chinese junks.

When his hands were not tucked under his outercoat, the insouciant City Hall type picked his teeth. Those who had achieved the ultimate in *savoir-faire* picked their ears with a toothpick. The toothpick also served as an economical substitute for a cigar, but the experienced public servant was easily recognized as the man who smoked a cigar in one side of his mouth, chewed a toothpick in the other, and held his hands under his coat. He was obviously somebody who had been around City Hall for a while.

During the long years of the Daley administration, the dress of these Swiss Guards of the municipality has changed considerably. Even The Mayor dressed like that in his younger days. Now he is chosen annually as a "best-dressed" man and he is credited with increasing the style consciousness of his followers. Some City Hall types wear two-button suits. Hats, if worn at all, are narrow, snap-brim fedoras. Sports shirts buttoned at the collar are out.

Styles have changed, but the motivation of the City Hall type has not. He comes to The Hall because the mere mouthing of the sentence "I gotta go down to The Hall" gives meaning to his life, meaning that is missing otherwise. Implied is the suggestion that he must be at The Hall, on call, because The Mayor himself might want to consult with him. "I gotta go down to The Hall" probably does not impress wife, children, neighbors or voters in the precinct, but it impresses the man who says it.

He spends his day saying, "Hello, Judge," "Hello, Commissioner," "Hello, Alderman," "Hello, yer Honor." If a hello is returned, his day is made. If his name is mentioned along with the hello, his prestige is enhanced. And if he should get a hello, a mention and a handshake from The Mayor, his importance, for himself, is assured forever.

18

Career

In 1968 young men stood on the fringes of the City Hall crowd and waited in hope of a friendly nod from The Mayor. They waited and the more hopeful among them idly daydreamed of a time when they might be the bestower of the nods. Even the black young men of City Hall could have those aspirations in 1968. Carl Stokes in Cleveland and Richard Gordon Hatcher in Gary offered proof that their time would come. The Mayor understood those dreams. He had been a young man in The Hall when everybody watched for the goings and comings of William Emmett Dever, the Democrat who had interrupted the reign of William Hale Thompson from 1923 until 1927.

Richard J. Daley has worked somewhere in the City-County Building for so many years most Chicagoans are convinced that he has been there since the day after he left De-LaSalle Institute at age seventeen. It is true that he has been a long time there, but it also is true that he was a long time getting there.

There was a formula for success, much tested and proved valid, that workingmen and their wives passed on to their sons in those days. Dick Daley followed it step by step. First, take the commercial course in high school. Second, get a job. Third, go to night school. Fourth, don't marry the first girl you meet. (This step is easiest for the Irish.) Fifth, if you aren't too old and you can stand it, go to law school.

Young Daley, who wasn't afraid of work, found a job with Dolan, Ludeman & Company, a commission house that still is operating in the Stock Yards. Although he was reluctant to mention this phase of his career in campaign literature, probably because he didn't want opponents to call him a "Stock Yards cowboy," The Mayor is proud of his years with Dolan, Ludeman. He had to be up at 4 A.M. to walk to the Yards from his parents' home at 3602 South Lowe Avenue. In the early morning hours he was on horseback, helping to move cattle from trucks to pens to the ramps that led to the slaughterhouses in the noxious Yards. When the "roundup" was finished, Dick went into the office, where he used the skills he had acquired at the Institute.

Three years later, when he was twenty, Daley had saved enough money to enroll in DePaul University night school. Before he could become a student in the undergraduate school, he had to work for the academic credits necessary to be certified as a high-school graduate. Eleven years later he was graduated from the university's law school. The discipline he imposed upon himself would be valuable in the future when he would be compelled to play the politician's waiting game.

During the first few years of this regimen, the youngster continued to work at Dolan, Ludeman, and he also was active in the Hamburg Athletic Association, the sports and social club in his community. His interest in sports brought Dick into the orbit of Joe McDonough, the youthful alderman of the Eleventh Ward. In 1927 the twenty-five-year-old Daley was hired by McDonough as a clerk in the alderman's office.

Among the Irish storytellers of the South Side, the athletic prowess of priests and politicians is magnified with each passing year, but Joe McDonough was truly a prodigious football player whose exploits demand no gilding. Howard Groeninger, a veteran of Chicago's semipro battles and the archivist of the Old-Time Football Players Association, attests that McDonough was an outstanding lineman.

"In 1916 I joined the Cornell-Hamburg team, which resulted from the merger of two powerful clubs," Groeninger recalled. "Joe McDonough had retired from active play then and was our coach. And our waterboy was Dick Daley."

Joe McDonough had gone to Villanova College in Philadelphia on a football scholarship, but the ties that bound him to his neighborhood in Bridgeport were too strong to be broken. After a year of college Joe returned to the South Side to stay. In 1917, when he was only twenty-eight years old, McDonough was elected alderman of one of the two wards that would later be combined as the Eleventh. Big Joe—he ultimately would weigh 280 pounds—served as alderman for fourteen years.

Joe's selection of Dick Daley to be a clerk surprised some Democrats in the ward. Especially surprised were handsome young men who had college degrees and were the pride of large Irish families which controlled many votes. They were dismayed to be passed over in favor of a stout little night-school drudge who also happened to be an only child. There were few of those in the ward. McDonough was not concerned that Dick and his parents, Michael and Lillian, had only three votes among them. Joe knew that the young man would be out hustling to find other votes in the ward. Dick was a precinct captain at twenty-one.

The Democratic party slated McDonough to run for Cook County Treasurer in 1930. This was before Chicago Democrats had Franklin Delano Roosevelt to carry them to victory, but Chicagoans were disenchanted by the inaction of President Herbert Hoover and fed up with the antics of Mayor William Hale Thompson, then in his third term. McDonough won easily, and his victory made him a power during that time of transition.

As clerk-secretary to McDonough, Dickie Daley had

worked in The Hall, as well as in the ward office. When Joe left the Council and moved to the treasurer's office in the County half of the building, Daley stayed behind. He served as a Council secretary.

"City Council secretary" was a high-sounding title when dropped into conversation out in Bridgeport, but down in The Hall there were aspects of the job that had to be demeaning to a man twenty-eight years old. The secretaries were referred to as "pages" and "gophers" by some patronizing aldermen. The gophers were so called because they were ordered to "go for" coffee and sandwiches.

One of the powers of the City Council then was John Clark, alderman from the Thirtieth Ward in the fashionable Austin district on the far West Side. Like McDonough, Clark also had been elected to his first term in 1917, but he had been even younger than Joe. At twenty-five, John had been the youngest man in the Council, and he held the office that had been graced by his father, one of the first aldermen to be elected from Austin. In 1930 John Clark was chairman of the finance committee, the most powerful position in the Council.

Clark liked to say that he never had had a sponsor for political office, a claim that was accepted by those who do not consider one's father a sponsor. Whether the claim was valid or not, John was extremely independent. He also was extremely volatile. Although he had a neutral-sounding name, he was very Irish, and although he had a gentle, almost pious appearance, he could be violent. Clark became so furious during a lively Council discussion with William Hale Thompson, he threw a copy of the City Council *Journal* at the mayor. That was before microfilming.

John Clark, who watched everything that went on within and without the City Council, kept an eye on the secretary from the Eleventh Ward. John was impressed by the energy, efficiency and politeness of young Dick Daley. John would remember.

19

Death

THERE would have been much for The Mayor to think about if he had walked with this crowd, on this day. He might have reflected upon the fact that there had been only two Negro aldermen in 1930 when he was a Council secretary. Now there are ten. And as he came down the other side of the slope, leaving the Dan Ryan behind him, he might have caught himself thinking that now he was going home.

This narrow street, much wider in the days before the Ryan was sunk below street level, is Wentworth Avenue. When The Mayor was a boy and young man, Wentworth had been the historic boundary line—whites to the west of it, blacks to the east of it. In his book *Black Chicago—The Making of a Negro Ghetto,* Allan H. Spear had written, "The black belt of 1920 had clearly delineated boundaries— Twenty-second and Fifty-fifth Streets, Wentworth and Cottage Grove Avenue." The Mayor was eighteen years old in 1920.

Negroes have lived west of Wentworth for many years, but their penetration was made in the area south of Thirty-fifth Street. This movement was helped along by Wentworth Gardens, a housing project along Wentworth between Thirty-seventh and Thirty-ninth Streets. This project of row houses and low-rise apartment buildings contrasted sharply with the mammoth high-rises of Stateway Gardens directly to the east. Although their vantage point was much closer to the ground, residents of Wentworth Gardens looked down their noses at the tenants in Stateway, whom they referred to as "project people."

Those who lived in Wentworth had another reason to feel superior. Their buildings were on the site of the original White Sox ball park, which had been the home field of legendary figures such as Ed Walsh, Billy Sullivan, Doc White and Fielder Jones. The ball park had remained there for many seasons after the White Sox moved north to their "baseball palace of the world" at Thirty-fifth Street in 1910. The Mayor's beloved Cornell-Hamburgs had played football in the old park. It also had been the home field of the American Giants, a fabulous Negro baseball team. Satchel Paige, the folk hero of black baseball in America, had played there many times.

Just south of the project, at 3924 Wentworth, is St. George Church, the parish directly east of The Mayor's parish, Nativity of Our Lord; and there is a priest at St. George who almost surely would have joined the crowd walking with The Mayor. The priest, the Reverend William Hogan, has walked often with and for Dr. Martin Luther King Jr. The priest has walked at Selma, at Gage Park in Chicago, and on the sidewalk outside the home of The Mayor.

Bill Hogan, tall and burly at 43, is one of the oldest of Chicago's activist priests. He is a product of the white South Side, and he has been an assistant in Negro parishes since his ordination in 1952. "I volunteered for what was called 'Negro work' in those days," Hogan has said. "I'd been all stirred up by the talks given at the major seminary by priests who then were assigned to Negro parishes. I went to Holy Angels parish right out of Mundelein [the seminary]. When I got there all seven public schools within the parish boundaries were on double shifts. That's the Kenwood-Oakland community, where, in a matter of a few years, 13,000 whites were replaced by 80,000 blacks. And then people ask why the grass doesn't grow."

The home of The Mayor and the rectory of the priest are just a few blocks apart, but these men never have had time to express their feelings to each other. Perhaps on this day, as they were marching west, Bill Hogan could have got the ear of Dick Daley long enough to say, "A lot of people say that Martin Luther King failed when he came north to Chicago in 1965, but I don't think he failed. He exploded a lot of myths. What he did here led to the Kerner Report. He and his movement awakened the conscience of so many persons."

Perhaps, too, The Mayor and the priest could have mourned, together, for the one that was gone. Death would have been walking with The Mayor this day and reminders of death are everywhere in these environs. There is Comiskey Park—the present owner can call it White Sox Park if he chooses, but it always will be Comiskey Park in the heart of a true South Sider—where he and Joe McDonough had watched so many baseball games.

As soon as Dick Daley earned his law degree at DePaul, he moved into the county treasurer's office as administrative assistant to Joe McDonough. That was in 1932, when Dick was almost thirty and Joe was forty-three. The nation was in the darkest period of a great economic depression, but the future looked good for young Daley and for his robust patron. Everyone knew that Joe would go a long way. Why, he might be mayor of Chicago one day. And that day could be soon.

On April 25, 1934, Joe McDonough died of pneumonia. Joe died broke. He left his wife with seven children. In this time before the ornate "funeral parlor" had become familiar on the American scene, the Irish held their wakes in the living room of the home or apartment of the deceased. Bridgeporters were accustomed to the wreath on the door or the flowers in the cane vase on the outside porch, but nobody had expected to see the bouquet of death at the home of robust Joe McDonough. So many times Dick Daley had made the short walk from his parents' home at 3602 South Lowe

Avenue to McDonough's residence at 551 West Thirty-seventh Street. The distance seemed greater on those late April nights of 1934 as Dick walked over to be one among the twenty thousand who filed through the home to say farewell to Big Joe.

Cynics estimated that each of the twenty thousand owed Joe at least a dollar. If some had paid their debt, it would not have been necessary to take up a collection for Mrs. McDonough and the children.

20

Dear Helen

IT WAS an exciting and scandalous time. Chicagoans were sitting in on the preliminaries to the kind of probate court case they dearly love. David Shanahan, seventy-five-year-old bachelor legislator from Bridgeport, had died and well! Dave Shanahan, as it turned out, hadn't been a bachelor a'tall, a'tall. He had given up his single status on his deathbed, where he was wed—in the church, mind you—to his secretary, Helen Troesch, who was no more than forty-one years old. Dear Helen had worked for Representative Shanahan since she was a girl of twenty and had been at his side, stenographic notebook in hand, during the five terms he served as speaker of the Illinois House.

Dave's first cousins, Mary and Margaret Flynn, didn't necessarily object to his wedding. After all, as the Irish say, there's no fool like an old fool. What upset Mary and Margaret, maiden ladies, was that Helen Troesch was the beneficiary in Dave's will. Mary and Margaret had been given every reason to believe that they would be the lucky ladies to share the bulk of Dave's estate, considering that they were the closest of kin. The sisters sued to have the will set aside.

Chicagoans chose up sides. Some were certain that Dave was a typically sweet and bighearted old Irish gentleman who had decided to do something very nice for a poor working girl who had come to his office as a young woman and served him faithfully into her middle years. They were sure

that Dave had never touched Dear Helen. Others, whose
memories of the recent "whoopee" era had not been dulled
by the Depression, were sure that Dave and Helen had been
lovers for all those many years. Anything she received in the
will she had coming to her, they argued.

Helen was astonishingly blasé for a woman who had been
made beneficiary of an estate estimated at more than a half
million dollars. (The estimate was extremely conservative.)
Helen emphasized that she hadn't been especially wild about
the idea of marrying good old Dave when he had been hale
and hearty. She finally did it when he was on the verge of
shuffling off, out of her concept of what might be termed
sportsmanship, for want of a better word. Helen broadly implied, again and again, that she could take Representative
Shanahan as an employer, but that she preferred to leave
him alone as a marriage partner. Until virtually the last minute.

The trial was superb entertainment. Louis Emmerson,
former governor of Illinois, was summoned to testify on behalf of the Widow Shanahan. Louis told the court that he
had heard Dave speak many times of his intention to marry
Helen. A priest assigned to St. Bridget's Church on historic
Archer Avenue charged that an attorney for Margaret and
Mary had tried to bribe him to change his testimony.

While the trial was warming up, Democrats of the Ninth
Legislative District followed it, laughed at it and plotted.
The Democrats, particularly the young Democrats, were vi-
tally interested, because Dave Shanahan had been a Republican. Dave, who had worked his way through the Chicago
College of Law by delivering ice with a horse and wagon,
had been in the state legislature longer than anybody. He
had served in Springfield for forty-two years without interruption and had been a cinch to be returned by the voters in
the November, 1936, election. Then he made the mistake
that even the wiliest of politicians sometimes cannot avoid.

He died before election day—fifteen days before, to be precise.

Shanahan had been conceded reelection despite the fact that the magic name Franklin Delano Roosevelt would be at the top of the Democratic ticket. The Democrats found room on the fringes of the Roosevelt coattails for Dave, who had proven that he could work both sides of the aisle in the legislature. The Democrats had named only two candidates for the three seats available to the Ninth District. The Republicans had slated only Shanahan. Three would be elected.

That's all there would have been to it, but Dave's departure changed the picture. The Republican committee announced that one Robert E. Rogers would run as a substitute for the late Representative Shanahan. Wait a minute, said the state election certifying board, which happened to be controlled by Democrats. Rogers could not be certified. Why? It was too late to get the ballots reprinted. Rogers would have to run as a write-in candidate.

Over in the Eleventh Ward the Democrats had a write-in candidate of their own—but his name would have to be written on the Republican side of the ballot. He was Joe McDonough's protégé, Dick Daley, eager for his first try at elective office. He couldn't have picked a more opportune time in Chicago history or a more splendid place. The Ninth District was the Democratic stronghold of the entire state. The only way a Republican could have won was the way Dave, poor Dave, would have won. By forfeit.

As proof of how the Democrats brought in the votes, William Gormley was the choice of 49,984 partisans. Peter Jezierney, who must have incurred the displeasure of 109 constituents, received 49,875 votes. Dick Daley was given no more than 8,539 write-in votes, but that was much more than enough to defeat Rogers, whose name had been written in by 3,321 of the electorate.

If Rogers was surprised by his destruction at the hands of the Democrats, he should not have been. Rogers understood the way politics was played along Archer Avenue, the street that was immortalized by Mr. Dooley, Finley Peter Dunne's fictional historian and social commentator.

"Polytics," said Mr. Dooley, "ain't bean bag. 'Tis a man's game; an' women, childher, an' pro-hybitionist'd do well to keep out iv it. As Shakespeare says, 'Ol' men f'r the council, young men f'r the ward.'"

It was thirty-four-year-old Dick Daley for Springfield to sit in the old man's seat. And in time the July and December romance was given the official seal of approval by the Probate Court. Helen Troesch Shanahan was awarded Dave's estate, worth more than $850,000. Helen took her bequest and disappeared into the fastness of the forgotten that is peopled by principal characters in Chicago's spectacular court cases.

21

‖‖‖‖‖‖‖‖‖‖‖‖‖‖‖‖‖‖‖‖‖‖‖‖‖‖‖‖‖‖‖‖‖

The Musketeers

RICHARD J. DALEY, the "instant Republican," was not the first politician to be elected on the wrong side of the ballot nor would he be the last. On January 6, 1937, the House voted to allow Daley, Dave Shanahan's substitute, to sit with his colleagues on the Democratic side of the aisle. To do this the Republicans cut their number to 66 and built the Democrats' strength to 86 but the totals made no difference. The new man from the Eleventh Ward would vote with the Democratic majority whether he sat left side, right side or in the visitors' gallery.

The motion to restore Daley's Democracy was made by Benjamin Adamowski, a bright young fellow from Little Poland on Chicago's near Northwest Side. The irony in this would be recalled often in the future.

There was no comparing Daley and Adamowksi in those early Springfield days. Adamowksi was in a class by himself. Only twenty-nine years old when he made the motion that removed the Republican stigma from Daley, Adamowski had served in the legislature for five years. Ben was intelligent, able and combative. When he thought he was right, which was always, he would fight the leaders of his party as well as the opposition.

Stout and stubby Dick Daley was what political perfectionists describe as a party hack. He also was what political scientists recognize as a bulwark of the party system. Daley was neither colorful nor sensational. As an orator he left the impression that he had neglected his elocution lessons. But he did his homework when he was away from the floor.

Ben Adamowski was accustomed to being referred to as "a power to be reckoned with in Springfield" by correspondents for Chicago newspapers. Ben saw himself as precisely that and was determined to use his power. Ben was the eldest of nine children of Max Adamowski, a 300-pound Polish immigrant who had been a saloonkeeper before Prohibition. From that liquid base, Max successfully ran for alderman. After he became alderman, the elder Adamowski sold his saloon and entered the real-estate business.

Son Ben, who had studied at DePaul University, received his law license in October of 1928. While he was in school, he had worked as examiner of titles, a job that had been provided for him by Clayton Smith, Cook County Recorder of Deeds and an important man in the Democratic organization. After young Adamowski was elected to the legislature in 1931, he told Smith that he would resign as examiner of titles. The powerful sponsor said that a resignation wasn't necessary, emphasizing that many members of the legislature held appointive political jobs to augment meager salaries paid to representatives and senators.

"I told Mr. Smith that I didn't want to do it that way," Adamowski said. "I preferred to open a law office and start practicing."

With typical confidence young Adamowski rented an office on prestigious LaSalle Street. He knew where the concentrations of power were.

Adamowski never thought of himself as "too young" for LaSalle Street or for Springfield. In the legislature at twenty-five, Ben realized that his age did not matter nearly as much as the fact that he represented the Twenty-fifth District, then the most populous in the state. He did not sit there and listen as boy legislators were expected to do. He made his presence felt and, especially, heard. From the beginning he confounded his elders. Not all of them saw him the same way.

Elmer Schnackenberg, a veteran Republican legislator, described Adamowski as a "political parvenu suffering from megalomania." University of Chicago philosopher T. V. Smith hailed Adamowski as the "Daniel Webster of the West." Judge John Gutknecht, who had been a law professor at DePaul, extolled Adamowski as the brightest student he had taught.

Ben's loyalty to the Democratic organization had been dramatized by one of the most agonizing experiences of his life. In July of 1929, huge, powerful Max Adamowski had been stricken by appendicitis. "My father was only forty-nine years old," Ben recalled, "but after he went into the hospital I overheard three separate conversations in which men were talking about the possibility of their succeeding Dad if he died. Death seemed unlikely, but peritonitis, which wasn't rare in those days, developed and my father died. I was bitter toward those three men for a long time, but I realized much later that there had been no cruelty in what they said. In politics you have to think about such things."

Ben's next emotional jolt came when he learned that his brother-in-law, John Kaleth, intended to run for Max Adamowski's City Council seat as a Republican. "I pleaded with John to stay out of the race," Adamowski said, "and tried to make him see that he could have a chance on the Democratic side a couple of years later. I told him that if he would stay out, I would stay out. But he ran anyway. I was infuriated by his campaign sign: 'John Kaleth, son-in-law of Max Adamowski.' I worked hard against him and we won easily.

"The saddest part of it was that my mother, burdened as she was with grief, was brought into the fight. She had signed a letter endorsing John, and she was quietly angry with me because I wouldn't support my sister's husband.

Mother and I did not speak for some weeks. And then I came downstairs on my birthday, and Mother said, 'Happy birthday, son.' I burst into tears."

Although Ben Adamowski rejected a job on a political payroll, Dick Daley had to have one. Daley did not practice law, as did so many of the legislators for whom "going to Springfield" was neither more nor less than an interesting and profitable sideline. Daley would have been hard pressed to support his small family on a representative's salary, which then was $1,750 a year. Within seven weeks of his election to the legislature, however, death, kindly death, provided another opening. Michael O'Connor, who had been chief deputy comptroller for Cook County for twenty years, had died on December 9. Eight days later County Clerk Michael J. Flynn appointed Daley to the vacancy.

Under the Illinois statutes the clerk of Cook County is the comptroller. In day-to-day operations of the county government, however, the clerk, often a popular politician without training in matters financial, usually is comptroller in name only. The work is done by the man who fills the chief deputy comptroller's position, an appointive job. Dick Daley's experience under four county treasurers, whom he served as secretary, enabled him to bring unusual knowledge to the position.

Daley proved to be an able deputy comptroller and a studious legislator. His reputation for honesty and integrity long since established, Daley was treated with diffidence, if not with respect, by the con men, thieves, hacks and venal lobbyists who infest Springfield. Some of the more brazen grafters were sure that the quiet man from Bridgeport was naïve but they were certain that he was not dumb.

Even before the methodical Daley had decided to move into the ghostly footsteps of Dave Shanahan, the mercurial Adamowski had launched the first of his intramural battles, the first in what would be a long series. The Webster of the

West wanted to be Speaker of the House, and when Chicago Mayor Ed Kelly, the leader of the Cook County wing of the Democratic party, did not offer to push Adamowski's home-built bandwagon, young Ben turned away from Kelly. Adamowski allied himself with Henry Horner, the first Jewish governor of Illinois, who was grappling with Kelly for control of the Democratic party.

Adamowski did not become speaker, but he was elected majority leader and functioned in the void left by older Democratic leaders, who could not or would not go along with Horner's legislative programs. During Daley's brief service in the House, he and the pyrotechnic Adamowski spent much time together. They found a boon companion in another young fellow, Abraham Lincoln Marovitz, a legislator from Chicago's West Side.

"The Three Musketeers in Springfield were Daley, Marovitz and Adamowski," Ben was to recall. "We were very friendly. Together a lot. Being in Springfield when the legislature is in session is a lot like traveling with a professional baseball club. Men who are friends spend much of their leisure time together."

Although the young legislators were constant companions away from the floor of the House, they weren't always teammates on the floor. Adamowski, in revolt against Kelly, was Horner's man. Marovitz was a protégé of Jack Arvey, a powerful ally of Kelly. Daley, the rookie, was a member of the Kelly team.

22

Another Rung

IF THE Illinois House of Representatives had been a professional baseball club, to borrow Ben Adamowski's figure of speech, it would have been in a Class D League, the lowest classification of that time in baseball history. Early in 1938 Dick Daley was given an opportunity to move up to Class C, the Illinois Senate.

Again, death was the Great Political Sponsor. In January Patrick J. Carroll, the senator from Daley's home district, died. Dick was named February 1 as a candidate for the vacancy. He ran and won.

With plenty of evidence available to prove their case, critics of the legislature argued that the quality of the Illinois Senate was no higher than the quality of the Illinois House. Those same critics had to admit, however, that the Senate had an advantage in quantity. There were 103 fewer members of the Senate, a numerical fact that enabled the critics to keep a much closer watch on the 48 senators. Many Chicago voters believe that their representative goes to Springfield to hide until the next election. Some representatives have been in the state capital so long their younger constituents have never seen them. Senators are more visible. Senators also get more exposure, and this can be helpful to a man who has political aspirations.

Exposure came to Senator Daley but his personality was such that his last name sometimes was misspelled throughout a newspaper story. A few Springfield correspondents didn't seem to know that there was a Dick Daley. A few others were sure that he was Dick Daly.

Daley's sentiments were with the workingman, as they had to be if he expected to be elected from a district so close to the Stock Yards. This was a time in political history when all thinking Democrats, and nonthinking Democrats, were on the side of the workingman.

On May 10, 1939, Senator Daley, whose strength was with figures rather than with words, proposed a bill. Had it been passed then, the fiscal woes that have plagued Illinois every biennium might have been alleviated. Daley's bill would have imposed a 2 percent tax on the gross income of individuals and corporations. There would be irony in this too, many years later, but in 1939 it was a provocative proposal. The Senator from Bridgeport argued that his income tax would be a replacement for the state sales tax that came down so disproportionately then, as it does now, upon the poor.

Daley's bill was beaten in the Senate, the place where most of Illinois's progressive legislation has gone to die.

23

‖‖‖‖‖‖‖‖‖‖‖‖‖‖‖‖‖‖‖‖‖‖‖‖‖‖‖‖

The Sox

As HE crossed Wentworth Avenue The Mayor would have looked to the northwest to Armour Square, one of Chicago's oldest and most hallowed parks. The park system is dear to the heart of The Mayor because the parks were so important to him and to his friends while they were growing to manhood. He had spent many hours on the playing field of Armour Square. He never had been much of a ball player, but in sports as in politics, he discovered that the man backstage could become as prominent as the star in the spotlight. He built his image by serving as a manager or as a coach for teams that represented the Hamburg Club.

Lawrence O'Neill, an official of the International Typographical Union, lived near Armour Square during his childhood and became the mascot for the Hamburg baseball team. "Dick often came to practice carrying his books," O'Neill recalled. "He was either coming home from classes at DePaul or going down there. He was a very busy guy, but he took his job as manager seriously. He made the lineups, booked the games, and ran the team on the field during games."

Teams of the caliber of the Hamburg Club played for money during that period in the late Twenties and early Thirties. The players of a team bet on themselves but the heavy wagering was in the form of "side bets." These were bets by partisans in the crowd and it was not uncommon for a game to be played for $1,000 a side. If a team had a politi-

130

cal sponsor, he was expected to bet heavily upon his athletes. When the team won, the sponsor usually made a large contribution to the club treasury. When the team lost, the politician accepted the departure of his money with grace, which was more than could be said about the way he reacted to the umpire's decisions. O'Neill insists that the Hamburg Club once scored a victory over the legendary Leroy (Satchel) Paige, greatest of the Negro pitchers before baseball was integrated in the late Forties.

Whether or not the Hamburg Club had prevailed against the pitching of the immortal Satchel and his black teammates, there could be no doubt that Paige had performed in the larger park that towers above Armour Square. The heart of a man who came out of the environment of The Mayor leaps at the sight of this structure. This is White Sox Park, west of Wentworth, the home field of Chicago's American League baseball club.

Chicago has had two teams since 1901, the year the American League was organized as competition for the established National League, and the man who is dedicated to being "the mayor of all Chicago" must cheer impartially for both baseball clubs. His inner commitment, however, is to the White Sox. He and they are from the South Side. He and they are from "the Old Neighborhood." The Cubs belong to the North Side, and no self-respecting Bridgeporter would sincerely espouse the cause of the Cubs.

Long before 1955 and his first victory in the mayoralty election, long before a section of box seats were reserved in his name, Dick Daley had attended White Sox games with the regularity of the faithful. He loves baseball, loves all sports. But the Sox are something special. He can walk over here to the ancient stadium—it was dedicated in 1910, when he was eight years old—and bring with him his sons, his neighbors, his political allies and subjects, and distinguished visitors from other cities of the world.

He is not a "professional fan." He doesn't go to the baseball games to be seen. Being seen doesn't hurt his image, and this was especially true in 1968, when the White Sox were having a summer almost as distressing as The Mayor's. Eddie Stanky, the manager of the ball club when the season opened, had been deposed, and he had been replaced by Al Lopez, a courtly Spaniard from the Ybor City section of Tampa, Florida. In 1959, when life was simpler and Dick Daley was in the first year of his second term, Lopez had directed the White Sox to the only American League championship the club had won over a span of forty years. Chicagoans are not accustomed to championships in professional sports, so there was nothing blasé about the municipal reaction within minutes after the White Sox had clinched the championship in Cleveland. The Mayor's dear friend, Fire Commissioner Robert Quinn, ordered the sirens to be sounded in fire stations throughout the city. Only then did it occur to anyone that not everyone in the city was aware of major-league baseball. Some citizens, upon hearing the wail of the sirens, concluded that (a) the Russians had finally attacked, or (b) the world was coming to an inglorious end.

There is nothing political about The Mayor and baseball at White Sox Park. He does the expedient thing only when he attends games played by the Cubs of the National League in Wrigley Field on the North Side. Even then he enjoys the baseball for its own sake and smiles good-naturedly, if not roguishly, through the cascades of boos that fall upon his box seat section.

Now the Sox had fallen upon evil days and the aggressive young Cubs, managed by Leo Durocher, were in the ascendancy. The Mayor hoped that the Sox would straighten out and make a better showing during the rest of the summer. A better showing for Chicago. The Sox still had time. So did he. The Democratic National Convention was only a few days away, and then Chicago would prove anew that it is the greatest city in the world.

The Sox Park. What a magnificent location this would be for Chicago's new sports stadium. The city needed a new stadium if it intended to keep pace with Houston and its Astrodome; New York and its Shea Stadium and Madison Square Garden; Kansas City and its imaginative sports complex; with Oakland and Anaheim, California. Oakland and Anaheim!

The Sox Park. So many memories. Big Joe McDonough had played football here with the Cornell-Hamburgs. This park had been the home of the Cardinals, Chicago's pioneer professional football team, which long since had transferred to St. Louis to play in the sparkling new stadium there. The departure of the Cardinals was a failure for Chicago, a failure that left a scar upon the psyche of this sports-loving mayor.

He had seen so many immortal football players here. Ernie Nevers, Marshall Goldberg, Paddy Driscoll, Phil Handler, Charlie Trippi, Pat Harder, Paul Christman, Ollie Matson—Cardinals all. He had watched their great games with the Bears, the archrivals from the North Side, and had marveled at the wonders of legendary Bears like Red Grange and Bronko Nagurski. Long after Nagurski's playing days had ended, his name would have a ring of tragedy for Dick Daley and his contemporaries in Chicago politics.

24

Clarence

IT WAS coincidence of the kind that the fatalistic Irish collect and save and preserve as assiduously as autograph hunters, stamp collectors and butterfly fanciers cherish their trophies. Clarence Wagner, the most powerful and the most charming member of the Chicago City Council, had died in an auto accident near Nagurski's Corner.

The name of Bronko Nagurski, a larger-than-life fullback for the Chicago Bears, was part of Americana. For those of his generation and for younger students of professional football, the word Bronko was a synonym for power, fearlessness and virility. Places and things were named for him in and near International Falls, Minnesota, the home area to which he had returned after his retirement from athletics. This man was International Falls's primary tourist attraction. Motorists drove to the gasoline service station operated by Nagurski, for no other reason than to look upon this legend or to have their sons meet "The Bronk."

Nagurski was well known to forty-eight-year-old Clarence Wagner and to forty-year-old Donald O'Brien, Chicagoans en route, with their young sons, to a fishing lodge on an island in Lake of the Woods, Ontario. The men were of Nagurski's generation. They had seen him play against their beloved Chicago Cardinals in White Sox Park; they had read hundreds of stories about his exploits, and they had been in his presence at sports dinners and rallies.

At approximately 7 A.M. Wagner's Cadillac, moving at 60 miles per hour, inexplicably left the blacktop road at a turn near Nagurski's Corner, plunged thirty feet through the air (according to police estimates), touched down on a soft shoulder, plowed for sixty yards along the side of the road, struck an embankment and turned over.

O'Brien's eldest son, Donald Junior, fifteen, suffered cuts. Terrance O'Brien, nine, came out with an injured back, as did Patrick Wagner, fifteen. The right leg of eleven-year-old Michael Wagner was fractured. O'Brien escaped with arm, shoulder and back injuries. Clarence Wagner, who had been driving, was killed.

Few could believe that death had come looking for Clarence Wagner, filled as he was with the joy of life. Those who knew him preferred to reason that he had lost control of his car because he had been blinded by the early-morning sun or that he had been stricken by a heart seizure.

Many years later Donald O'Brien, a judge in the Circuit Court of Cook County, would say, "It wasn't the sun. It's hard to know, even now, what actually happened, but those highways up there are full of curves, and I think that Clarence mistook a small dirt road that went off into the woods for a turn in the highway."

As is true of most men who go fishing together, Don O'Brien and Clarence Wagner were friends. They also were neighbors and political teammates. Wagner, chairman of the City Council finance committee, and O'Brien, a member of the Illinois Senate, lived in the Fourteenth Ward. They were protégés of Thomas D. Nash, one of Chicago's most powerful and unforgiving political leaders. Wagner and O'Brien were members of Nash's prestigious law firm. Dick Daley had had his name on the entrance door to Nash's law office, but Daley's stay with the firm had been extremely brief. The reasons for his hasty departure are obscured by the deaths of many principals and by convenient memory lapses of those who have learned that forgetfulness can be a politician's most valued trait.

Whatever the reason, there was something about Dick Daley that Tom Nash was not willing to forgive. And now, in July of 1954, Nash was doing his relentless best to mine the political roads that Daley was attempting to capture on his way to the top. The prize at the summit was the chairmanship of the Democratic Central Committee of Cook County.

Municipal Court Clerk Joseph L. Gill had served as sort of caretaker county chairman since the resignation of Colonel Arvey in December of 1950, a month after the Cook County Democrats had endured disastrous defeats. It was expected that the aging Gill would serve through the mayoral election in April of 1955. This schedule might have been followed but for the fact that the party leadership had become disenchanted with Mayor Martin Kennelly. The committeemen had given the power to Kennelly. He had done nothing with it. Now they would take it back, and to do that they needed a vigorous man at the command post in the Morrison Hotel headquarters of the Central Committee. Dick Daley, first vice-chairman of the Committee, was expected to get the job by right of succession. Tom Nash had other ideas.

Nash, a distant cousin of Patrick Nash of Kelly-Nash notoriety, had made major contributions to the colorful legends of Chicago. Tom's law firm, Nash and Ahern, provided legal counsel for Al Capone, the city's bad name, and for Al's brother, Ralph. Nash and Ahern had defended Terry Druggan, a beer runner, against charges that Terry had dared to violate the Volstead Act, a most unseemly accusation to bring against someone named Druggan. Tom and his law partners had earned the everlasting gratitude of South Side sports lovers by winning an acquittal in court for the eight members of the 1919 White Sox team who had been charged with prearranging the 1919 World Series.

Nash had been on the political battle lines through cam-

paigns too numerous for him to recall. He had powerful
protégés and he had strong alliances. His lieutenant, Clarence Wagner, committeeman and alderman of the Fourteenth Ward, was the acknowledged leader not merely of the
City Council but of City Hall. It was said that Wagner was
running the city because Kennelly did not know how to run
it. The Fourteenth Ward was a stopping-off place for those
Irishmen whose dear old mothers spoke with pride after Sunday Mass of "my Mike, the lawyer" or "my Pat, the union
leader." The main thoroughfare of the Fourteenth was Garfield Boulevard (Fifty-fifth Street), and to have a home or an
apartment along "The Boulevard" was a status symbol beyond measurable monetary value.

The Fourteenth was the first outpost of those referred to as
"lace-curtain Irish" by less fortunate brethren who had
stayed behind in the Eleventh Ward and other inner en-
claves. When the lace-curtain Irish boasted too much of life
on The Boulevard they were catalogued as "bicycle Irish."
They are the Irish who make your ass tired.

Later, the Irish who had become "well-to-do" pushed on
from The Boulevard or bypassed it entirely to invade the
Nineteenth Ward, a stronghold of the WASP in fashionable
Beverly Hills. The Protestants who had dwelled in Beverly
Hills for so many years viewed the trespassers with displeasure and distaste and made their own plans for migrations
into Hinsdale, Palos and other western suburbs. As the
WASPs departed just a step or two ahead of those who had
fled from the Negroes (the hilarious aspects of this were lost
on all), an Irish-Catholic ghetto developed in surroundings
that were tasteful, conservative and almost subversively Republican. The major difference between Beverly Hills and
the old neighborhoods that were "going" is that there are no
taverns in Beverly Hills. This did much for the gentility of
the community.

The Irish were not without leaders in Beverly. The colo-

nists had been preceded by Tom Nash and another of his
protégés, John Duffy. Like Wagner, Duffy was several cuts
above the average for Chicago politicians. Duffy, an urbane
citizen who could become pugnacious when pushed too far,
was the committeeman of the Nineteenth Ward. He was a
native of the Fourteenth Ward and operated a florist shop on
Halsted Street, north of The Boulevard. He became known
throughout the Midwest as a sponsor of semiprofessional and
amateur sports teams. Although the Nineteenth Ward had
been solidly Republican in national elections, Duffy had
served as alderman from the ward from 1935 into 1950. John
was Wagner's predecessor as chairman of the City Council
finance committee.

Wagner, tall, bespectacled, witty and unusually sophisticated for a product of Chicago's political school, had been
elected finance chairman after Duffy resigned to run for the
presidency of the Cook County Board. It is one of the peculi-
arities of the Cook County election system that the candidates for County Board president must, in effect, run for two
offices. They are candidates for the board and, additionally,
for the presidency. In the 1950 election even the popular
Duffy could not prevail against the disaster that overtook the
Democrats. John was elected to the Board but the voters
chose a Republican, William Erickson, as Board president.

That election may have been the turning point in the fortunes of the Nash team and of Richard J. Daley. Had Duffy
won the County Board presidency and the thousands of jobs
that go with it, Nash and his young friends would have held
almost complete control. They could have done anything
they chose in either end of the City Hall-County Building.
Their man, Wagner, had power without parallel in the City
Council. Clarence was floor leader for the Kennelly administration. Martin Kennelly, quite unlike the dictatorial Ed
Kelly, permitted the aldermen to run the Council. Wagner,
in turn, ran the aldermen.

John Duffy and other qualified Democrats lost in that 1950 election. Dick Daley, the party's candidate for County Clerk, won by 147,000 votes over Nicholas Bohling, Seventh Ward alderman, and the most respected and rational Republican in the Council. In this election, as in two previous elections and one appointment, Daley had been the death-watch candidate. The familiar pattern had been repeated in January of 1950. County Clerk Michael J. Flynn, who had appointed Daley to succeed the deceased chief deputy comptroller, Michael O'Connor, in 1936, had died. Even after death Mike Flynn had a job for Dick. Flynn's job.

In March Daley returned from Springfield, where he had been serving as revenue director in the cabinet of Governor Adlai E. Stevenson, to be appointed county clerk. Never long away, even during his Springfield years—he had been Democratic committeeman for the Eleventh Ward since October of 1947—Dick Daley was back at the nerve center of Cook County politics. While he served out the unexpired months of Mike Flynn's term, Daley consolidated his power. After he had defeated Bohling so handily, against the trend, there were whispers that Daley had been the beneficiary of a "trade" whereby the Democratic and Republican organizations each conceded an important office to the opposition.

The whispers never have died, but they are no more than the romantic political nonsense Chicagoans love to place upon the graves of lost political causes. No Democratic candidate for sheriff in a county of Mississippi or Georgia had a free pass to victory any more valid than that of the Democrat who ran for clerk of Cook County. A Democrat won the office in 1910 and no Republican has held it in sixty years.

Duffy's defeat and Daley's victory had been eating away at members of the Nash group for more than three years when fifty Democratic ward committeemen and thirty township committeemen assembled at the Morrison Hotel on July 8, 1953. They had come to accept the resignation of sixty-eight-year-old Joe Gill and to praise him fulsomely. They would elect a new county chairman who would revitalize the party for the national and state races in 1954 and for the mayoral and aldermanic elections in 1955. Dick Daley was "in," according to the insiders.

Then Clarence Wagner arose and in his deceptively nonchalant manner moved that the committeemen postpone the election of the county chairman until July 21. Wagner's motion carried. Now the Nash faction had thirteen days in which to do something about Daley. Perhaps they could not stop him, but they were willing to give it a rousing try. Wagner would not be without help. One of his most powerful associates was Alderman Thomas Keane, a calculating man who would try to pick the winner. Alderman P. J. (Parky) Cullerton, who had lost the finance committee chairmanship to Wagner, had grown close to Clarence and would listen to reason.

For a change the battle lines were clearly drawn, as they rarely are in Chicago politics. This would not be guerrilla warfare. This was out in the open where the public could enjoy it. Everyone was aware that Nash and Wagner wanted the county chairmanship for one of Chicago's most dynamic and controversial figures. Their man was James J. McDermott, judge of the Superior Court.

"Big Jim" McDermott, his Gaelic features soft and fine, his hair white, himself tall and robust, resembled a matinee idol to whom nature had been generous. Jim had joined Nash and Ahern in 1920, soon after his graduation from DePaul University law school. He became committeeman of the Fourteenth Ward in 1932 and was elected alderman in 1933. During ten years in the council—he resigned in 1942 to become a member of the Board of Tax Appeals—McDermott used charm, physical presence, bluff and vocal power to impose his will upon that pliable body.

It also was written that Big Jim's big voice had been stilled

only once during a decade of thunderous and acrimonious
debate. That was on October 6, 1937, the day that the bottom fell out of his chair. Even then his admirers and his enemies suspected that the crashing collapse of the chair had
been arranged to illustrate a point. They thought it more
than coincidence that McDermott, chairman of the City
Council building code subcommittee, was listening to complaints from operators of small lumberyards when his chair
fell apart.

In 1940 Jim offered a five-word opinion of a city ordinance
that prohibited home owners and apartment building jani-
tors from sprinkling lawns during certain hours. "To hell
with that law!" McDermott said. It was in 1940, too, that
McDermott threatened to smash the cameras of self-
appointed vote-watchers who had said that they would record history in Fourteenth Ward polling places. On election
day the vote-watchers came but so did Big Jim, the vote-
watchers-watcher. There were no cameras.

Everyone was aware that if McDermott were to be county
chairman, the party would be run with an iron hand and
with an explosive temper. Political writers could anticipate
two stories, at a minimum, each working day. The first story
would be from McDermott. The second would be from
McDermott's enemies. The fact that a Superior Court judge
was actively participating in partisan politics upset some
Chicagoans, but it did not disturb Wagner, Duffy, Nash or
McDermott.

The master plan was that Wagner would step down as
committeeman of the Fourteenth. McDermott would be
elected by the precinct captains, thereby becoming eligible
to be elected county chairman. After he ascended to that position, he would resign as judge. And in the spring of 1955,
Wagner or Duffy would be the organization's candidate for
mayor.

Two days after Wagner made his motion for postponement, he drove north with O'Brien and their children. At Lake of the Woods Clarence and Don would leisurely plan their strategy while they fished. On the morning of July 10, a reporter asked Tom Nash about Wagner's reaction to the suggestion that he give up the ward committeeman's job. "He would be willing and happy to do so," Nash said. Neither the old politician nor the reporter knew that the man they were discussing had died.

Later in the day Judge McDermott walked swiftly through the sands of the Indiana dunes near Long Beach to a resort home not far from his own. He had been asked to tell Mrs. Wagner that Clarence was dead.

25

‹‹‹‹‹‹‹‹‹‹‹‹‹‹‹‹‹‹‹‹‹‹‹‹‹‹‹‹‹‹‹‹‹‹‹‹‹‹‹

The Myth

IF THERE had been contemporary art in the Roman Catholic Church during the 1950's, saints-in-business-suits would have been modeled after Martin Kennelly, mayor of Chicago. Many of the faithful believed that sweet-faced, white-maned, innocent-minded Martin was indeed a saint. Many of the cynical were convinced that Martin would have served the public better on a stained-glass window than in City Hall.

The forty aldermen, give or take a few vacationers and chronic absentees, who sat with bowed heads during City Council memorial services for Clarence Wagner on July 13, 1953, privately referred to Kennelly as "Snow White." The allusion stopped there, because students of the Council thought of four fifths of the aldermen not as dwarfs, Grumpy and Dopey and the rest, but as the Forty Thieves.

Martin Kennelly, whose inbred sentimentality sometimes spilled over into emotion, wept twice during the Council's tribute to Clarence. The realistic thought that ran through the minds of some as they watched Kennelly put his grief on the record was, He *should* cry. Wagner did all his work.

Robert Merriam, a sometime Democrat who was the self-appointed leader of the antiadministration aldermen and a self-propelled hopeful for mayor, hailed the departed as "an able and capable protagonist who loved a good fight." The language itself did honor to Wagner, because Clarence would have understood that protagonist was not a dirty word.

Friends in the gallery remembered with fondness one of the most hilarious moments in the life of the whimsical Wagner. On a night in March of 1947, when Kennelly was campaigning for his first term as mayor, Clarence left the Democrats to their well-planned stratagems and stole into the ancient Coliseum, where the Republicans were rallying on behalf of their mayoral candidate, Russell Root. Wagner's frolicsome intention was to make a speech on behalf of Kennelly. Although the Wagnerian lantern jaw and high forehead were familiar to any Chicagoan who could afford to buy a daily newspaper, his political adversaries, demonstrating typical Chicago Republican lack-of-awareness, actually permitted the mirthful saboteur to reach the speakers' platform. Clarence was about to stride toward the microphone when a Republican worker, who probably was a defrocked Democrat, identified the spy in the ranks.

After the eulogies in the City Council chambers and in Visitation Church on Garfield Boulevard, Clarence Wagner's last battle was renewed by Tom Nash and Jim McDermott. The allied Fourteenth and Nineteenth Wards expected help from the older committeemen who had fought along with them against the power of the mayor's office during the dictatorial days of Ed Kelly. McDermott was at his vituperative and bellowing best. "I know that they [the Daley backers] have the shiv out for me," Big Jim said, "but I think it looks pretty good for us."

McDermott and Nash looked again and pragmatically concluded that they could not hold the younger men who had been Wagner's friends. A dead politician has no friends. Dave Shanahan's people had understood that in 1936. Dick Daley and his allies, most of them stalwarts in the Kelly-Arvey organization, held the positions rich with patronage. Daley was the county clerk. Joe Gill was municipal court clerk. Al Horan was municipal court bailiff. With Wagner gone, the Nash-McDermott forces had no power base to build upon. They had no inducements to offer the ward leaders who might have been willing to listen to Clarence.

McDermott had been scheduled to be elected Fourteenth Ward committeeman on the night of July 20. That afternoon the Judge withdrew. His cause was hopeless. The next day fifty-one-year-old Dick Daley was elected county chairman. Big Jim had been beaten, but he never compromised with the Daley group. He did not "go our way," as a Chicago political expression has it.

With the passage of the years Clarence Wagner has grown in stature as do soldiers who have fallen in battle. He has become a folk hero to those who dwell in the land of Might-Have-Been. "If Clarence had lived, Daley never would have been mayor," they say.

Some practical politicians believe this. "The Tom Nash crowd would not have let Daley be county chairman in the first place, I'm convinced of that," Benjamin Adamowski said. "They had a blueprint that was perfect. The whole plan was to have Wagner as candidate for mayor, or John Duffy. The Gill-Horan group would have gone along with Clarence, because he was chairman of the [City Council] finance committee. It was the cleavage between the Tom Nash forces and what was left of the Kelly-Pat Nash organization that forced Arvey to give up the county chairmanship."

Nicholas Bohling, the Republican who has been in the Council longer than any other member of his party now serving as an alderman, said, "This is just my opinion, of course, but I think John Duffy would have been the candidate for mayor. The point is that the entire political picture would have had a different focus if Clarence had lived."

Some practical politicians do not believe. "Wagner would not have stopped Daley, but he would have tried," Colonel Arvey said. "We had Al Horan and Joe Gill. We had too many votes [among the committeemen]." The Colonel might have added that "we" also had Jack Arvey.

John Dienhart, the newspaperman to whom politicians have confided secrets for almost a half century, said, "Clarence wasn't strong enough to stop Daley in 1953."

The Mayor, who has not always managed to hide his irritation with the cult that has kept green the memory of the popular Wagner, has said of the Tom Nash rebellion in '53, "They didn't have more than four votes."

In the cold light of reality it seems probable that The Mayor and Colonel Arvey are right. From the opening of the battle, Tom Nash, Wagner and Judge McDermott fought a rear-guard action. They might have prevailed for a few more weeks but in the end they would have done no more than harass Daley, who had planned with meticulous care.

All who might have testified for the losing side are gone. Wagner died near Nagurski's Corner. Cancer took Tom Nash and John Duffy. "Big Jim" died of a heart attack on the doorstep of a sister's home a block from The Boulevard. Death frequently has favored Dick Daley with a macabre smile.

26

||||||||||||||||||||||||||||||||||||||||||||||||||

Going Home

McCuddy's and Danny O'Brien's. The old and the relatively new. These are the watering places across Thirty-fifth Street from the white-painted outside walls of White Sox Park. McCuddy's, with its white-tiled front, has been there since the Mayor was a boy. Danny O'Brien's, bright-face-brick façade to welcome the parched, is a local "in" joke. There is no Danny O'Brien. The place is owned by Italian and Croatian men from the old settlements north of Armour Square.

When the baseball team was bringing thirsty customers into Thirty-fifth Street by the tens of thousands, the owners of McCuddy's and O'Brien's could make a pleasant profit merely by being open on the days and nights that the White Sox were playing. It's different and more difficult now. The fans of the South Side, having lost interest in the White Sox, no longer attend in great numbers, and the word has gone out that the neighborhood around the ball park is not safe. The Mayor deplores such talk, because this neighborhood is adjacent to his neighborhood. McCuddy's and O'Brien's, however, are in the area that belongs now to the black citizens who would have been walking home with The Mayor after the memorial services for Martin Luther King Jr.

The tempo of his very own, personal M.L.K. march picking up, The Mayor would have sped past the Shields Avenue parking lot that once was not large enough to contain the cars that arrived for night games and late on Sunday morn-

147

ings but now is almost empty a lot of the time. He would have entered the eastern end of the viaduct that carries the tracks of the Chicago and Western Indiana Railroad over Thirty-fifth Street. This is one of the widest underpasses in the city and until Bill Veeck, the master showman of sports, had taken over the White Sox in 1959, the underpass had been one of the darkest in the world. Veeck had painted the walls and girders, and the city had provided the lighting to bring cheeriness to what had been a dank cave.

This viaduct is something else now. It is the line of demarcation that Wentworth Avenue had been for so many decades. The Negroes had spilled across that old border long since and occupied homes as far west as Shields. To the east of the viaduct is the black world. To the west, which would be beckoning just about now, is the white world. The Mayor, who insists upon being the mayor of all the people of Chicago, would have preferred that none of his fellow marchers refer to the vista ahead of them as "Dick Daley Country." The Mayor would not take kindly to Warner Saunders' allusion to "the womb."

Here on the other side of the tracks is the place where The Mayor's heart is. Here he was born. Here he has lived all the days of his life. Here he has raised his family. Here he will die. This is "The Neighborhood."

To call this section of Bridgeport "modest" is to understate. Distinguished visitors from other cities, their curiosity whetted by stories they have read of Chicago's mayor living in a simple bungalow on a quiet residential street, are not prepared for this. Chicagoans from other areas, including the ghettos and the slums, are shocked by the hodgepodge of coal yards, garages, taverns, bakeries and residences. It is as though the zoning ordinances for the community had been drawn by a panel of madmen.

There are the yards of the Virginia Coal Company. And over there is the Emergency Traffic Patrol garage for the Illinois Division of Highways. Back on the north side of Thirty-fifth is Lee's Towing Service, and here on the southeast corner of Thirty-fifth and Wallace Avenue is the George B. McClellan School. Named for the Civil War general who was the Democrats' Presidential Candidate against Abraham Lincoln in 1864, the school was built while the General was alive. It was eighty-seven years old in 1968.

When he was little Dickie Daley, The Mayor had attended the McClellan, briefly. Then he had transferred to the Catholic School, Nativity. The McClellan hardly had been a "new" school when The Mayor attended it, and he was sixty-six years old in 1968. The building, four stories high, with great wide windows, is something out of the comic-page panel "The Good Old Days." Some who have been startled by the decrepitude of the McClellan wonder why The Mayor permits this school, his old, old school, to remain in his neighborhood. Why, they ask, hasn't he suggested that the Board of Education build a new school on this site?

Those who ask are not in the business of politics. To replace the McClellan would not be the political thing to do when so many other communities have a desperate need for new school construction. How would it look if The Mayor's own neighborhood were given a new school? The last thing the administration needs is a new school at Thirty-fifth Street and Wallace. The very last thing. Besides, many of the children of the neighborhood attend the Sisters' school at Nativity of Our Lord.

The Mayor and his neighbors do not have a modern public school, but they are afforded excellent protection by the Police and Fire departments. Here at the southeast corner of Thirty-fifth Street and Lowe Avenue, The Mayor's own block, is the small, compact building that houses Engine Company 29 of the Fire Department and the Ninth District Station of the Police Department. The district is referred to not by its official number but as Deering. Long before The

Mayor was born, there had been a police station on Deering Street, which is now Loomis Street. When the police station was moved the familiar place designation was retained. Important guests, on seeing the fire-police building, assume that it was built because The Mayor lives up the street. It was there long before Dick Daley thought of being mayor.

Proudly The Mayor would have led his marching ensemble, its numbers increased now by his neighbors, south on the east side of Lowe Avenue. The simple homes, many of them old and many wearing aluminum or imitation siding over the wood that had withstood Chicago's weather for generations, have sunken yards and high stairways that ascend from the sidewalk. These are examples of the historic "Chicago cottage," so named because the mud of the streets in the early city made it practical to have the main entrance to a residence on the second floor. The homes are neat and the yards are green.

Near the end of the block, a few feet north of Thirty-sixth Street, the crowd would have gathered at the "Servicemen's Honorarium." This is the board upon which are inscribed the names of neighborhood boys serving in Vietnam and in other places to which the military services had assigned them. During World War II almost every block in Chicago had one of these boards—in most neighborhoods it was called an "Honor Roll"—but many fell into disrepair in the days of tortured peace and ultimately were removed or rotted away. That this one remains on Lowe Avenue, near Thirty-sixth Street, should be no surprise. Patriotism continues to be a virtue here. Draft cards are not burned by the young men who live on this block. No one here questions the propriety of the war in Vietnam except, perhaps (and only perhaps), the parents who remember those youngsters whose names are marked by a gold star. The Mayor supported President Johnson's position on Vietnam and would continue to support it during the Democratic National Convention, which was to open, a few days later, a few blocks from this Service-men's Honorarium.

"Honorarium" has a pretentious ring until one considers the meaning of the word. An old *Webster's Collegiate Dictionary* defines *honorarium* as "an honorary payment or reward, usually in recognition of gratuitous or professional services on which custom or propriety forbids any price to be set."

There can be no price for what these young men have been asked to do. And look at the names. Italian, German, Polish, Lithuanian, Irish. Those who live far from here believe that The Mayor's neighborhood is Irish. It is not and has not been for many, many years.

Now The Mayor would have led the crowd across to his side of the street, and he would have been aware of the possibility that some of the black citizens trailing in his wake had been among those who had marched to 3536 South Lowe Avenue on other occasions, for other purposes.

27

Skip-a-Rope

THEY came through the night, in July and August of 1965. Night after night they came, approximately one hundred of them, black and white, to picket the bungalow at 3536 Lowe Avenue. They were there to protest the policies and programs of Schools Superintendent Benjamin Willis. Usually they were led by Dick Gregory, the track athlete from Southern Illinois University who had polished his locker-room gags about black-white interrelationships until he had worked up a monologue that earned him $5,000 a week from nightclub operators. The white world's insatiable and uneasy curiosity about the black man's mind made black comedian Gregory one of the most-in-demand acts in show business. He was especially successful when his audience included a large delegation of conventioneers from the Deep South. The laughs came from the belly, even if the heart and the conscience of the listener were wounded, and the fact that Gregory's black humor was black in another sense sailed over the heads of many who were willing to give him a standing ovation.

There was daring and foolhardiness in these nocturnal processionals in The Mayor's own neighborhood. Some police were surprised that any civil-rights leader had dared to think seriously of demonstrating on the sidewalk in front of The Mayor's home. For years it had been said and believed that Bridgeport would never "go," that the residents of this community would not turn away, run away when the Negroes came. Neither would the citizens accept the westward movement of the blacks and attempt to compromise with them. Bridgeporters would stand and fight, and those days, whenever they came, would be the summer of 1919 again.

The stories of the race riot of 1919 have been passed along here, from generation to generation, just as they have been told and retold in the Black Belt from which The Mayor and his entourage would have walked. There are men here in Bridgeport, just as there are men in the Belt, who contributed their thoughtless hate to the horror of 1919.

The marchers, white priests and nuns among them, came at 10 P.M. "We had gone to Selma," Father Bill Hogan said. "We had to go to Bridgeport." The angry confrontation was expected on the first night. It did not come. And on the second night. It did not come. And on the third night. And those who were watching, the observers from press, radio and television, began to comprehend that it would not come.

Lois Wille, an excellent reporter-writer for the Chicago *Daily News,* was there. For the August 30, 1965, issue of *The Nation,* Mrs. Wille wrote: "The one overwhelming impression you get is this: Here are two teams of superbly disciplined, fiercely determined combatants. Neither is going to yield—ever."

Neighbors of The Mayor would assemble on their porches to watch in almost total silence. Community leaders and Eleventh Ward Democratic workers—most were both— were there to make certain that there would be no heckling. The demonstrators were equally mute. The residents surely could have driven out the pickets. The pickets surely could have provoked the residents. But each side had its reason for maintaining the peace. The residents feared the ugly publicity that would be brought to bear upon The Mayor. The pickets feared for their safety.

The Mayor, his wife and their children stayed indoors, blinds drawn, and waited.

Below the calm of the eerie surface silence, hatred and bitterness maneuvered like submarines in a wartime wolfpack. During daylight hours, on a playground four blocks from the Daley family bungalow, little girls played jump rope to this singsong: "I'd like to be an Alabama trooper,/That's what I'd truly like to be./'Cuz if I were an Alabama trooper,/I could kill the niggers legally." The singsong was a takeoff on a singing commercial that advertised the hot dogs produced by a Chicago meat packer. The little white girls had learned the rhyme from older brothers and sisters. All had been taught to hate by their parents.

And those parents are good people, good by the standards set by themselves, by their environment and by their churches. They are good people, too, by standards established by those outside Bridgeport who judge the good from the bad. These people, the Italians, Germans, Poles, Lithuanians and Irish, whose sons' names are on the Honorarium across the street, stick together; but they also understand, better than many who live on the Gold Coast and the North Shore understand, that they must be their brother's keeper.

These good people have one blind spot. Race. It is so deep within them it has become reflexive. They do not know precisely why they hate. Many would deny that they hate. Some go to Mass and Communion almost every morning—as The Mayor does—how could they hate? They go to Mass and Communion in the morning, and during the day they refer to Negroes as "shines." This is the vernacular. Of course, there are good shines. They are those who stay in their place. They don't try to move into white neighborhoods. The good people of Bridgeport would not mind living on the same block with a good shine, but the good people fear the shines who live in Stateway Gardens and Taylor Homes.

"Look at the way we take care of our homes," the good person says. "These are all old homes, but they look like a million because we take care of them. The people around here care about their homes, about the neighborhood. Why don't the shines take care of their homes and their families and themselves the way we do?"

This is an argument guaranteed to win the affirmation of almost every patron of any Bridgeport tavern—oh, a few smart-aleck college guys might come up with a wise-guy answer, but you know how they are—because few Bridgeporters would dare to make the point that the good people choose to ignore. The point is that an Italian, a German, a Pole, a Lithuanian, an Irishman can buy a home anywhere in Chicago, if he has the price, and move into that home without asking for police protection. A Negro cannot.

A few of the good people are aware of the weakness of their position, but they are as silent as The Mayor's neighbors who are standing guard there on the porches while Dick Gregory leads his motley following up and down, up and down.

Why don't they stay where they belong?

As is true of many Chicago communities, Bridgeport is very proud of its "melting pot" tradition. "Look at all the nationalities living here in peace," the good people say, forgetting again that the melting process was very slow and that the pot had been heated often beyond the boiling point by bitterness between the nationalities. Forgetting that families here were torn apart not more than a generation ago because a Lithuanian girl with lovely legs, an exciting bust and fair hair asked for her parents' approval of her marriage to a burly Irish boy with red hair, freckles and the beginning of a beer belly.

Everybody has melted here except the Negro. He and his sister have been kept out of the pot. That there has been no room in the pot anywhere in Chicago does not absolve the good people of Bridgeport. They have worked harder than most to keep the Negro out, and the presence of The Mayor and his family at 3536 South Lowe Avenue is an assurance that this neighborhood shall not change. The good people believe implicitly that as long as Dick Daley is mayor of Chicago, the black people from east of the tracks will not over-run Bridgeport.

The fifty-some Negroes marching in front of The Mayor's bungalow were approximately one third as many as live in Bridgeport. The 150 dwell in the southeast corner, not far from Father Bill Hogan's church, and they are contained there by the iron will of the good people. Lois Wille quoted Al Raby, a thin, agonizing young schoolteacher who burns like a black candle in the wind. "They wouldn't dare cross the street to the white section after sundown," Raby said of the 150 who live in Bridgeport.

Al Raby is one of the good people, too, and as such he is not above deliberately ignoring the point just as his white adversaries do. Raby knows better. He knows he overdramatizes when he charges that the 150 are in danger. White Bridgeport does not fear the 150, who are isolated politically as well as geographically and racially. White Bridgeport fears the thousands of Negroes behind the 150.

"If you let a few come in, this neighborhood isn't going to last three years," a white Bridgeporter explains.

28

~~~
‹‹‹‹‹‹‹‹‹‹‹‹‹‹‹‹‹‹‹‹‹‹‹‹‹‹‹‹‹‹‹‹
~~~

Bless Me, Father

DAN MALLETTE, the little priest who looks like a street fighter, also thinks like a street fighter and talks like a street fighter. He will forgive you your sins if you come whispering to him in the dark-brown box of the confessional but he will not excuse you for your social transgressions. The social sinner cannot beg for understanding from Father Mallette. The sinner cannot say, "Father, I tried, really tried, but it's beyond me. I've tried to change my ways, and I'm just not strong enough to do it." "Come back when you are heartily sorry," Dan will say, "but before you do, go and make amends to those you have offended. They must forgive you before I can absolve you in the name of the Father, and of the Son and of the Holy Spirit."

When one is immersed daily in the crucible of Chicago's race relations, one changes, outwardly and inwardly. Danny Mallette was plunged into that caldron, day in and day out for eleven years. Fresh-faced he was, almost sweet-faced he was, in 1957, the year he was assigned to St. Agatha parish, at 3147 West Douglas Boulevard, in Lawndale. He soon was known throughout the Archdiocese as the "Inner City Shepherd," an ostentatious designation that would make him smile sardonically in 1968. That was the title of a column he wrote for *Novena Notes,* a well-edited pamphlet published weekly by the Servite Fathers, who conducted a weekly novena in their huge old church at 3121 West Jackson Boulevard. The novena had been tremendously popular during World War II, when Chicago's Catholics prayed anxiously for peace on earth, but the novena and its spiritual purposes were no longer sufficient to draw the multitudes to Our Lady of Sorrows Basilica in 1957. Catholics still were willing to pray the rosary for their very special intentions, but not if it meant traveling through a Negro ghetto to do so; and, alas, the neighborhood around the vast church had changed. Our Lady of Sorrows.

Many who no longer made the trip to the West Side for the Friday services continued to receive *Novena Notes,* and they were captivated by the column written by the dear young archdiocesan priest. Especially appealing was the picture that ran with the column, a picture that made Danny look young enough to be an altar boy. For a year or so the column reflected the faith, hope and charity of the young priest, who was carrying the banner of Catholicism to the non-Catholics of the newer Black Belt.

In 1968 the face of Father Mallette was marked by lines of despair, and his soul was scarred by the wounds of barbarism. As he prepared to leave Chicago for "leave-of-absence" assignment at Fordham University, this thirty-seven-year-old priest said, "I feel that I haven't accomplished a damn thing in eleven years here. It's like being at the bottom of a pit."

Or a caldron, Father?

There are those who believe that Dan was railroaded out of the city, that persons of power persuaded John Cardinal Cody, Archbishop of Chicago, to remove this latter-day rabble-rouser from the hair of the body politic.

The Reverend Shelvin Hall, fifty-three-year-old black pastor of Friendship Baptist Church, is Father Mallette's friend. They fought together for so many dreary years against the injustices of life in Lawndale.

"I had the feeling that if you keep a man on the front line —what is it?—battle fatigue sets in," the Reverend Hall said slowly. "He worked sixteen hours a day. Danny lived sixteen hours a day for the people, sometimes twenty-three hours a day. It was weighing on him. Then when the administration of his denomination changed, things did not seem to be as cordial for him as they had been before. That began to weigh on him even more.

"No man can work sixteen hours a day, seven days a week, for nine years without wearing down to a shred. Dan probably should have been promoted up to a bishop or an archbishop or a cardinal or a pope or something, instead of being transferred."

The Reverend Hall smiled slowly and sadly. He has known the bottom-of-the-pit frustration much longer than Father Mallette had, and Shelvin Hall still is there, still going into battle, sixteen hours a day, seven days a week, forever.

Mallette left fighting. Of The Mayor and his efforts in the ghetto, the acrimonious priest said, "Daley failed because he is a racist. In bald language, I mean that black lives are not as important as white lives. It is built into our system, and Daley is a perfect product and reinforcer of the system. Daley is sentimental and can look at the concentration camp of public housing and say it's better than the rat-infested slums that were there before. So what? Can you tell an eighteen-year-old in the Taylor Homes that he should be happy that he is not a slave? Public housing was perverted by the system that Daley lives by into a system perpetuating serfdom in the style of the American 1960's."

There have been examples in Bridgeport of the inexorability of that system. For years the Chicago Housing Authority had owned a small site in Bridgeport, less than a mile from the bungalow of the man who then was serving his first term as mayor. In November of 1957, three years after Elizabeth Wood's enemies had taken her job away from her, the C.H.A. announced that this "surplus" site would be sold to an organization known as the Near South Side Development Associa-

tion. The Near South Side Development Association proudly
announced plans to build on the site twenty-six single-family
homes to sell from $15,500 to $16,700. Friends and neighbors
of The Mayor arranged the financing for this real-estate
coup.

In fairness to the good people of Bridgeport, it must be
said that this was the approved way of operating in those
days if a community organization was determined that the
C.H.A. would not build public housing within the domain of
that organization. The men and women of Bridgeport were
not the first Chicagoans to erect a wall of money to keep out
the Negroes. Instead of one hundred or so apartments for
Negroes there would be twenty-six neat homes in the tradition of Bridgeport. The maneuver was transparent, but there
was no outcry against it in Chicago's daily newspapers.

In 1961 eighty Negroes were burned out of an apartment
building near Bridgeport. Red Cross officials, seeking shelter
for the fire victims, obtained permission to house the Negroes
in facilities of Bridgeport's Holy Cross Lutheran Church at
3116 South Racine Avenue. The homeless were brought to a
hall of the church, and soon thereafter representatives of the
good people appeared in sizable numbers. The Negroes and
the good Samaritans of Holy Cross Church were threatened
by angry witnesses to Christianity. The Red Cross workers
quickly decided that a fire was sufficient terror for one night.
The Negroes were taken to another church, this one in their
neighborhood. The victory was complete. They had gone
"back where they belong." Eugene Dibble, a Red Cross volunteer, angrily said, "The mob won."

The Mayor proclaimed his indignation about what went
on outside Holy Cross Lutheran, but those who reported to
him evidently had not seen "the mob" that had incensed
Dibble. "It's regrettable," The Mayor deplored, "that a small
group of teen-agers should conduct themselves disgracefully
and cast false shadows on the reputation of the city and that

community. I know that I speak for the entire community in expressing our regret for this incident."

In 1962 a Negro couple who lived on neutral Bridgeport ground—they dwelt out of sight in a lumberyard—convinced themselves that nobody would mind too much if their five-year-old daughter attended kindergarten in the community. The white folks might not like it, but they wouldn't put up a big fuss over one tiny black girl. After all, the parents reassured one another, we're not the pushy kind. Pushy Negroes don't live in lumberyards. Accordingly, the parents enrolled the child, and the principal accepted her. A series of phone calls, threatening or obscene or both, convinced the couple that they had given too much credit to the good people.

This episode was contemporaneous with James Meredith's determination that he would rewrite history at the risk of his life. Meredith was trying to enroll at the University of Mississippi. "Meredith made it," Lois Wille wrote. "The little girl didn't."

In October of 1964, John Walsh, a thirty-seven-year-old white high-school teacher whose curiosity was surpassed only by his courage, chose to buy a two-family house three blocks from the home of The Mayor and rent one of the apartments to twenty-one-year-old Paul Jones, a Negro student at Loyola University. "I just wanted to see what the mayor would do," the teacher said later.

He did not necessarily learn what The Mayor would do, but after the Negro student moved in on Friday night, along with a friend, nineteen-year-old Ovalda Buntin, also a Negro, the teacher learned what the friends and neighbors of The Mayor would do. They would gather around the two-flat for three successive nights and throw things. Heavy things, sharp things, things that break windows.

On Tuesday furniture and clothing were removed from the building. These objects, lo and behold, turned up in protective custody within the walls of the Deering Police Station at Thirty-fifth and Lowe. Later in the day two white gentlemen from the neighborhood appeared with a lease attesting that they and not the Negro were the legal tenants of the apartment. On the fifth day after the original move-in, the new tenants celebrated with a house party to which the good people were invited.

There was bitterness in Bridgeport, but it was not directed against those who took the Constitution into their own workers' hands and twisted it to suit their concepts of the art called freedom. "That troublemaker of a teacher was fronting for somebody," the freedom-lovers proclaimed indignantly. "Where would a teacher get the money to buy a two-flat? The En Double-A Cee Pee must have been behind him."

The logic of this argument was irrefutable. Everyone was sure that the schoolteacher couldn't afford that building. A Stock Yards worker could buy a two-flat, or an employe of the City of Chicago forestry department, or a fireman, but not a schoolteacher.

There was laughter, too, in Bridgeport, laughter that was joined by whites throughout the city. "They" would never get into The Mayor's ward. Other wards, maybe, other wards, surely, but not The Mayor's ward. The people in Bridgeport knew how to handle the shines, and if threats didn't work they had plenty of political clout to keep out the undesirables.

There was something else about Bridgeport worth a big laugh. It hardly would look right if Bridgeport didn't have a Chicago Housing Authority project, so it has one at Thirty-first and Lituanica Streets. It was built on the site of Finley Peter Dunne's gashouse. The project, properly enough, is called Bridgeport Homes, and in the spirit of the times, it is integrated. One Negro family lives in Bridgeport Homes.

Father Dan Mallette was infuriated by the cynical laughter of his white brothers, many of them communicants of the church he served. He believed that the good Catholics of Bridgeport, the daily communicants and those less regular in their worship, would be better Christians if there were more than one Negro family living in Bridgeport Homes.

In collaboration with his friend the Reverend Shelvin Hall, Father Mallette prepared a complaint to be presented to Robert Weaver, then the head of the United States Public Housing Administration. The clergymen charged that the Chicago Housing Authority discriminated against Negroes. The priest and minister asked that federal funds be withheld from the C.H.A.

The request was denied, but the two clerical Davids of the ghetto, one black, one white, had put their projectile in the air and there was no way to stop it. The Reverend Hall and Father Mallette took their case to the American Civil Liberties Union. The A.C.L.U. filed a suit in federal court on August 9, 1966.

When tough Danny Mallette departed Chicago for New York and the campus of Fordham, he left the Daley administration with something to remember him by.

29

⁗⁗⁗⁗⁗⁗⁗⁗⁗⁗⁗⁗⁗⁗⁗

A Trinity of Mayors

WITH a wave of his hand, The Mayor would have invited his followers, some of them newly converted disciples, surely, to the west side of Lowe Avenue. The bungalow, the world-famous bungalow, is there at 3536, with a policeman on duty at the sidewalk in front of the house. In many Chicago communities, including some in which middle-class Negroes live, this home would house a family that was not quite keeping up with the Joneses. Here in Bridgeport, where the Daleys provide day-to-day proof that nothing is impossible for a neighborhood boy, provided that he has a good wife and well-mannered children, the home is exceptional.

There are no Joneses here for the Daleys to keep up with, but even if the family lived in another community, it would not be part of that social competition. Neither The Mayor nor his wife cares for the pretentious or the ostentatious, and their children seemingly have been immunized against the affectations that make the offspring of so many big-name politicians dreary and boresome. This, thank God, is a real old-fashioned American family, as they say in Bridgeport.

The Mayor would have had to leave his fellow marchers soon to get back to the decisions that awaited. But before the crowd dispersed he would have introduced "Mother," if she was at home—a likely probability, because Mrs. Eleanor Daley, the wife of The Mayor, prefers to be at home. Efforts were made by the Chicago newspapers to glamorize Eleanor, but she was too knowledgeable to fall into the trap of pseudo

164

sophistication. She is the kind of woman described by catty women as "oh, so sweet," by men as "a good Joe," and by parish priests of the old seminary as "a loving wife and devoted mother."

And if any of their five children still at home had been around the house this afternoon, The Mayor would have asked them to meet the crowd. The Daley youngsters, all seven, are "good kids" and "a credit to their parents." They are attractive, wholesome, bright and dutiful. Except for the occasion when a traffic ticket was issued to twenty-six-year-old Richard junior—he didn't say, "My father is The Mayor and I'm going to have your job"—the Daley children are in the news only when they graduate from school or are married. By the standards of 1968 it might have been said that the Daley children are underinvolved.

The family strives for privacy and usually achieves it. Because the Daleys, parents and children, do not make extracurricular news, the newsmen do not watch the family on a day-to-day basis. Mrs. Patricia Thompson, the Daley's eldest child (born on St. Patrick's Day, 1936), had been a mother for five days before the press learned of the arrival of infant Courtney Ann Thompson. The Daleys simply had not bothered to make an announcement.

After the introductions—Mother and the children would have impressed this crowd as they did all others—The Mayor would have had time for a brief, informal, off-the-cuff talk to the crowd. He is at his best in this situation, particularly if he has a microphone that enables him to speak slowly and softly, and especially if he can be assured that he will not be distracted by impertinent questions from what he refers to as "the media."

What might he have talked about? He could have told the crowd a success story. Such stories always appeal to the poor. He could have cited his Eleventh Ward, which is so close to their wards in place if not in time, and of the opportunities that unfolded for three hard-working young fellows

from the ward. In his modest manner he might have reminded them that the two men who preceded him at the
mayor's desk also were from the Eleventh.

He knows the history of those men, and he could have
started with the first of the trinity of mayors—Edward J.
Kelly, who was born on Finley Peter Dunne's "Archey Road"
in 1875. (Archer Avenue, which angles across the north and
west of the Eleventh Ward, just inside the Adlai Stevenson
Expressway and the Sanitary District Drainage and Ship
Canal, once was one of Chicago's most impressive thorough-
fares.) Ed Kelly's father, Stephen, was Irish, and his mother,
Helen, was German. Finley Peter Dunne knew all about
Archer Avenue and he knew much about the German influ-
ence upon the original Irish settlers of the area.

Archey Road stretches back for many miles from the
heart of the ugly city to the cabbage gardens that gave
the maker of the seal his opportunity to call the city
"urbs in horto" [Dunne wrote]. Somewhere between the
two—this is to say, forninst the gas-house and beyant
Healey's slough and not far from the police station—
lives Martin Dooley, doctor of philosophy.

There was a time when Archey Road was purely Irish.
But the Huns, turned back from the Adriatic and the
stock-yards and overrunning Archey Road, have nearly
exhausted the original population—not driven them out
as they drove out less vigorous races, with thick clubs
and short spears, but edged them out with the more bit-
ing weapons of modern civilization—overworked and
undereaten them into more languid surroundings remote from the tanks of the gas-house and the blast
furnaces of the rolling mill.

Out of Archer Avenue, storming, came young Ed Kelly,
gifted with the wit and the looks of an Irish father, the deter-

mination and stubbornness of a German mother, and the strength of both. Those were the only gifts he possessed, but they were sufficient to provide him, in time, with an estate that would be fought for in the courts. The eldest of nine, Ed found a job in the Marshall Field department store as a cash boy, when he was twelve years old. That was not his first job. He had left elementary school after the fourth grade to assist in feeding and clothing his brothers and sisters.

The "patch" in which Ed Kelly grew up was part of the "true" Bridgeport, according to keepers of local traditions. The historical name for the section in which Dick Daley has spent a lifetime is Dashiel. Before 1890 the road between 24th and 39th Streets that is now Union Avenue was Dashiel Street.

When he was seventeen Kelly traveled to the far South Side of Chicago to look for work at the site of what would be the World's Columbian Exposition, Chicago's first extravaganza of a fair. There was plenty of work anticipated. A visionary wanted to erect a 3,000-foot tower. Another who made no small plans said he would build a 400-story building. Plunging off in another direction, a futuristic city developer suggested that a suite of apartments under Lake Michigan would be a prototype for the dream Chicago of tomorrow.

Neither the lofty, the massive nor the watery idea was to be projected beyond the brains of the star-struck beholders, but there was to be a Manufacturers and Liberal Arts Building that could seat 300,000 fair visitors if anyone were to round up sufficient lumber to build the stands. Ambitious projects such as that captured the imagination of young Kelly as he made his way through the muddy chaos out of which the Columbian Exposition would arise. When he saw a crew of engineers at work, husky Ed shouted, "Do you work for the fair?" One of the surveying crew bellowed, "Work for the fair, hell. We're *buildin'* the fair, kid."

Kelly decided that he would become an engineer. He enrolled at the Athenaeum, the classical name for a Gay Nineties night school. Engineering might have seemed beyond the potential of a youth who had dropped out of school before the fifth grade, but Kelly surprised his teachers by his almost instantaneous grasp of the math, the formulae and the layouts. His mind seemingly photographed numbers. He was working then in the yards of the Santa Fe Railway. His job was described as "number grabber" and it meant that he read and wrote numbers of freight cars rolling past him at high speed. A good number grabber could read four cars ahead and still think about the pretty girl he would take to a dance or about the opportunities offered to a poor boy by politics.

Kelly's first job as an apprentice engineer was with a crew that was building the Sanitary District Drainage and Ship Canal. The Irishman with the strong back worked as an axman, clearing trees from the banks of the canal near Lemont, Illinois. In 1905 big, rugged Ed Kelly, an experienced engineer, caught the eye of big, not-so-rugged Robert Rutherford (Bertie) McCormick, a 25-year-old Republican who had been elected president of the Sanitary Commission. McCormick recognized Kelly as a man who could get things done. Both would get things done, together and in opposition. There was a newspaper in McCormick's future—the Chicago *Tribune*.

The shy, aristocratic, Calvinist McCormick and the outgoing, lower-class, Catholic Kelly organized a mutual admiration society. Both were physical giants in their time. McCormick, 6 feet 4, and 215 pounds, was believed to be capable of felling a man with a punch. Kelly, 6 feet 2, and 190 pounds, was known to be capable of knocking down an opponent. In 1908 Kelly, who had been a Democratic committeeman when he was twenty-one years old, ran for trustee of the Sanitary District. His opponent was Robert R. McCormick. Bertie won, but this "go" in the political arena did not diminish the affection between the two big men.

Kelly, who became chief engineer of the Sanitary District in 1920, was to remain with the District for thirty-nine years. Always active politically, Big Ed was more effective when he campaigned for others. He ran for office frequently, but always was defeated. Then in 1933, when he was fifty-seven years old, the most important office in Chicago opened for him. He would be mayor and he would not have to run. The position would be given to him.

The benefactor was seventy-year-old Patrick Nash, who had been brought out of retirement in 1931 by Anton Cermak, the Bohemiam mule skinner from the strip mines of Braidwood, Illinois. Cermak, victor over bombastic William Hale Thompson in the 1931 mayoralty, did not choose to function as county chairman and asked Pat Nash to take over as administrator of the Democratic organization of Cook County. Pat was willing.

Despite the herculean efforts of McCormick and Kelly to build the Drainage Canal that provided the citizenry with water fit to drink, it still was possible in 1932 for Chicagoans to contract amoebic dysentery. That was what happened to fifty-nine-year-old Tony Cermak when sewage seeped into the water supply of the fashionable hotel in which he lived on South Michigan Avenue. Weakened by the bug, Cermak traveled to Miami Beach to recuperate early in 1933. While he was there Chicago's mayor was summoned to a mammoth reception for the new Democratic President-elect, Franklin Delano Roosevelt.

Cermak belonged at that reception on February 15. Anton was the kingmaker who had delivered the vital Illinois delegation to Governor Roosevelt of New York during the Democratic National Convention in the Chicago Stadium in June of 1932. When Roosevelt arrived at the Chicago airport after a flight from Albany, the nominee was transported to the Stadium by Mayor Cermak. Roosevelt was indebted to Cermak as John F. Kennedy one day would be indebted to Richard Daley.

It was to be a great day for Chicago in Miami's waterfront park. There would be a chance during this gala for the mayor to invite the President to attend Chicago's Century of Progress Exposition, which was to open late in the spring. The fair would celebrate the one hundredth anniversary of the Town of Chicago; it would recall the fortieth anniversary of the World's Columbian Exposition, and it would restore the spirits of millions who were struggling through the economic depression.

Cermak was moving toward the car of the crippled President-elect just as one Giuseppe Zangara dashed from the crowd to fire revolver shots at close range. Cermak's body stopped a bullet that might have struck Roosevelt, and the severely wounded mayor fell into the arms of F.D.R. Tony Cermak lingered until March 6. His elaborate funeral was in the Chicago Stadium, scene of his consummate triumph the previous June.

Romanticists believed that Zangara intended to kill Roosevelt, a thought abhorrent to most Americans, who were sure that a President of the United States never again would be murdered in cold blood. Cynics said that Zangara was the hired gunman of irate Prohibitionists, who were out to get Cermak, one of the most ardent "wets" in the nation. Realists insisted that the fanatical Zangara didn't have any preference as to targets.

Chicago's preferred legend is that when Roosevelt came to Cermak's bedside soon after the shooting, the mayor said, "I'm glad it was me, instead of you." Some veteran newspapermen argue that the quote came out of the lively imagination of John Dienhart, Cermak's confidant who scooped the nation with deathbed interviews, but Dienhart has no intention of revising legend. Thirty-five years later Dienhart continues to harbor the suspicion that Zangara was a paid killer, hired by the Syndicate. This supposition is scorned by students of the era who categorize Cermak as an ally of the Ca-

pone syndicate, but in the convoluted politics-crime relation-
ships of that violent time, anything was possible. Dienhart's
theory is reasonable to those who remember that in December of 1932 Frank Nitti, a leader in the Capone apparatus,
had been wounded three times. Nitti's assailant was not another gangster, in the grand tradition, but a Chicago police
sergeant. Everybody who patronized the gambling rooms in
the Loop had heard the rumor: The word had gone out from
City Hall that the tough cops were to frighten the mobsters
across the city limits.

Whatever the explanation, there can be no doubt that
had it been "you" instead of "me," the course of world history
would have been altered. A generation later, in Dallas, there
was no Tony Cermak to step into the assassin's field of fire.

With Tony gone, Pat Nash could have been mayor simply
by nodding his head, but the old man said, "It's not for me,
boys. I'd rather stay where I am, but I have the man for the
job."

Everybody in city and county politics knew the man Nash
had in mind. Big Ed Kelly. The friendship of Nash and Kelly
was deep rooted. Ed was chief engineer for the Sanitary District, a body which spent millions on sewers. Pat and his
brother, Dick, were sewer contractors.

As it usually does, violence provided a precedent for selection of an interim mayor of Chicago. During the World's Columbian Exposition of 1893, the city's first world fair, a disgruntled political job seeker was granted an audience by
Mayor Carter Harrison Sr. in the latter's home on Ashland
Avenue. Minutes later Harrison, who was serving his fifth
two-year term, was shot and mortally wounded.

On November 6, nine days after the assassination, members of the City Council elected George Swift mayor pro
tem. A special mayoralty election was set for December 19,
and the Democrats regained the mayor's office when Swift
was defeated by John Patrick Hopkins.

As far as Pat Nash was concerned, and he was totally concerned, that 1893 precedent had gone quite far enough. He would borrow from it, but it hardly suited his purposes. Ed Kelly was not a member of the City Council and there were two years remaining on Cermak's four-year term.

"I'll tell you what we'll do, boys," Nash said in conference with the Democratic aldermen, "we'll elect Frank Corr as acting mayor, and then we'll get the state law changed."

Corr, best known even in his own Seventeenth Ward as the sponsor of a rousing local football team, was elected by his fellow aldermen on March 14, eight days after Cermak died. Good old Frank served for one day less than a month. A bill was introduced in the legislature at Springfield that would make it possible (and legal) for the City Council to elect an outsider. One of the co-sponsors of the legislation was Benjamin Adamowski, majority leader in the House. Back in the City Council Ed Kelly was nominated to be acting mayor by Alderman Jack Arvey of the Twenty-fourth Ward. The debate that followed was stormy and bitter, but Pat Nash was not concerned. He understood that some of the "boys" on the other side wanted to get their names in the papers. He knew, too, that Kelly could not lose.

The schoolteachers of Chicago had been paid only once during the nine months preceding Kelly's election. Big Ed quickly found cash to provide a payroll for the teachers and within a year he had the city on a paying basis. As Robert Rutherford McCormick had observed many years before, Kelly knew how to get things done.

The White Knight

"HE's no saint," Chicago's citizens said of Ed Kelly as they attempted to explain their affection for him. And they loved him, truly loved him for a very long time. What appealed to them was that he was almost as villainous as he was virtuous. They understood him, and he understood them. He gave them the type of mayor they wanted, the kind of town they wanted.

Chicagoans always had preferred a Carter Harrison Sr., who advocated a "wide-open town"; a Carter Harrison Jr., who promised "the fullest measure of personal liberty consistent with the maintenance of public order"; a William Hale Thompson, who echoed the bluntness of Harrison the Elder. Those three had been elected and reelected. Big Ed Kelly, splendid as a LaSalle Street banker, turned his soft, warm gaze upon the citizenry and boasted of their "liberal town."

"Liberal" did not mean what liberals thought it meant. "Liberal" meant that there were lavish gambling rooms downtown within short walking distance of City Hall. "Liberal" meant that every ward had one completely equipped *handbook* (an ornate establishment, with wall sheets, with announcers giving vivid descriptions of the races and with armed guards at the doors) and several miniature books, which were nothing more than phone-in operations in milk stores. "Liberal" meant houses of prostitution out on South

173

Federal Street and strippers on South State Street giving their all for conventioneers. "Liberal" meant political control of the Police Department. And "liberal" meant votes in great numbers for the organization.

When Ed Kelly made his first official run for mayor in 1935, his liberality was liberally rewarded. The voters returned him to City Hall with 798,150 votes as compared to 166,571 for his Republican opponent, Emil Wetten. Some civic groups were offended by Kelly's incredible plurality, but if the Democrats actually stole votes in that election, they stole them just to keep in practice. There weren't many Republicans in Chicago that April.

Big Ed had his vote total on his license plate in 1936, and although he could not be expected to be returned to office by such a staggering margin, he won comfortably in the elections of 1939 and 1943. He had served for thirteen years, longer than any mayor in Chicago history, when Jack Arvey and other powers in the party came to the conclusion that the Kelly magic had run out.

Perhaps the problem was that as he moved into his seventies and saw the years dwindling down, Edward Joseph Kelly became liberal in the fullest sense of the word. Arvey had said it best: "Roosevelt made a liberal out of Kelly, an inflamed liberal."

Jack Arvey was a liberal, too, within his definition of the term, and during his war service in the South Pacific, Colonel Arvey had publicly vowed that if he returned to Chicago he would devote the balance of his life to serving humanity.

While he was working for humanity, Arvey also had to perform on behalf of the Democratic party of Cook County, and in 1946 the decisions were his to make in partnership with Kelly. Since the death of Pat Nash in October of 1943, Arvey had been county chairman.

"You have to put this in perspective," Arvey was to say twenty-three years later. "Kelly had taken a firm stand on open occupancy, which was a daring thing to do in those days."

The iconoclastic Ben Adamowski, also looking back, said, "I think Kelly could have been reelected in 1947. If he had had Pat Nash with him then, Kelly probably would have run and won. But Kelly was an easy guy to frighten."

Arvey tends now to agree with Adamowski. "In retrospect, I think now that Kelly would have won. Considering the Republican candidate and the good will that had accrued to Kelly during the war years, through the Servicemen's Centers, he would have won. It would have been a close election."

Dismayed by the very thought of a close election, party leaders Arvey, Joe Gill and Al Horan prevailed upon Mayor Kelly to step down. To replace him they tapped another self-made man from the Eleventh Ward, Martin H. Kennelly.

At the beginning of life, little Marty Kennelly was granted an advantage that had been denied to little Eddie Kelly. Instead of being the eldest of nine poverty-stricken children, as Kelly had been, Marty was the youngest of five poverty-stricken children. Jeremiah Kennelly, the father, had died when Marty was two years old, but Margaret Kennelly, whom her son loved to describe as a "down-East Yankee," was an unusually strong person.

Marty was born on August 11, 1887, at 3035 Poplar Street, in a house that would be described in campaign literature as "a cottage virtually in the shadow of the packing plants." Poplar is one of fifteen truncated streets that are unknown to millions of Chicagoans because these streets begin and end in the Eleventh Ward. The names—Lock, Broad, Arch and Quarry—were familiar to Finley Peter Dunne and his Mr. Dooley when the streets carried traffic to the Drainage Canal. They were important then, but they are part of history now, and there is no Mr. Dooley to sing their meaning to the Hennessys of the world.

The Kennellys, like the Kellys, were "true" Bridgeporters in a time when the political sector that later became the Eleventh Ward was two wards—the Fourth and the Fifth— with no fewer than four aldermen (two to a ward) in the City Council. An old-timer who insists that his memory is infallible said, "The Fourth Ward ran to the river on the north, and west to just the other side of Deering Street where Frank McDermott's brewery was." The dominant Democrat in that old Fourth Ward was a colorful citizen named James "Bull" Dailey.

By the time "the baby," Martin, was ready to be enrolled in the Holden Elementary School at 1164 West Thirty-first Street, Margaret Kennelly and her older children had won the important battles. The family could allow Marty the luxury of finishing grammar school. Only then did he have to take a full-time job, and following the pattern of Eddie Kelly, Marty found work with Marshall Field. Instead of working in the department store downtown, Kennelly went to the wholesale house west of the Loop, where he was paid two dollars a week.

Fourteen months later young Kennelly did something that most boys from his environment could not or would not do. He quit his job and went back to school. He wanted to continue his education at DeLaSalle Institute, which his biography would describe as "the poor boys' college," but before he left the employ of Marshall Field, Martin asked for and received a note stating that he had been a dutiful and conscientious worker. He would save that note.

He took the business course at DeLaSalle, as Richard Daley would, some years later, and when Kennelly was graduated he was announced as a winner of a Christian Brothers medal for scholarship. The medal did not hurt his cause when he applied for a job at the Becklenberg Warehouse, Sixty-third Street and Wentworth Avenue. Marty was hired as an office boy, which was precisely what he and his mother had in mind for him, but the youngster from Poplar Street wanted to do more than file correspondence and move messages. He spent as much time as possible in the vast, high-ceilinged building behind the office. He had decided that he would be a warehouser.

Marty's mother could say in truth that her son was a "big man" with Becklenberg when America's entry into World War I interrupted the careers of many young men from the Eleventh Ward. Kennelly went into the Army as a private, served in France with the Supply Corps and was discharged as a captain. Years later he was credited with originating the zone system for Supply. If this was true, one wonders why the West Point graduates who were paid to think about such things had to wait for a product of Poplar Street to draw lines on a map for them.

Whatever his contribution to American success in the Great War, Captain Kennelly was thinking thoughts of his own along about the time that Colonel Robert McCormick and one of his cousins were making postwar plans. McCormick's scheme was to start a newspaper in New York City. Kennelly's dream was to have his own warehouse business in Chicago. Both local boys made good.

In partnership with his cousin, Joseph Patterson, McCormick started the New York *Daily News.* In association with his two older brothers, Martin established the Kennelly warehouse in 1919, the year that Chicago's South Side was being ripped by racial hate. By 1923 the Kennellys had sufficient capital to buy out Werner Brothers, a widely known firm, which had a warehouse near Wrigley Field, the Cubs' ball park on the North Side.

By 1923 Martin Kennelly also had sufficient political influence to obtain the contract for storage of the city's ballot boxes and voting booths between elections. Martin had something else which enabled him to land a moving job much more prestigious than a city contract. The trustees of

the Field Museum of Natural History were accepting bids
for the moving of priceless exhibits from the museum's old
building in Jackson Park to a new structure in Grant Park.
Martin searched in his files, found what he sought, and en-
closed it with his bid. The enclosure was the "well done"
note he had been given when he left Field's wholesale house
in 1903. To Stanley Field, the man who would make the decision, Kennelly wrote, "This is what you thought of me
then."

The Kennelly brothers were awarded the job, and they
moved the exhibit so efficiently and gently, Stanley Field was
moved to write another note of commendation.

Almost six feet tall, 190 pounds and handsome in a baby-
faced way, Martin was the answer to the prayers that were
said in front of the vigil lights of St. Bridget's Church by the
mothers of so many marriageable daughters. What's more,
Dear Lord, he's well-to-do and could provide a fine home
and educations for Mary's children. But Marty had neither
the time nor the inclination for matrimony. He loved his
warehouse as a pastor loved his church, and he shared a
hobby with many of the clergy—politics.

Kennelly worked in politics for others, rather than for himself, and although he was a Democrat, he usually was
aligned with the Democrats who were fighting against Kelly-
Nash or Kelly-Arvey. In 1939 he had been a major financial
backer of his great friend, State's Attorney Thomas Courtney, and managed Courtney's campaign against Mayor Kelly
in the primary.

Martin was perfect for 1947. Invariably cautious to the
point of timidity, Kennelly did not agree to run for mayor
until Arvey assured him that there would be no intraparty
feuding or fussing. The Republicans, suffering from their traditional myopia, cooperated beyond Arvey's wildest hopes
by slating a candidate whose presence on the ballot guaranteed no contest. It was thought that the Republicans would
go to C. Wayland (Curly) Brooks, a proven vote-getter, but

for reasons best known to Republican Governor Dwight
Green and to Robert McCormick, the Grand Old Party of
Cook County chose as its candidate one Russell Root of the
Seventh Ward. Root, a shambling lawyer, had been sponsored for committeeman of the ward by the aggressive and
articulate young alderman Nicholas Bohling. Nick Bohling
would have been a much stronger candidate for mayor, but
the Republican lemmings were determined to take another
bath.

What was needed in 1947 was a reform candidate. Russell
Root chose to campaign against Joseph Stalin and Harry
Truman. That presented Kennelly with the opportunity to be
the reformer, a role for which his experience and his way of
life had prepared him totally. Kennelly, the Democrat, ran
against the record of Kelly, the Democrat. Ah, those were
crazy days, and they would have been crazier still if Kelly
had listened to his inner voices, rather than to Arvey, Gill
and Horan, and forced Kennelly into a primary. Big Ed
might have won everything, and free of any obligation to
the organization, he could have spent the next three years of
his life strengthening the Chicago Housing Authority and
other programs dear to his heart.

During an inexplicable lapse in their two-fisted attack
upon Truman, Chicago's Republicans took notice of Kennelly long enough to suggest that there was chicanery and
skulduggery in his long service as keeper of the city's ballot
boxes and voting booths. The Democratic candidate had
been paid $907,957 by the city for those services, the Repub-
licans asserted.

Martin lifted his handsome white eyebrows toward
heaven, turned his pale, sad eyes upon the electorate, *tsk-
tsk*ed a time or two, and said, "I took that contract from year
to year as a civic duty, not to make profit. And my annual fee
to the city is the same in 1947 as it was in 1923. I've never
raised it a penny."

Voters in the Eleventh Ward, where Martin had been

raised, and those on fashionable North Sheridan Road, where he had lived for so many years, put pencil to paper, divided $907,957 by twenty-four and wondered why he had bothered to dirty his hands with those dusty booths and ballot boxes.

"Why, he's a living saint," they said.

And the living saint was endorsed by more than one thousand business and civic leaders, the great majority of them Republicans. The leading endorser, though, was a Democrat, eighty-seven-year-old Carter Harrison the Younger, he who had been elected mayor five times because he had given Chicagoans "the fullest measure of personal liberty consistent with the maintenance of public order."

ıııııııııııııııııııııııııııııııı

The Portables

AFTER The Mayor had spoken with fondness and humor of his predecessors from the Eleventh Ward, he would have shepherded the crowd north on the west side of Lowe Avenue until all were at Thirty-fifth Street again. As his new friends strolled through the August afternoon, they would have noticed, as he did, the broken sidewalks on this side of Lowe. They would have wondered about that cracked and shattered concrete, as he wondered, and they would have gone back home to tell family and neighbors that The Mayor took care of a lot of things in Chicago before he had the walks repaired on his own block.

He would have arranged with the police captain at Deering to provide an escort for these good Chicagoans, these good, black Chicagoans, until all had cleared the viaduct of the Chicago and Western Indiana. It would have been a shame to have had such a meaningful afternoon marred by an incident precipitated by a thoughtless high-school boy shouting a racial insult. There could be no hatred on this day of all days, this day dedicated to the memory of Martin Luther King Jr. All here assembled knew that The Mayor and Dr. King shared the conviction that "hate accomplishes nothing."

He would have sent them on their way with a smile and a wave, they returning to their neighborhoods as he had returned to his. With this mayor the neighborhood is everything. It is the ciborium for family, home, church and friends. In April of 1955, just before his turn to be the third mayor from the Eleventh Ward, Richard Daley wrote these words at the invitation of the Chicago *Daily News:* "I love my neighborhood and my city. My neighborhood to me is the symbol of all the neighborhoods. My neighbors are all the people of this city."

The candidate for mayor meant to be sincere, but every native-born Chicagoan recognized in 1955 that the second and third sentences contradicted each other. The incompatibility between the sentences had not been resolved by 1968. Chicagoans who were reared in other cities or in country towns do not understand the distinction as natives do. To comprehend one must define "neighborhood." It is not a community or an enclave. It is not a ghetto or a Shangri-La. It is a state of mind; a set of attitudes.

The neighborhood begins to be built in the mind of the Chicago child as soon as his mother believes that he is old enough to be trusted out of the yard or off the porch. First, the neighborhood is the sidewalk in front of the home or apartment building. Then it is down the street. Across the street. Up the block. Around the corner. Past the alley. Under the viaducts.

By the time the boy is in high school, it is all those who look at life very much as he does. Two successive blocks might be part of "the neighborhood," but the third block will be excluded in favor of the fourth, because the boys on the third block are "different."

A neighborhood is not something that a father can pass on to his son, although each has spent his boyhood on the same block. The father's neighborhood might have moved from north to south and the son's from east to west. Asked about a street that is thought to be in his neighborhood, a Chicagoan frequently will say, "Nah, I never hung out on that corner," or, "We stayed away from that street."

The man who says that his neighborhood is the symbol of all the neighborhoods is much too insular to be a good neighbor to all the people of the city, no matter how hard he might try. The bitter truth is that all the neighborhoods are portable, except one. Clarence Wagner fought in the City Council to save the neighborhoods of the Fourteenth Ward and some of Clarence's constituents fought with fists, rocks, bottles and fire bombs, but fifteen years after Wagner's tragic death, the black citizens were invading the Fourteenth in ever-increasing numbers.

All the neighborhoods are portable, except one. Many white Chicagoans who have moved three or four times in advance of the Negroes during the last quarter-century huddle now in taverns on the west side of Western Avenue, far to the south of the Eleventh Ward. These taverns are directly across the street from Beverly Hills, which has no taverns. The late John Duffy fought in the City Council to keep Chicago Housing Authority projects out of the Nineteenth, but six years after John's death the Nineteenth is a refugee center for the Catholics, who have fled before the black invaders, and a staging area for the Protestants, who are planning their moves to distant western suburbs.

Together they huddle in the taverns on the other side of Western, Catholics and Protestants, singing the old songs of the old neighborhoods, watching and waiting. These people know that a neighborhood is something that can be packed into a van and moved to another location. So many of them have had so much experience.

Cynically and realistically they confide that the neighborhood that is spoken of with such fondness by The Mayor has remained inviolate because he is there. If he were to go, as Ed Kelly and Martin Kennelly went after their fortunes improved, the neighborhood would go as so many other neighborhoods have.

As Mrs. Wille wrote in *The Nation,* "Bridgeport is what

Daley trusts." And because he trusts it, he believes he must give it his support. Committed as he is to his neighborhood, The Mayor is locked in by his neighborhood. He can't escape from there to be a neighbor to all the people.

That may have been one of the reasons why The Mayor did not walk down Thirty-fifth Street from Dr. Martin Luther King Jr. Drive to Lowe Avenue.

Part Two

THE RUN

A Hippie Laughs

EVEN if he had wished to do so, The Mayor could not walk. The leisurely approach was not for him. Not now. He had to run, or the days would get away from him. Thursday, August 8—the date of the dedication of Dr. Martin Luther King Jr. Drive—had to be X'ed out on his calendar. He had no more than sixteen days to ready himself and the city he loves for the Democratic National Convention, which was to open in Chicago on Sunday, August 25.

He had to do so much and he was aware that some were saying that he had to do too much. His critics were saying that the fact that he was trying to do everything himself was proof that he no longer trusted the men he had chosen to be his aides. As the Stock Yards Irish of a generation earlier had put it, he was "everywhere, like horse manure."

The Mayor had a stock answer for those critics. "It's easy to criticize," he said. He had on his hands a strike that had to be settled before the Convention opened in the International Amphitheater. It simply had to be settled, because it was a strike of the International Brotherhood of Electrical Workers, the union of linemen, cable splicers, installers and repairmen who work for the Illinois Bell Telephone Company. It was almost impossible to visualize a political convention without adequate phone service and without—may the Lord have mercy on the soul of the man who invented it—television. The I.B.E.W. had crews in the Amphitheater during these early days of August, working under a sort of armistice; but if the strike was not settled soon, the Convention would be chaotic.

The Mayor knew that many persons were predicting chaos for Chicago during convention week. Some delegates who were coming to the Convention were said to be seized by a fever of fear. They were afraid of a repetition of the April riot. Prominent persons within the party were agitating to have the Convention moved out of Chicago. Miami, they were talking about. Miami, where the Republicans had nominated Richard M. Nixon a few minutes after midnight on this very day, the day of the street signs that changed South Parkway to Dr. Martin Luther King Jr. Drive. Miami, where blacks were rioting and where the National Guard was called out during a national political convention. Miami, instead of Chicago!

He was convinced that no city could handle a political convention as efficiently and as hospitably as Chicago would. In 1952 both parties had convened in Chicago. In 1960 Chicago had hosted the Republicans at the Amphitheater.

Chicago would prevail and Chicago would be triumphant, he was sure, although he had solid reasons to suspect that there were some who were planning to make the predictions of chaos come true. His suspicions were directed not to the ghetto of Chicago—he did not fear his own—but to many places in the nation where the young and the not-quite-young were assembling to make a trip to Chicago.

One hundred thousand hippie-Yippies were said to be coming to the city for convention week. One hundred thousand? Well, things were so depressing and the sense of doom so urgent that Chicagoans desperately wanted to believe that a hundred thousand hippie-Yippies would be willing to come and make things ludicrously miserable for everybody. Chicago felt a need for smelly goats to scape, for hairy heads to knock. Nobody seemed to understand that there probably were not one hundred thousand certifiable hippie-Yippies in all the world.

Movements, fads and manias come late to Chicago unless the "new thing" originates in Chicago. Skirts, for example, go up and down more slowly in Chicago than in New York, Montreal or San Francisco. The geographical location of the city has something to do with this unwillingness to adapt, but the basic reason is the conservatism that has prevailed for generations. Chicagoans have a constitutional aversion for being like people from other places. Thus, there was resistance to the miniskirt, although it was generally known that Chicago women had thighs like women elsewhere. Style-conscious Chicagoans ultimately got around to the mini at about the time that women in New York and San Francisco had been sold on the micro-mini. By the eighth month of 1968, as the Convention delegates and the "demonstrators" began to close in on Chicago, the skirts of the native girls had reached mid-thigh. Chicago's approach to expressway construction is almost identical to the women's attitude on skirt lengths. Chicago was the last of the important American cities to get around to building expressways, but once The Mayor had thrown all the resources at his command into highway construction, Chicago had the best expressways in the land. The Mayor, like the ladies of his great city, was reluctant to accept change.

Those who charged that The Mayor was too far "out of it" to comprehend the changes all around him overlooked the fact that he had married late in life. In 1968 his seven children ranged in age from teens to young-marrieds. None of his kids was a hippie or a draft-card burner or a demonstrator for causes (other than the Democratic party), but the winds of religious and social change had blown through the bungalow at 3536 South Lowe Avenue. His eldest child, Patricia, Mrs. William Thompson, had been a nun for almost five years; she had taken the veil of a Sister of Mercy on the feast of the Assumption of the Blessed Virgin Mary in 1955, but had left the order in August of 1960, before taking her final vows.

The Mayor's second daughter, big-eyed Mary Carol, is married to Dr. Michael Vanecko. The doctor's brother, the Reverend Richard Vanecko, served in the West Side ghetto during the early years of his ministry. The occasions were infrequent, perhaps, but there had been informal family gatherings that presented young Father Vanecko with an opportunity to express his views in the presence of The Mayor.

By the standards of the Sixties, the Daley children were underinvolved. Patricia had worked briefly as a teacher in Chicago's school system. Mary Carol too had been a public-school teacher, but instead of working in a ghetto school, where her presence would have enhanced the Daley image with the black citizens of Chicago, she taught at Logan School in Wilmette, a virtually lily-white suburb north of the city. Daughter Eleanor also taught in Wilmette. There was sufficient family exposure to the world outside, however, to enable The Mayor to understand "where it's at."

That's why he had said that Chicago would welcome the hippies, Yippies and flippies. Conscious as he was of the Midwestern, Protestant-Catholic, Irish-Middle European, conservative traditions, he knew that there were few hippies within the city limits, suspected that there was not one Yippie, and threw in flippie as a whimsical invention of his own. He didn't fear the kooks. What worried him were the *provocateurs*, the assassins.

Intelligence sources convinced The Mayor and his administrative assistants that enemies within and without were determined to wreck the convention by killing, burning and bombing. Five of nine examples of intelligence that would be cited later in the Walker Report "exposed" the activities of black-power groups, black nationalists, black militants and black street gangs. The most absurd item of information re-

ported plans of various organizations to put LSD into the
Chicago water supply. Experts in the city's Water and Sewers Department recognized this threat as the most outra-
geous kind of adolescent put-on, but days passed before anyone bothered to explain that LSD would have to be shipped
to Chicago in hundreds of tank cars if the saboteurs seriously
intended to send delegates, candidates, city officials, the police and The Mayor off on an unscheduled trip by infiltrating
the water filtration plants with vials of LSD. Meanwhile, the
"water protection brigade" was strengthened and nobody
gave a thought to the reality that the hippie-Yippies would
have to drink the same water that the straight citizens would
be drinking.

Somewhere a hippie was laughing, a not altogether bad
thing because hippies don't laugh quite as often as politicians do.

33

‖‖‖‖‖‖‖‖‖‖‖‖‖‖‖‖‖‖‖‖‖‖‖‖‖‖‖‖‖‖‖‖

The Spirit

IN CHICAGO nobody told The Mayor that he could not do something that he felt he must do for the good of the city. Getting things done was his strength. Not-doing things had been the weakness of his beloved city prior to 1955. For so many years, while he was rising so slowly from the lower echelons of politics, Chicago's slogan had been proud, defiant, boastful. "I Will!" the city thundered. Then came the decade that began in 1945 with the decline of Ed Kelly and the slogan in effect became a whimpering "I cannot." By the time Richard J. Daley had won his struggle to become county chairman, Chicago was moving as its river moves—backward. Chicago could not get anything done. This city that had been so energetic dawdled for fourteen years over something called the Congress Expressway and did not move it more than a few blocks beyond the Loop. Chicago needed a mayor who understood the meaning of "I Will!"

During an interview in 1966, Ed Lahey of the Chicago *Daily News* asked Richard Daley when he began to think of being a candidate for mayor in 1955. The Mayor said, "I guess, maybe, in December 1954. Martin was letting the Council run things. Some of the labor fellows like Steve Bailey [Plumbers], Bill Lee [Teamsters] and Bill McFetridge [Building Service Employees] came to me to talk about it."

What the labor fellows wished to talk about was Chicago's

192

lack of progress during Kennelly's two terms as mayor. "Progress" meant *jobs.*

"Martin could have had the nomination if he had done the right thing," Ben Adamowski said with asperity. Kennelly did not do the right thing, because Martin, unlike Kelly, did not know how to get things done. The Democrats had to get a new boy.

The decision to change was arrived at during a routine meeting to choose the slatemakers. County Chairman Daley called this meeting soon after the November elections of 1954. Joe Gill, Daley's predecessor as chairman, was appointed chairman of the slatemaking committee. Other members were William Dawson, Negro Congressman; Barnet Hodes, Jack Arvey's law partner; Al Horan, representing the West Side; State Senator William (Botchy) Connors, representing the North Side, and Alderman Joseph Rostenkowski, a stalwart of the Polish bloc. The ethnic-racial-neighborhood "mix" was churning and bubbling.

On December 18 Mayor Kennelly walked into the meeting of the slatemaking committee with chin out and hat in hand. Not so many days ago he had expected renomination by acclamation. Even now he obviously harbored the hope that the good Democrats in this room would not follow a course that would lead to defeat (he was sure they could not win without him).

The mayor was allowed three minutes, fifty-six seconds to make his presentation to the committee. "In that brief interval I saw the county chairman sitting in at his own draft," Kennelly said, much more sardonic than was his nature. When Martin walked through the door of the committee room, he was out of the organization and off the ticket.

The committee listened to other would-be nominees— John S. Clark, former alderman and assessor; Stephen Mitchell, national chairman of the Democratic party during the Presidential campaign of Adlai Stevenson; John

Gutknecht, state's attorney. And the committee chose—surprise! surprise!—the stout fellow who had been sitting on a couch in the back of the room.

"It's a great honor and I never dreamed it would happen to me," Richard J. Daley said.

Not quite two months earlier Daley had promised the electorate that what happened in December would not happen. Speaking at a businessmen's luncheon in his campaign for reelection as county clerk, Daley said, "I am not and never was a candidate for mayor." The county clerk emphasized that he wished to "get the record straight, once and for all."

That was not the kind of promise that is held against a politician by other politicians. Ben Adamowski understood. "They were interested in getting the right kind of candidate to knock out Kennelly," Adamowski explained. "They had to have an Irish candidate. If they had run anyone other than an Irish candidate, they would have raised the ethnic question. And you never raise the ethnic question in a primary."

Ed Kelly had been the spiritual father of the trinity of mayors from the Eleventh Ward. Martin Kennelly was the redeemer. And December of 1954 was the time of the spirit. The pragmatic Democrats picked an Irishman from Kennelly's old ward.

34

‖‖‖‖‖‖‖‖‖‖‖‖‖‖‖‖‖‖‖‖‖‖‖‖‖‖‖

I'll Stand With You

IF THE MAYOR had deigned to respond to those who thought Chicago could not handle the Democratic National Convention, he might have said, "Look at Miami! Is *that* where you want to take it?" A few hours after The Mayor had told the crowd at the dedication of King Drive, "I dream of a city with a program like that which Dr. King dreamed of," the Republican party nominated Spiro T. Agnew to be its Vice-Presidential candidate at Miami Beach, and across Biscayne Bay National Guardsmen were patrolling streets of Miami, where three Negroes had been shot to death during a riot.

The Mayor did not bother to talk with those who lacked faith in Chicago's power to do. He knew what they were. They were the doomsayers, the same kind as those who had been so sure, in 1955, that Richard J. Daley could not be elected mayor. They were like Martin Kennelly, the mayor who had not known how to get things done.

Less than twenty-four hours after the December 18, 1954, announcement that the Democratic slatemakers had tapped their county chairman to run for mayor, Kennelly denounced "the bosses" and declared that he would run against Daley in the February primary. If he did not, Martin warned, the bosses would wreck civil service, demolish central purchasing, demoralize the Police Department and return politics to the schools.

The next day Candidate Daley clucked sadly and said, No, he wouldn't do things like that.

There was to be a third candidate in the primary. Ben Adamowski was willing to raise the ethnic question. Adamowski, who had resigned in disgust in 1950 from his position as corporation counsel in the Kennelly administration, had said 'way back in November that he would go for mayor no matter what the slatemakers chose to do.

Adamowski had joined Kennelly's team because Ben had expected Martin to be a great improvement upon Ed Kelly. Adamowski, who hit Kelly harder than Big Ed was accustomed to being struck, had said of Kelly in 1940, "Why, he could even give a lesson in bossism to Hitler and Stalin." Soon Adamowski had been as disappointed in Kennelly as he had been furious with Kelly. "In the business world, Martin was a success," Adamowski said in 1969. "Dollarwise, he was one of the most honorable men I have known. But my argument—to his face—was that he was morally dishonest, because he let the boys at Democratic headquarters use him as a front."

By statute Chicago has a "weak mayor, strong council" form of government, a legal fact that was hilariously overridden by the Harrisons, by Big Bill Thompson, by Tony Cermak and by Ed Kelly. These mayors made no requests of the aldermen. They issued orders. Kelly put it succinctly. "You run the organization or it runs you," Big Ed said.

Dick Daley understood the truth in that, and so did Ben Adamowski. Fifteen years later many Chicagoans continued to wonder whether malice had been Adamowski's only motive for leaping into the battle, but Ben remains convinced that his reason for entering was politically sound. He had expected a two-man race. The other man would not be Kennelly but the organization candidate.

"I didn't think Kennelly would run," Adamowski explained, "and if he did declare, I didn't expect him to stay in. My experience with him was that in a contest, he'd back off. If he had backed off that time, it would have been two people—Adamowski and Daley."

There were three people. Kennelly decided to stay in. As the incumbent and the man who still carried the keys to City Hall, Martin had no reason to doubt that his name would be first on the Democratic side of the ballot. How would it look, after all, if the mayor, himself, was second in the Democratic column? Accordingly, Kennelly instructed his man to bring the mayor's nominating petitions into the city clerk's office long before the office opened. The order was carried out to the letter, and the Kennelly petitions, which had been dropped on an outer counter while the clerk's office was empty except for the Kennelly man, had been time-stamped at 8:19 A.M. Candidate Daley's petitions were time-stamped at 8:13 A.M.

The unofficial explanation was that the wily Daley messenger had made his delivery through a rear door. This version was accepted by the press, but the old fellows in the big fedoras with the broad brims turned up all around told stories of how easy it is to turn back time when it is being kept on a stamp. Kennelly was beginning to comprehend that when the organization turned on one of its own, that "own" was quite alone.

Ben Adamowski also filed his nominating petitions that morning, but he didn't send his emissary out to foot-race a time stamp. Ben had been around long enough to know that his name wouldn't have made the top of the ballot even if his messenger had come through that back door at three o'clock in the morning.

The primary presented Adlai Stevenson with an opportunity to repay two debts. Stevenson, national standard-bearer for the Democrats, owed Kennelly the back of his hand. Always above the battle, the saintly Kennelly virtually had sat out Governor Stevenson's campaign for the Presidency against General Dwight Eisenhower in 1952. Stevenson owed the Democrats of Cook County a debt of gratitude. Their leader emeritus, Jack Arvey, had chosen Adlai to run for governor of Illinois, and the organization always had gone all the way for Stevenson. Additionally, the Governor had reasons to like and to respect Dick Daley. During his service as director of revenue in Stevenson's administration, Daley had been efficient, effective and loyal. The urbane Adlai paid off both debts by announcing his support of Daley in the primary. The liberals howled, and Stevenson unabashedly admitted that he was doing something he never had done before. But he knew what he was doing.

Soon Kennelly had only one powerful politician with him. Tom Nash still was fighting the battle that Clarence Wagner had intended to wage. But John S. Clark, the former assessor, and P. J. Cullerton, chairman of the City Council finance committee, had turned away from the mayor after indicating earlier that they might be kept in line by Nash. The sixty-four-year-old Clark, whose influence on the West Side had not waned although he had retired from office, gave Daley much more enthusiastic support than had been expected. As the primary campaign was nearing its climax, Clark told an audience that Daley has "one of the most beautiful records of any of the thousands of men I have known in public life."

Daley also was given rousing help by John Clark's son, Bill, a member of the Illinois legislature. In father-son conversations John fondly recalled how Dick Daley, that wonderful young fellow from the Eleventh Ward, would go for coffee and sandwiches for John and other members of the City Council back in the good old days. Bill Clark would remember his father's nostalgic story.

If Daley then was not the worst public speaker in the history of Chicago politics, he was bad enough to convince his advisers that he should be kept out of sound, as much as possible, if not out of sight. The organization candidate campaigned to, and for, the men he called "pre-sint" captains. With forty-eight wards committed to him, the county clerk knew there was no way he could lose in the primary as long as the doorbell pushers did their jobs.

When he did make an appearance Daley gave his audience the "I'm witchoo" treatment. To four thousand party workers assembled in the Civic Opera House, Dick said, "Ladies and gentlemen of the Democratic party of the City of Chicago, let them be the State Street candidate. Let others be the LaSalle Street candidate, I'm proud and happy to be your candidate—the candidate of the Democratic party. . . . I'm a kid from the Stock Yards and I say to all of you, I'll stand with you."

In that last sentence, which was syntactically superior to the first sentence, Daley struck a chord that would be sounded again and again for four terms. He did not ask the audience to "stand with me." He said, "I'll stand with you." The Prince of Wales never put it better.

Daley won the primary with 49 percent of the vote. Kennelly, running well, considering that he had no base, received 36 percent. Adamowski, strong in the Polish wards, had 15 percent. Some Chicagoans, including many Poles, suspected that the maverick Adamowski had run in connivance with the organization. The strategy, as the suspicious interpreted it, was that Adamowski would cut into Kennelly's strength. The weakness of that argument is that the Polish vote invariably is an organization vote. Adamowski probably hurt Daley more than Kennelly.

"I would doubt that Kennelly could have won if I had not been in the race," Adamowski said in 1969. "Daley beat us both."

35

‖‖‖‖‖‖‖‖‖‖‖‖‖‖‖‖‖‖‖‖‖‖‖‖‖‖‖‖‖

By Appointment

OUTSIDERS ASK, "How are mayors elected in Chicago?" Insiders smile at the question. Everybody knows—well, everybody who cares knows—that Chicago's mayors are not elected. They are appointed, by the party in power. There is an election every fourth year, but this is a matter of form to satisfy the requirements of the municipal charter. For almost one hundred years the mayor has been either a Democrat or a Republican. The last successful candidate who did not carry the banner of the donkey or the elephant was Harvey Doolittle Colvin. He represented the People's Party and defeated Lester Legrand Bond, the Union party's standard-bearer, in the election of November 4, 1873.

In the election just prior to Harvey Doolittle Colvin's memorable triumph, the winner had been Joe Medill, who ran on the Fireproof ticket. Joe actually was a Republican, but a nonpartisan "Union-Fireproof" slate had been agreed upon by the combined central committees of Republicans and Democrats. This unprecedented display of cooperation and good sportsmanship in Cook County politics was inspired by the fact that the election of November 7, 1871, followed not long after the historical event that Martin Howan had referred to in his limp attempt at humor in August of 1968. Mrs. O'Leary's cow or something or somebody had started a little fire and within hours most of the wooden city was ablaze. "Fireproof" was the magic word in the autumn of '71.

Before Medill came on the scene with his asbestos image, fifteen of the previous eighteen mayors had been Republican or Democrat. Chicago, which boasts that it has had everything, had a Know-Nothing mayor in 1855, a good year for that sort of approach. He was Levi Day Boone, who had been a Democrat before he became militant.

William Stratton, a Republican who was governor of Illinois from 1952 through 1960, summed up the reality when he said, "In Chicago there is hardly even a second political force. I'm speaking now of formal party organization. In New York City, to cite an example, there are and have been effective third parties. Many big cities have effective second and third forces."

Chicago's first force, its one and only force, is the Democratic party. The voters have not elected a Republican to be mayor since April 5, 1927, when Big Bill Thompson won his third term in a contest with the Democratic incumbent, William Dever. The only other Republican to be mayor in the twentieth century was Fred Busse. He served from 1907 into 1911, and "good fellow" Fred was elected with the blessing of Democratic leader Roger Sullivan.

County Chairman Richard J. Daley understood the Chicago reality even better than did Bill Stratton, a downstater from Morris, Illinois. Once Daley had fought his way through the 1955 primary, he knew that he was in unless something or somebody went terribly wrong. The county chairman was confident although he also was aware that the Republicans were sending out their strongest candidate since "Big Bill" had gone peacocking around the town. The Republican choice for the mayor's office was Robert Merriam, Fifth Ward alderman and leader of the antiadministration bloc in the City Council.

Merriam, who had been a Democrat, tossed his convertible hat into the Republican ring 'way back in the autumn of 1954. Grand Old Party members with long memories thought this a case of turnabout being fair play. Merriam's father, Charles, a political-science professor at the University of Chicago, had run a gallant but losing race for mayor as a Republican in 1911, against Carter Harrison the Younger. During the Roosevelt years Charles Merriam renounced the Republicans and became a showcase Democrat.

Robert Merriam's greatest advantage over Daley was that Bob didn't look or sound like a politician, although that is what he was. Daley, wide, stubby, jowly and cursed with that weak *t* that makes everything sound like *tuh*, was a cartoonist's stereotype of the Irish politician. Merriam was slender with concave cheeks, deep-set eyes and heavy brows. He was so literate he had written a book, *Dark December*, a study of the Battle of the Bulge, in which he had served during World War II.

Merriam, by golly, looked like a public servant, and that's what he had striven to be since 1947, when he had been elected to the City Council in the Kennelly landslide. The Republicans, out of power since 1931, saw in Merriam a chance to recapture Chicago. They already had Illinois in the person of Governor Stratton. Merriam agreed to stay out of state and national politics, after the mayoralty, and his conversion was ratified by the hierarchy of the Republican party.

The blessing of the Cook County Republican organization sometimes is worse than a curse. Merriam was restricted by two major handicaps. First was the disarray of the party. Many within it were repelled by the thought of a Democrat-turned-Republican, and instead of giving Bob a push, they dug in their heels. Second was the disaffection of the undecided voters who were suspicious of a turncoat candidate.

"If Merriam had run as an independent, I'm convinced he would have won that election," Ben Adamowski said. "That's why the [Democratic] organization had to have a guy like Daley with sufficient strength to get the citywide backing that would limit the electoral strength of Merriam. That's also why Kennelly didn't get the nomination. The party was afraid of Merriam beating Martin."

The party also was afraid of Merriam beating Dick, but one who did not tremble at the thought was Donald J. Walsh, business manager of the Hearsts' Chicago *American*. An old hand in Chicago politics, Walsh had started, as Daley did, as a secretary. "Eventually I became secretary to Victor Lawson, publisher of the *Daily News*," Walsh said. "I usually worked from 8 A.M. until 7:30 P.M. and it was very interesting. If a politician had the endorsement of the *Daily News* in those days, that politician didn't have to make a speech, didn't have to have a campaign card printed. He was in."

Early in 1948 Walsh resigned as circulation director of the Chicago *Sun* to guide the Senatorial campaign of Paul Douglas, economics professor and Marine war hero. During his years in the City Council Douglas had been another anti-Kelly alderman, a sort of University of Chicago polished counterpart of Big Jim McDermott. Douglas had been succeeded, in time, as Fifth Ward alderman by Bob Merriam, and because the two had so much in common, Merriam was expected to be a tremendous asset in the Douglas campaign.

"In my opinion Merriam was all talk and no action," Walsh said acidly. "As far as I was concerned, Merriam was as light as a cork."

The Republican candidate was heavier than that, but Walsh obviously was unimpressed. The newspaperman was convinced that the Democrats had a winner in Daley. "I had known Dick since the early Forties," Walsh said. "I particularly remembered our trip to the national convention in Philadelphia in 1948. Arvey and others on the train were campaigning for General Eisenhower as the Democratic Presidential candidate, but Dick Daley got hold of Martin Kennelly on the train and tried to convince the mayor that he should stick with Harry Truman."

From April of 1949 into January of 1950 Walsh and Daley

had worked together as members of Governor Stevenson's cabinet, Don as director of public safety and Dick as revenue director. When Walsh left the state government he returned to Chicago to become circulation manager of the *American*, a Hearst newspaper, and it was from this base that Walsh operated on Daley's behalf in 1955.

"William Randolph Hearst had died and his sons had taken over the chain," Walsh said. "The local papers were given more freedom to endorse candidates, because the younger Hearsts wanted us to be involved in community affairs. We had backed Bill Stratton, the Republican candidate for governor in 1952, and he had won. I convinced our publisher that we could have another winner in Dick Daley."

Although Walsh was desirous of helping an old friend, he was more interested in having the endorsement stand up. The *American* came out for Daley, but the *Sun-Times, Daily News* and *Tribune* supported Merriam. The *Tribune* was for Merriam, the candidate, but it was not unkind to Daley, the man.

Daley's reputation for honesty and integrity was such that he managed to turn bad breaks and a near-scandal to personal advantage. The Democratic ticket seemed to be in serious trouble on March 8 when Benjamin Becker, a reform alderman who had been running for city clerk, was cited by the Chicago Bar Association. Becker was charged with splitting fees with lawyers whose clients had sought the alderman's help in obtaining zoning variations and was later censured for misconduct by the Illinois Supreme Court. Becker quit the ticket, but Daley came out from under the cloud holding hands with Morris B. Sachs, a wealthy clothing merchant.

Sachs, who had gubernatorial aspirations, had been Martin Kennelly's candidate for city clerk in the primary. "Morrie B.," as he was known to thousands of Chicagoans, was one of the few men in the city who could be referred to as "beloved." The most famous picture of the primary was of the short, dumpy Sachs weeping upon the shoulder of the tall, erect Kennelly after the mayor had conceded to the organization candidate.

Daley announced that he would add Sachs to the ticket as candidate for city treasurer and that John Marcin, who had been slated for treasurer, would run for city clerk. Daley had masterfully attacked a problem that could have meant disaster for him and used it to enhance his "nice guy" image.

Adlai Stevenson was out campaigning energetically for Daley, thereby giving the liberals another reason for reexamination of conscience, and Tom Keane, the sardonic humorist of the City Council, did the hatchet job on television. During a eulogy of the Daley family—"that enchantingly adorable mother . . . and those seven children kneeling at the side of their bed at night in family prayer . . ."—Keane said what Daley never would have been able to bring himself to say.

Tom subtly added that "Daley has seven children and they are all his own." Merriam had been married twice and two of his three children were born to his wife during her first marriage.

Daley was pilloried as a hack who would conspire with the elements that desperately wanted a wide-open town again. Dick fought back, jowls aquiver. In a speech at a meeting of the Church Federation of Greater Chicago, Daley said: "When I walk down the street where I live, I see every street in the city of Chicago. When I walk into my church, I see every church and temple in the city of Chicago. When I look at my children, I see every child in the city of Chicago. And I promise you here and now that if elected, I shall be mayor of all the people."

Liberals were shaken again when they read, just before the election, of the woman who rose to speak for Daley in a rally at the Windermere East Hotel in the Hyde Park district.

"I have learned to distinguish between those who make headlines and those who carry out programs," she said snappishly. "I have learned to distinguish between those who come to our help when aid is needed and those who have other business at the moment when a crisis is at hand. That is why, in distinguishing between the two candidates, I speak for Mr. Daley."

The speaker was Elizabeth Wood, deposed head of the Chicago Housing Authority.

⸻⸻⸻⸻⸻

36

Back to the Yards

As THE first full week of August, 1968, neared its end, the kid from the Stock Yards was turning his attention back to the place where he had ridden herd on cattle for Dolan, Ludeman. That's where the Democratic National Convention was to be, thanks to the imagination of those vigorous Chicagoans who had decreed that the city's convention hall should be adjacent to the municipal abattoir.

Perhaps because they are so perverse and so violent, the natives are sentimental about the stinking Stock Yards. This nostalgia is reflected in the songs Chicagoans sing. Citizens who react so adversely to the standard commercial songs about their city—"Chicago, That Toddlin' Town" and the more recent "My Kind of Town, Chicago Is"—that they have been known to throw up in public places, get all dewy-eyed when a baritone in a neighborhood tavern wails his way through "Back o' the Yards." The lyrics of this ballad begin with, "Back o' the yards,/Back o' the yards,/In old Chicago town,/Where an ace is an ace,/Any time, Any place," and then soar to even more evocative musical images. During World War II millions of Americans learned this song, most of them against their will, and in certain sections of Chicago, particularly where Irish-Americans huddle together, "Back o' the Yards" is the municipal anthem.

The International Amphitheater, which was to be the convention hall, actually is in front of the Yards, as is Mayor

Daley's neighborhood, but tens of thousands of Chicagoans who have never set foot in the muck of a cattle pen will inform a stranger, at the tops of voices and with gestures, that "I'm mighty proud to be shoutin' out loud, that I come from in Back o' the Yards." So The Mayor is far from alone when his eyes brighten, his shoulders jiggle, his jowls quiver and his feet shuffle at the first notes of the South Side's very own fight song.

Built at Thirty-ninth Street during a time in history when Chicago hadn't pushed that far south, the Union Stock Yards had been an anachronism for generations, but truth to tell the Yards didn't smell nearly as bad in 1968 as they had in 1948. The Mayor and his administration deserved no credit for that, unfortunately. Although there are dozens of reasons why a stockyard should not be located within a city, there are other reasons why politicians don't put pressure on Swift and Armour and Wilson. Things like jobs, political contributions and the prestige of meat-packing families.

What City Hall had been reluctant even to contemplate was accomplished in time by the militant members of the United Packinghouse Workers and by time itself. The locals of the Packinghouse Workers, their memberships increasingly black, applied economic pressure with strikes that rarely were orderly. Pressing in from another sector was the obsolescence of plants and equipment. Confronted with major rebuilding projects and with what management described as the intransigence of the union, the major packers took their slaughterhouses to cities where the labor pool might not be so roiled.

As the daily receipts of cattle, hogs and sheep declined, so did the level of smell that frequently permeated the entire South Side and sometimes infiltrated the Loop as a reminder to the bankers on LaSalle Street and the merchants on State Street of what Chicago was all about. Not that many Chicagoans complained about the smell. The effluvium of the Stock Yards was so overpowering at times the entire city smelled as though all the drunks in town had lost control of their stomachs simultaneously. But permanent residents of the city pretended to be oblivious to the pungent odor of burning hides that made visitors stop breathing for long moments.

Some Chicagoans persuaded themselves that the acrid perfume of the Stock Yards was beneficial, if not downright therapeutic. "It clears the sinuses," they said, "and it enlarges the lungs. Nobody who lives near the Yards or works in 'em ever gets the pneumonia." None of this was true, but merely talking about it was good for the residents of the immediate Stock Yards area, because when they talked they were using their mouths for a purpose other than breathing. Stock Yards dwellers did not breathe through the nose, and that may have been the reason why the sinuses were not assailed.

Anyone from The Mayor's Eleventh Ward or from the neighboring Fourteenth Ward invariably took the offensive when the odor of the Stock Yards came blowing up. The worst they would say about it was, "It's not so bad." One of its most vigorous advocates was Donald O'Brien, Clarence Wagner's good friend and political ally. During a 1953 discussion of the future of the International Amphitheater somebody in the General Assembly, probably a downstater, had the temerity to mention "the stench." Moving to the counterattack like the loyalist he was, O'Brien put these immortal words into the record: "I was born within a sniffle of the stench and it hasn't hurt me."

Only too well did The Mayor remember why the Amphitheater had been under discussion and under attack in Springfield in 1953. The subject of heated and acrimonious debate was not the Amphitheater but another building that Chicago had been contemplating for housing conventions, exhibitions and shows. The problem was that some powerful interests wanted to put this new convention hall on the lake front, the worst possible place for it.

The Chicago *Tribune* especially wanted the hall on the

shore of Lake Michigan, a compulsion that desecrated the memory of Daniel Burnham, father of the "city beautiful." As always, officials of the *Tribune* had the memory of another man uppermost in mind. 'Way back in 1925 Colonel Robert McCormick had envisioned "the best convention hall in America" for his city. The Chicago *American,* guided by Executive Editor Edward Doyle, fought effectively in the middle Fifties to prevent the hall from being built on what was meant to be park land. The *American* had a lively ally in the *Southtown Economist,* the community newspaper then under the direction of John Dienhart. Perhaps because he remembered when the lake front had been a mess, Dienhart was a self-appointed protector of Chicago's front yard. On Saturday, October 20, 1956, the *Tribune* paid $13,000,000 to buy the *American.* Nothing more was printed in the pages of the *American* about the lake front being a poor place to throw up a convention hall. Dienhart was alone in the fight, and this was another time when might prevailed over right.

The convention hall opened on November 18, 1960, and it was named McCormick Place to honor the publisher and editor, who had died on April 1, 1955. The hall cost $35,000,000, almost three times as much as the *American* had cost. Although The Mayor and others professed to see it as a thing of beauty, McCormick Place was another architectural grotesquerie. If City Hall had indeed been designed after the forts at Verdun, McCormick Place surely was inspired by German fortifications at Utah Beach during World War II. It was an especially disconcerting sight when viewed from a boat out on the lake. On the inside its floor plan was such that experienced arena managers doubted that McCormick Place could house a national political convention.

Ugly and impractical though it was, McCormick Place had a built-in advantage that comforted practical-minded citizens. It was fireproof. At approximately 2 A.M., Monday, January 17, 1967, a fire started in an exhibit set up for the show of the National Housewares Manufacturers Association. The heat of the fire warped the structural steel and the roof and walls of the fireproof hall fell to the floor.

With McCormick Place still a modern ruin in August of 1968, the Democrats had to return to the Amphitheater, the site of the Republican convention in 1960 and of both national conventions in 1952. On Friday, August 9, 1968, the Amphitheater was something it had not been during those other conventions. It was a sealed-off fortress. A high steel-mesh fence was in place to the west of the building, extending from Exchange Avenue (4124 South) to Forty-fifth Street. The irony of this barricade, installed especially for convention security, was that it faced toward the legendary Back o' the Yards. It was as though somebody feared invasion by Upton Sinclair's rabble from out of the past. Only the barbed wire was missing from Chicago's "Berlin Wall," but John Meek, convention coordinator for the Democratic National Committee, had been assured that the wire soon would be strung atop the fence.

Federal and local officials met Friday to perfect the security plans that were symbolized by that fence. James Rochford, a deputy police superintendent, was one of Chicago's representatives at the meeting. Rochford had returned from Miami, where he had been assigned as an observer of security precautions at the Republican convention. Nobody was sure of the direction from which the invasion would come or of who the invaders would be, but there were reasons to be apprehensive.

Throughout the week the hippie-Yippie advance guard had been making threatening sounds. David Dellinger, fifty-two-year-old chairman of the National Mobilization Committee to End the War in Vietnam, had declared on Monday that a coalition of antiwar and black-liberation forces was determined to stage a "dramatic, militant and massive" demonstration during convention week.

Dellinger's warning was embellished somewhat on Thursday by Abraham Peck, editor of *The Seed,* one of Chicago's "underground" newspapers. Flower children who had been thinking of coming to Chicago for five days of fun, frolic and lovemaking were advised by Peck to stay where they were. Peck said that only those hippies, Yippies and non-ippies who "deemed change necessary" would be welcome at the Festival of Life, which was scheduled for Lincoln Park on the Near North Side.

The Yippies and hippies were on their way, no doubt about that, although there was consolation in intelligence reports that their numbers would not be nearly as staggering as the one hundred thousand that had been predicted. When antiwar groups started to talk about converging on Chicago, one hundred thousand protesters did not seem to be an unrealistic figure. This was in October of 1967, however, only a few days after the National Mobilization Committee had rallied some fifty thousand to march on the Pentagon and a few months after one hundred thousand or more had paraded to United Nations Plaza in New York on April 15, 1967. The withdrawal of President Johnson from public life had accomplished a major objective of the peace groups, with the result that the loose coalition had lost much of its thrust. By August 9 realists within the peace movement were conceding it was unlikely that more than ten thousand outsiders would come to Chicago. If an impressive show of protest was to be made, the numbers would have to be supplied by Chicago-area residents and, given the conservatism of the city, that probability did not seem likely.

There were so many other problems that concerned The Mayor. The International Brotherhood of Electrical Workers still was on strike, despite his yeoman efforts to bring union and management to a settlement, and as a result, the McCarthy people were screaming "favoritism" at the Humphrey people and at the Convention coordinators. On one front The Mayor had sweet-talked the adversaries into a temporary cease-fire that permitted the installation of 3,200 telephones and 200 Teletype machines within the Amphitheater, but this agreement did not include the Conrad Hilton Hotel, which would be headquarters for Humphrey, McCarthy and the Democratic National Committee.

As of Thursday the McCarthy headquarters had two telephones—the two that normally were in a suite—and this brought an old Daley critic, who was more bitter than most, charging into battle. Steve Mitchell, who had been Democratic national chairman in 1952 and who had gone into the Illinois gubernatorial primary in 1960 against The Mayor's slated candidate, Otto Kerner, was serving as chief of convention arrangements for McCarthy. Mitchell blamed McCarthy's telephone shortage on John Bailey, the national chairman, and demanded that Bailey resign.

The Mayor reacted like the big brother of a quarreling family. John Bailey, he said with traditional hyperbole, was "the finest chairman in the history of the Democratic party," and added, "No one has been fairer." The Mayor dismissed Mitchell's complaint as "a self-serving statement."

The Mayor also took time to say that rumors of the Convention being transferred to another town were "completely unfounded and a fabrication." John Criswell, national treasurer of the Democratic party and chief planner for the Convention, said, "Yes, sir." One Martin Howan, described as a spokesman for the National Committee, unleashed a historical allusion that made Chicagoans grimace and mutter. "Even if Mrs. O'Leary's cow kicks over another lantern, we're going to have the Convention in Chicago," Howan said more hysterically than historically.

Down in the Loop a phone cable in the Field Building was cut for the third successive day. And in the bus barns around the city the Negro drivers were making plans to go out on strike again on August 25, the day the Convention was to open.

The Mayor had to worry about all these problems, because

214 DALEY OF CHICAGO

everything that went on during convention week would be his responsibility. Inside the Amphitheater he would be the local party leader. Outside the convention hall he would be mayor of the host city. He had volunteered for this double helping of grief almost fourteen years earlier.

37

A Word to the Outs

INTO the City Council chambers on April 20, 1955, jammed relatives, friends, politicians and jobholders to witness the evening inaugural of Chicago's fortieth mayor and to pay homage to him. The holder of the cornucopia had changed; there was a new dispenser of favor.

The election had been reasonably close. The difference had been that Bob Merriam had the "volunteers"; Daley had the doorbell pushers. The party faithful had performed effectively and Merriam conceded victory to Dick Daley at 8:58 P.M., election night. Merriam had 581,555 votes. Daley won with 708,222, and Dick would do as the first of the Bridgeport mayors had done. Daley's license number for 1956 and for years to come would be 708-222.

In the front row at the evening inauguration were Mrs. Eleanor Daley and six of their seven children. The seventh, Sister M. Richard, a novice in the order of Sisters of Mercy, watched the ceremony on television at the novitiate in a Chicago suburb. Also present in the front row was The Mayor's proud father, Mike Daley, the old sheet-metal worker who had had a word of encouragement for his only son after the only significant defeat of Dick's career. This had been in 1946 when Sheriff-candidate Daley conceded victory to Elmer Michael Walsh. "Forget about it, Dick," Mike had urged his son. "The Lord never slams a door in your face without leaving a window open."

There had been a window slightly ajar, and now all the doors to all the offices in City Hall, as well as in the County Building, were wide open. Dick was everything now. He was county chairman and in a matter of moments he would be The Mayor.

Traditionally, the former mayor swore in his successor, but this time bitterness revoked tradition. Martin Kennelly was present but not participating. The oath of office was administered by Superior Court Judge Abraham Lincoln Marovitz, one of the "three musketeers" of Springfield days. The other musketeer, Ben Adamowski, was absent. This was a day of prophecy-come-true for Marovitz. 'Way back in 1943 at the farewell party that sent bachelor Abe swinging off to the Marine Corps, Marovitz made a prediction and asked everyone there to remember it. He predicted that Dick Daley would be mayor of Chicago one day.

Then it was time for The Mayor's speech, a prospect that edified only the most loyal. The party faithful had heard Dick often enough during the campaign, and if they didn't have to hear him again for a while that would be all right with them. They were familiar with the slurred words, the swallowed words, the mispronounced words, the extra syllables, the *t*'s that sounded like *d*'s, the malapropisms, the subjects and predicates that didn't match. The only thing they missed in critiques of Daley's speeches was that he spoke very much as most of them did.

Aware of his weakness on the platform, The Mayor spoke for no more than fifteen minutes. Nothing he said of himself or of his plans was deemed worthy of applause, even by this captive audience. The only applause came when he mentioned Martin Kennelly. The crowd gave Martin a one-minute ovation before the jobholders realized that they might be overdoing the sentiment and gradually brought their palms together with less gusto.

Daley's speech was not inspiring, but it was far more

meaningful than was imagined by many who were nodding sagely as he droned on. The Mayor did not speak well, but he had something to say. Those who had been close to him for years realized that he almost always had something to say. They were listening closely and they came to the conclusion that he was giving the word to the "outs."

In Chicago and Cook County the Republicans are not thought of as the "outs," because they are so rarely in. The "outs" in late April of 1955 were the fifty aldermen who had been running the city for eight delirious years. The fact that most of them were Democrats made no difference. Their ride on the golden merry-go-round was over.

Daley spoke some seemingly conciliatory words that were in fact a warning. "I have no intention of interfering in any way with the proper functions of the City Council," he said. "But as mayor of Chicago, it is my duty to provide leadership for those measures which are essential to the interests of all the people and, if necessary, to exercise the power of veto against measures which would be harmful to the people."

It was not the threat of veto that shook the aldermen. They knew that Martin Kennelly, in eight years, and Ed Kelly, in fourteen, never had vetoed an ordinance passed by the Council. It was Daley's implication, thinly veiled, that The Mayor would decide which measures were "essential to the interests of all the people," just as Ed Kelly had done. During the primary and the campaign, the aldermen and ward committeemen had given the ball to Dick Daley. They knew now that he was not going to give it back. This man meant to be mayor.

Daley had public opinion running with him. Not so many months earlier the Chicago Home Rule Commission, its members appointed by Mayor Kennelly, had published a large book of recommendations. Ostensibly the purpose of the Commission was to provide a program that would strengthen the bargaining position of the City of Chicago in its never-ending conflict with the state government at Springfield; but there also was a secondary purpose, which Daley could use for his own ends. This was the streamlining and modernization of the city government.

During his speech The Mayor expressed the hope that the City Council would enact proposals of the Chicago Home Rule Commission "to relieve the Council of administrative and technical duties . . . and permit the aldermen to devote most of their time to legislation." This "expression" was nothing less than the new mayor's first demand.

The message came clearly to Nick Bohling, an old Daley foe who would become a Daley admirer. Bohling, one of the thirteen Republicans in the City Council in 1955—there had been seventeen in 1947—had been the only alderman of the opposition party appointed to the Home Rule Commission by Kennelly. Nick had helped to write the book and he knew that Daley would use it to the advantage of the mayor's office. "The newspapers thought that we aldermen shouldn't have any powers at all," Bohling said in 1969.

The Mayor would do what could be done to oblige the editors.

‖‖‖‖‖‖‖‖‖‖‖‖‖‖‖‖‖‖‖‖‖‖‖‖

38

Double-Header

IT WAS two minutes before nine when The Mayor walked into his office on the morning after his inauguration. His penchant for punctuality had become something of a legend in the County Building section of this seat of government. Old appointees in the county clerk's office, who had grown accustomed to sauntering in at their leisure, swore that County Clerk Daley, the ever-watchful, lurked in a hidden recess, from which he sprung no later than two minutes, thirty seconds prior to starting time.

During his first press conference as mayor, Daley repeated something that he had said during the campaign. He told press, radio and television reporters that he would insist on stepping out "soon" as county chairman. He made it sound as though he meant the sooner the better. Back on February 24 Candidate Daley had said, "Upon my election I will resign as Democratic chairman to devote my full time and attention to the duties of the mayor's office."

He also declared during the press conference that he would attempt to implement the recommendations of the Home Rule Commission by urging legislation that would reduce the size of the fifty-member City Council and permit the election of some aldermen at large, who would be responsive to all the voters of the city rather than to the citizens of a specific ward.

Almost fifteen years later Daley still was county chairman; fifty aldermen sat or dozed in the City Council and there was no alderman at large.

The problem in reducing the size of the Council, which is at least twice the size it should be, is the reluctance of the voter to admit that public-service agencies, federal and state governments, and the little round man in the City Hall now provide many of the services that were in the domain of the alderman thirty years ago. There is a magic ring still for middle-aged Chicagoans in the words, "I'll complain to my alderman."

As for alderman at large, there isn't much enthusiasm for that idea, either, because Chicagoans, practical politicians all, tend to see a citywide alderman as a "guy running around like a chicken with his head chopped off." There also is the fear that aldermen at large would be carbon copies of Leon Despres, the gadfly from the Fifth Ward, who quite adequately represents the world in City Council matters.

The intriguing question that remains is why The Mayor chose to, or was allowed to, continue as county chairman. This fascinates students of Chicago politics almost as much as the romantic speculation about what the future would have held for Daley if Clarence Wagner had lived.

After eight years of wonderful freedom during the Kennelly administration, the aldermen could see themselves being turned around and herded, like so many black sheep, back to the Kelly disciplines. Except that this time it would not be Kelly-Nash or Kelly-Arvey, with a responsive shoulder to cry upon occasionally, but Daley-Daley. Knowing this, the aldermen gave Daley the dual powers, or so it seemed, and he built upon those powers year after year.

Ben Adamowski laughs off these interpretations as nonsense. "No alderman or ward committeeman 'gives' anything to the mayor," Adamowski said. "The mayor gives things to them. Or he takes them away."

Nick Bohling, the Republican, puts it another way but just as succinctly. "Your popularity as a person increases with other committeemen when you are elected mayor."

Colonel Arvey, the elder statesman, said he had been opposed to Daley's seeking the county chairmanship because Arvey feared that Dick would eliminate himself as a mayoral candidate if he became party leader. "Dick came to see me— Joe Gill still was chairman then—and Dick told me that Joe had talked to him about taking over as chairman. Dick and I had talks on the subject even before that. There were some reactionaries in our party then—I don't want to mention their names, because they are dead now—and at that time there were some rumblings that those men were going to take over our party.

"Dick asked then if I would be for him for county chairman," Arvey continued. "I said, 'Don't you want to be mayor? If the mayor's office is your ambition, don't take this job, Dick. If you ever want to run for mayor you'll be attacked as a political boss and that will be a great burden. But if the alternative to that other group is you, I'm for you.' "

Dick Daley had become party leader. He had been attacked as a political boss. Now he was The Mayor, and if he ever had had first thoughts about surrendering the county chairmanship, he began to have second thoughts soon after his inauguration. The word was around The Hall that the committeemen would meet before April to elect a new chairman to succeed Daley. But on April 27, John Dreiske, political editor of the *Sun-Times,* wrote, "One of the reasons Mayor Daley is reported wanting to remain [as chairman] is to have close supervision over the 1956 slatemaking."

The Mayor had closely supervised the slatemaking in 1956, in 1960, in 1964 and in 1968. Now he would prepare for the Democratic National Convention, which would be held in the International Amphitheater, a mile and a quarter from his home.

The Yippies were coming to Chicago for the Convention, he had been warned. Let them come, he told America, his round face wreathed by smiles. Yippies, hippies, flippies, they could all come, and Chicago would make them welcome.

39

Summerdale

CONFIDENT though he was that Chicago would divert the invasion of hippie-Yippies, The Mayor yearned in August, as he had during the terrible days of April, for the almost magical presence of his most celebrated former aide. If Orlando W. Wilson had not chosen to go into retirement in May of 1967, The Mayor would have been able to concentrate on matters within the convention hall. Orlando Wilson would have handled the streets, the parks and the rest of the city outside the walls of the International Amphitheater. In his dry, pedantic manner Orlando would have controlled the hippie-Yippies without leaving his office. Come to think of it, Wilson would have been the perfect man for this season of madness. He had been a professor from, of all places, the University of California at Berkeley.

Professor of police administration, to be sure, but a professor nonetheless. The young protesters who were threatening to come to Chicago could identify with Wilson. As has been true of so many fortuitous changes in the course of Chicago history, disaster created the vacuum that was filled by Orlando Wilson. The void began to spread from the lively mind of one Richard Morrison, who awakened one morning in January of 1960 to the realization that the thing missing from life was he. Richie was in a jail cell, an accommodation not unfamiliar to him. Morrison was not a common thief like some of the guys who worked in City Hall. His vocation demanded more daring and skill than were needed by those who stole from the taxpayers. Richie, at twenty-five, was a career burglar, reasonably competent in his field. It was said of him that he would take anything that wasn't screwed down and some things that were.

Richie, a toy man with delicate features and the sallow complexion of the night worker, felt lonely in jail. He also believed that he had been double-crossed by his partners. The loneliness bothered him more. He had expected to be double-crossed. He was in jail because that is where his business associates wanted him to be. He meant very little to them, he understood. He was the "little creep," the "little goof," the "little jerk."

Morrison knew what professional burglars did in a situation similar to his. They sat it out. They served time and kept their mouths shut. Richie knew that he should not be troubled by his injured feelings, but he was. When attorney Gerald Getty, a public defender, came to visit Richie, the lonely little burglar decided to reminisce about his recent past.

His partners were policemen, Richie said, simply but truthfully. There were twelve of them, Morrison told Getty, all assigned to the Summerdale district station on the North Side. Revealing this information to a public defender was one thing. Testifying in court would be quite another, Getty realized. Criminals often were afflicted by tightening of the larynx as court date approached. But Richie, his heart made heavy by the forgetfulness of his fellow men, insisted that he would be willing to blow the whistle on the cops before the grand jury. And he did.

Newspaper headlines cast Morrison as "The Babbling Burglar." His associates were "The Burglars in Blue." As the not-so-incredible story unfolded, little Richie was revealed to be much smarter than any of his partners, although one was the son of a high-ranking Police Department official and another had earned a degree in sociology from Loyola University. Richie, for example, never would have stored stolen goods in his apartment or garage. His police accomplices did precisely that stupid thing, thereby making seizure of evidence absurdly easy when other policemen raided the homes of the Summerdale moonlighters.

Richie was not notorious for telling the truth, but this time he—and all the evidence that had been left lying around in the form of television sets, radios, furniture, draperies, outboard motors, tires and sporting goods—were believed. An all-woman jury found eight of the twelve cops guilty, and five were sentenced to prison.

The "Summerdale Scandal" brought down Police Commissioner Timothy O'Connor, the symbol of Chicago's "honest cop." O'Connor, largely self-educated, had a rather simplistic approach to the conduct of the men serving under him. Because he was honest, he assumed that the great majority of policemen were similarly honest. Citizens might have warned him that his naïveté was hastening the day that would be referred to, with contempt, as "Summerdale."

Prevalent then within the Chicago Police Department was a philosophy that enabled an individual to make his own distinction between "honest graft" and graft. This deep-rooted philosophy went far back, beyond the time of Hinky Dink Kenna and Bathhouse John Coughlin, dictators of the First Ward at the turn of the century, to a day when the wide-open city made it almost mandatory that a cop ally himself with one side or the other, knowing that both sides were outside the law.

After World War II idealistic veterans, new to the force, attempted to buck the system, but by January of 1960, almost fifteen years after the end of the war, nothing much had changed. Some younger men long since had given up. They chose to go along with their elders, many of whom had obtained their jobs during the years of the Depression through a manifestation of "honest graft." They had bought their places on the eligibility list by paying off ward committeemen. Those who didn't go along became isolated and bitter.

The motorist who was stopped by a police squad car on

Lake Shore Drive and charged with driving ten miles over the limit understood the ground rules for the game of "honest graft." When the motorist handed his driver's license to the policeman, the motorist also added two or three singles or, if he could afford it, a five-dollar bill. The policeman then returned to the squad car, studied the driver's license for a minute or two, and said, "Mister White, I'm gonna give you a pass this time but be more careful in the future."

The motorist was a key player in the game, of course, but the citizenry's belief in the integrity of the police force was not bolstered simply because everybody knew that mutual corruption was necessary if "honest graft" was to endure.

The policeman excused himself with an explanation and a cynical smile. "If a guy drops me a deuce or a fin after I nail him for speeding, nobody gets hurt. He doesn't have to go to court and I've got a few more dollars for food and clothes for the kids. But if a guy causes a serious accident or is driving while he's drunk, he's got to go to the station."

Such explanations might have salved the consciences of some members of the Police Department's St. Jude League on the occasion of their monthly Communion Sunday, but everybody knew that "honest graft" could be stretched by the individual, or by two cops in a squad car, to cover almost any situation. The length of the stretch depended upon the living standard to which a policeman had grown accustomed. Some lived simply.

Nobody on the force was more austere than Tim O'Connor. For many years he did not own a home but rented an apartment. Tim would have no part of "honest graft"; but, street-wise as he was, he had to be aware that many of his men, including some top-ranking officers, were into it. He obviously trusted that they would not go too far. But if they did, there was no certainty that he would find them out, because honest cops, like honest doctors, have a compulsion to close ranks protectively around the venal in their ranks.

Thieves don't suffer from the same compulsion, as the aphorism makes clear. When little Richie Morrison, who had no honor to share with his thieving partners, told his cops-as-robbers story, The Mayor had to do something that he had talked about doing during his first campaign for mayor. He had to ask for the resignation of Tim O'Connor.

Just before he was elected in April of 1955, Daley had written these words at the invitation of the Chicago *Daily News:* "I shall seek the best advice and counsel in the country from recognized enforcement officials . . . in selecting the best qualified police commissioner available. I shall guarantee his complete independence to build an 'influence-proof' police force, improving morale and promotion opportunities."

There were two reasons why Dick Daley did not make good immediately on that promise. First, O'Connor had been Kennelly's man, and the new mayor had no intention of permitting press and public to seize upon the replacement of Honest Tim as proof that Daley intended to revert to the wide-open policies of Kelly, Thompson and the Harrisons. Second, Daley the hero-worshiper admired O'Connor. If Dick had gone on the police force instead of into politics, he would have tried to be the kind of cop Tim was—fearless, tough and honest.

Given the reprieve, O'Connor responded with the type of police administration Daley wanted. The department cracked down on gambling and dramatically cut the crime rate. The headlines were favorable, and O'Connor was in.

In January of 1960 and the months to follow, the headlines were unfavorable. A few cops had brought disgrace to Chicago and, therefore, O'Connor was out. Policemen reacted predictably. They hated Morrison for his vulgar display of "bad sportsmanship" that had undone good guy Tim O'Connor. They did not seem to hate the Summerdale Eight or other crooked cops who had been sabotaging their commissioner night and day.

40

Great Stoneface

REACTING vigorously as he always did when Chicago's reputation was blackened, The Mayor determined that his city would have the best police commissioner money could buy. To find that superior man, The Mayor appointed a committee of five, headed by eminent policeman-professor Orlando W. Wilson.

Wilson had the credentials. He was a book policeman, author of many volumes on police administration, but he also had been a street cop. He had become a patrolman on the Berkeley, California, force in 1921 to work his way to an A.B. degree from the University of California. He was to continue in police work, in wartime as in peacetime. During the wild days of Prohibition, he had cleaned up Wichita, Kansas. In World War II he served with the Military Police in Italy and England, rising to colonel's rank. Back at the University of California as professor of police administration, he had directed the reorganization of thirteen police departments. If he was not *the* authority in his field, he surely was one of the authorities.

This job that The Mayor was trying to fill would be the plum of plums, law enforcement's showcase to the world. During a month of exhaustive screening of applicants, Wilson and his fellow committee members conducted more than a hundred interviews. Despite this great care, or because of it, the right man could not be found. Finally, the other four members of the committeee recommended their chairman. After a long talk with The Mayor, Orlando Wilson did what County Chairman Daley had done when the Democrats were looking for a candidate for mayor in December of 1954. He took it himself.

Many Chicagoans, within politics and without, thought the selection of Wilson was too pat. They smelled a conspiracy. One whose nostrils were unusually sensitive to any situation in which Richard Daley was involved was The Mayor's former "musketeer," the Democrat-turned-Republican state's attorney Benjamin Adamowski. On the very day Wilson was named, March 2, 1960, Ben challenged the validity of the appointment on residency grounds. The police commissioner had to be a citizen of Chicago, Adamowski argued.

This challenge was repulsed easily by aldermen whose predecessors had found a way to make Ed Kelly mayor of Chicago. The City Council validated Wilson's self-designation, changed the job title from commissioner to superintendent, and made Chicago 67 percent more attractive to Orlando by raising his starting salary from the $18,000 O'Connor had been earning to $30,000.

Ten days after his appointment was rubber-stamped by the obsequious aldermen, Wilson met the more than ten thousand men of his command in two mass meetings. The policemen who had served in World War II were reminded of huge military buildings into which they had been herded to listen to commanding general or regimental colonel. This was not a get-acquainted session. This was an orientation lecture.

Wilson was a gray man. His hair was gray. His eyes were gray. His face was gray. His six feet seemingly extended by his slenderness, he towered over the policemen as he spoke to them. His words were as dry as the ash at the end of the ever-present cigarette that soon would be so familiar to every Chicagoan. He gave the troops the word. He said, in effect, what

Dick Daley had said after Adlai Stevenson had chosen Daley to be director of revenue for Illinois.

"The fix is out," Wilson said.

Policemen who didn't want to be honest cops understood immediately that this man would be a formidable foe to break. Policemen who wanted to be honest cops realized that Wilson meant to give them the opportunity. Realists all, the cops concluded that the plain talk of the military described their situation. Their souls belonged to God but their asses belonged to Wilson. From that moment they were to be privates, sergeants, lieutenants and captains in a military unit. It would be futile to turn to ward committeemen for help, because The Mayor was Wilson's ward committeeman.

Traditionally the police commissioner's office was in City Hall. That was one of the most obvious things wrong with the department, Wilson decided. The superintendent thought the place for him would be one far removed from politicians and one that made his presence, if not his person, highly visible to his men. He moved to the ramshackle Police Headquarters at Eleventh and State Streets, fourteen blocks from The Hall.

When The Mayor said he wanted the most modern police department in the world, Wilson reminded Daley that money would be necessary. Chicago's police would go first class for the first time in history. The superintendent was assured of a blank check. What Wilson wanted, Daley would want, and what Daley wanted, the City Council would approve.

Given almost unlimited authority, Orlando quickly accomplished for the administration of the Police Department what The Mayor had not been able to bring off for the administration of the city. Just as there were too many wards for efficiency, there were too many police districts. Many of the station houses were part of the fiefdoms of powerful ward committeemen. Wilson reduced the number of districts from thirty-eight to twenty-one. A few politicians screamed, others mumbled. Wilson did not hear the sounds of politicians. He did not need them. He did not want them. He was above them. He had The Mayor going for him. The superintendent's public-relations sense, an instinct that few policemen have developed, told him that he also had the people going for him.

Wilson proved himself worthy of the trust by demonstrating that he could save money as well as spend it. He found a thousand more policemen in, of all places, the Police Department. They were men who had been working for years as school-crossing guards and as clerks. Wilson replaced them with women at the crossings and with civilians in the clerical positions. Men who had not worn their police uniform for years had to hurry down to the neighborhood tailor to have the pants let out.

This gray man organized a gray unit, the Internal Inspections Division. The I.I.D. was referred to with bitterness as "one hundred spies," and that is precisely what the men of the unit were. Undercover agents within the department, they were assigned to every division and every squad to ferret out men such as those who had gone into business with Richie Morrison. The very next motorist who offered a little "honest graft" to a squad-car cop might be a member of the I.I.D. It was as though the gray man was everywhere without leaving his office at Eleventh and State.

As realistic and as cold as the toughest of his men, Wilson candidly admitted that his administration had not driven out all the crooks in the Police Department, but he added with his terrible directness, "We have made it a lot more difficult for them to be crooked." Wilson's dry words were applauded by the public, aware as they were that no other head of the Chicago police had admitted there was even one bad officer on the force.

Beyond the politicians though he was, Wilson had to cope with bitter opposition from within the department. The anti-

Wilson factions fought him conventionally in the newspapers
—some of his executive decisions, such as assigning only one
man to a squad car, were not popular with the public—and
the "anti" cops also waged guerrilla warfare against him with
"I.I.D." units of their own.

Men whose careers had been spent investigating persons
were certain that they could come up with damning evidence against Orlando Wilson. They tried very hard to "get
something on him," but managed to unearth no more than
two items of intelligence. "His name isn't even Wilson," they
whispered cryptically. Right, his name had been Vrälson.
This hardly shook those Chicagoans who knew that *Wilson*
was an Anglicization popular with many Scandinavians. One
could just as well challenge The Mayor because the name
Daley is something else in the Gaelic. "He divorced his first
wife and then married one of his students," the gossipmon-
gers revealed. True enough, but this revelation didn't shock
the public, either; Wilson had made no secret of his marital
history.

Wilson turned out to be too clean to be dirtied by those
who yearned for the bad old days, and with the passage of
time his policies began to win support within the department. He earned the appreciation of the younger men by announcing that there soon would be examinations for promo-
tions. The last such testing had been offered in 1948, and this
twelve-year delay in affording a glimmer of hope for advancement had been more responsible than any other factor
for killing initiative. Wilson said that the exams would be
held frequently in the future. Cops who had come on the job
since 1948 and those who had ranked far down the list after
that examination would be given a chance to make sergeant
before they were old men. Additionally, Wilson created
many new posts in the upper echelons, thereby speeding the
promotional process. His men no longer had to wait for the
ancient gaffers to retire or die.

More important than any decision he made or any investigation he ordered or any opportunity he offered was Wilson's determination to make the Chicago Police Department a professional force. For those who needed motivation even more than money, there could be pride in the job. Wilson understood that snob appeal had meaning for men who went to work in the blue uniform. When the superintendent traveled from his home to the no-longer-ramshackle headquarters building—Eleventh and State had been modernized at great expense and at his insistence—Wilson did not ride through the city in a squad car. He rode in a limousine. By impressing upon the public that the head of the Police Department was a very important person, Wilson put across his message that the police were important.

Unlike The Mayor's other dictator, Benjamin Willis, who had been wafted on sighs of relief from his position as superintendent of the Board of Education, Wilson became increasingly popular. Although he held the press at arm's length, Chicago's Number 1 policeman became a great favorite with the reporters. He met with them once a week, and they were won over by his dry and sometimes irreverent wit.

Wilson's success was still another example of The Mayor's coming out smelling like a rose after the Fates had dropped him into a dung heap. The lined face of the superintendent, which looked as though it had been etched by a jackhammer, was a symbol of security for the public. The citizenry was convinced that Chicago needed Orlando. The gray man conveyed the sense of being in control of a situation, whether he was or not, a gift that every great military commander has. Wilson might have remained forever as the top man at police headquarters, but a public servant who is held in such high esteem invariably is one who insists upon retiring.

When Wilson decided in May of 1967 that the Chicago Police Department would have to struggle along without him, one of his great admirers expressed regret and concern. Richie Morrison, still alive and still talking, plaintively asked a reporter, "Do things look like they might go back to the old days? That's what would happen if the higher echelon [of the Police Department] takes over."

But Wilson took care to avoid such a backslide. He chose as his successor a man who had served him well as an assistant, James Conlisk Jr.

41

⫿⫿⫿⫿⫿⫿⫿⫿⫿⫿⫿⫿⫿⫿⫿⫿⫿⫿⫿⫿⫿⫿⫿⫿⫿⫿⫿⫿

Moving Day

ONLY a few Chicagoans felt the terrible sadness of the week-end that was August 9, 10, 11, 1968. This was not a sadness that could be shared by all, as was the shroud that enfolded the city on the weekend of April 5, 6, 7, in the same year. This was not the sadness of fear that rode on flames through the West Side for all to cringe before. This was melancholy that insidiously worked its way into souls and submerged. For how long? For days. Surely, for days. And of the few who were sad during that weekend in August only a few of them understood why they were sad.

There was much movement during that weekend, and there were some meetings. Saturday was especially busy. In a restaurant downtown, Dave Stahl, administrative assistant to The Mayor, had a get-together with Rennie Davis, David Dellinger's man in Chicago. Davis was working as coordinator of the lively program that the National Mobilization to End the War was planning for convention week. Davis and Stahl talked about National Mobilization's request for permits for two large parades to be held on August 28 and additional permits for the use of ten parks as assembly grounds for the "delegates" to this other convention.

Nothing was resolved at this meeting.

Senator George McGovern of South Dakota announced on Saturday that he would seek the Democratic nomination for President. Now, as everyone had expected, there would be two Irish names for the delegations to consider. The name that Chicago's Democrats had in mind, however, was something else. It was the name that McGovern had mentioned so prominently when he entered the competition. The Senator from South Dakota said he would be "backing R.F.K. goals," as a newspaper headline put it.

A few blocks from the restaurant where Stahl and Davis had met to speak of permits there was a small office, dark now, that had been expected to be bursting with activity on this Saturday in August. It was the office that had been rented by the Chicago Kennedy for President committee. Robert Kennedy's last official words from the stage in the Embassy Room of the Ambassador Hotel in Los Angeles had been, "So my thanks to all of you and on to Chicago and let's win there."

Now the question was whether anyone would win there.

Some one thousand persons marched in the Loop on Saturday. Their purpose, they said, was to mourn the dead of Vietnam and of Hiroshima. There were speeches in Civic Center Plaza, across Clark Street from the City Hall-County Building, by Dellinger, the Reverend Ed Riddick of the Southern Christian Leadership Conference, and Bernardine Dohrn of the Students for a Democratic Society. When the program ended, the crowd applauded the police who were on duty.

This mass meeting was much different from another that had been held in the Civic Center Plaza late in April. On that other Saturday a crowd estimated at 6,500 had marched from the band shell in Grant Park to the Plaza to protest against the war in Vietnam. That program had ended with the police wading into the crowd, clubs swinging and batons flailing. Many persons were injured and eighty were arrested. This had been the kind of confrontation that had been predicted by University of Chicago Professor Hans Mattick in his comments on the "Shoot to Kill" order.

A report on events of April 27 in the Plaza had been released on August 1 by a panel of well-known Chicagoans, a panel that had not been appointed by The Mayor. This committee had been brought together at the urging of the Roger Baldwin Foundation of the American Civil Liberties Union. Again the police, city officials and The Mayor were the losers. The committee, headed by Edward Sparling, retired president of Roosevelt University, reported, "Allowing public officials the benefit of every doubt, the commission concluded that they sought to destroy the march."

The Mayor did not comment immediately upon the report, because he had been in Washington on August 1, lunching with President Johnson. Back in Chicago the next day, The Mayor responded with typical fervor. "Much of it is not true," he said of the report. "The Police Department did not create any incidents. The Police Department is always attacked. I had a long conversation with Superintendent Conlisk and I know it isn't true." Then The Mayor confessed that he was "sort of amazed" by "the constant effort of these people [the marchers] to confront the police."

There had been no effort to confront the police on August 10 with anything except a round of applause.

Stories in the newspapers told of unusual public improvements that were being made in Canaryville, the section just south of Bridgeport. From Thirty-ninth Street to Forty-third Street holes in the streets were patched, light poles were painted and redwood fences were raised in front of the vacant lots on side streets leading to Halsted Street. None of this would have been necessary if McCormick Place had not been combustible, but Chicago was determined to put its best face forward for the delegates who would be riding to the International Amphitheater, even if that face had to be lifted and remade like the façade of an aging movie actress.

That the face was false did not surprise a city employe named Fritz Etienne, who had been employed, quite ironically, in the transportation design section of the Public Works Department's Bureau of Engineering. In the Sunday editions of the *Sun-Times,* Etienne explained why he was leaving Chicago, with his wife and four children, after eleven years of residence. He was a native of Haiti who had come to the United States and to Chicago because he had been certain that the laws of the nation and the ordinances of the city would guarantee the freedom that had been denied to so many in his native country.

"You soon learn," he said, "that the Negro must have other special laws—laws that say you should be able to live where you want."

The Mayor of all the people evidently had not been the mayor for Fritz Etienne, who said he was moving to Montreal. He also said that he was a direct descendant of Jean Baptiste Point Du Sable, the black man who was Chicago's first resident.

If he had been Irish, instead of Haitian, Fritz Etienne might have stayed around to tell all who cared to listen, "I'd be on Easy Street today if the old man had hung on to that property down on the river." Etienne chose to leave Chicago, just as Du Sable had done.

42

Pablo's Dog

THERE had been a happy time when The Mayor's periphrasis
and obfuscation was accepted by the press, which expected
good-natured con from politicians, but that day was gone.
Since April and "Shoot to Kill," The Mayor no longer amused
those reporters who followed him on his meandering oratori-
cal trips around Mrs. O'Leary's Barn. Now the press had
been expanded to "the media" and an important division of
the media was madder than hell at Richard J. Daley.

The television networks, whose leaders were capable of
matching The Mayor or any other government leader in il-
logic, still were smarting because The Mayor had insisted
that the Convention be in Chicago, in spite of everything. On
Friday, August 23, with the opening of the Convention less
than forty-eight hours away, the networks went on the offensive. CBS led the attack against the security measures that
would seriously inhibit coverage of the Democrats' big show.
Eric Sevareid let Chicago have it during Walter Cronkite's
newscast early Friday evening. Sevareid had the temerity to
compare Chicago with Prague. This was the kind of thing
The Mayor had come to expect from his hard-hitting adver-
sary, Ben Adamowski, but the blows hurt even more when
they were thrown by an outsider. In Prague that day Russian
troops had machine-gunned a student dormitory. That sort
of thing never would happen in Chicago.

Television officials were seething because their large, mobile equipment and transmitting vans had been ordered off

the streets Friday. Earlier in the week the networks had been told that their cameramen would not be permitted to work from rooftops or from windows at the Amphitheater or near Convention headquarters.

In United States District Court that day the National Mobilization Committee was a loser in its suit to obtain a permit for a march to the Amphitheater during the Convention. The antiwar organization also failed to obtain a ruling that would have forced the city to allow peace demonstrators to sleep in city parks. Providing sleeping accommodations for visitors was not a city responsibility, said Judge William (Billy) Lynch, The Mayor's boyhood pal, political ally and former law partner.

While the National Mobilization was losing in the Federal Building, those who professed to be members of the Youth International Party, if there was a Youth International Party, were performing in the Civic Center Plaza. Chicagoans who knew something of the zany history of their city and were aware that there once had been a "Bughouse Square" which attracted the soapbox philosophers of far left and far right were shaken by the sudden realization that Civic Center Plaza, one of The Mayor's dreams-come-true, was the modern "Bughouse Square." Most shook with indignation. Some shook with laughter.

On the east end of the Plaza, a few yards from Dearborn Street, stands the most famous "whatsit" in Chicago history. This is the Picasso, which most Chicagoans refer to as "The Mayor's practical joke." The second question is whether the joke was perpetrated by The Mayor or was on him. The first question is, "What in God's name is it supposed to be?"

Permission to mount this Picasso in the Plaza was obtained from the eighty-five-year-old sculptor by a whimsical and public-spirited Chicago architect named William Hartmann. Because Picasso professes to be a Communist and has been an advocate of free love, among other things, most of The Mayor's friends and all of his enemies were astonished when he agreed to accept Pablo's gift. Big John Hoellen, one of the few opposition aldermen in the City Council, denounced the Picasso project and suggested that Chicago should erect a statue of Ernie Banks, the venerable and venerated black first-baseman of the Cubs, in the Plaza. Hoellen expected no support for his idea and got none. His North Side constituents, most of them partisans of the Cubs, thundered that Ernie Banks was old as first-basemen go but he was far from rusty.

The Picasso had to be rusty to match its backdrop, the thirty-story Civic Center. The Picasso, $300,000 worth of rusty steel, five stories high, was unveiled on August 15, 1967, and an entire city said, "Huh?" After inspecting it from every angle, Chicagoans decided the pile was one of three things—the face of a woman or the face of Picasso's Afghan hound or a heap of junk. The initial reaction of many citizens was to disown the sculpture as another example of modern art gone mad, but when Chicagoans read that tourists were coming from all over the world to gawk at Chicago's prize, the natives went back for a closer look. The Picasso was the perfect centerpiece for the Yippies.

Seven Yippies and their "Presidential candidate," a pig named Pigasus, had been arrested in the Square. They had been, that is, if one were willing to concede that a pig could be arrested. Nobody was terribly upset, just then, by the screwball tactics of the Yippies. Jerry Rubin and his unwashed followers were comic relief when compared with other problems confronting convention city.

The Mayor seemed especially disturbed by a murder-plot story that came out of the Cook County Jail, Chicago's center for advanced sodomy. Three jail inmates, each supposedly acting independently, circulated "inside information" that black gangs would collaborate in attempts upon the lives of Vice-President Humphrey, Senator McCarthy and Senator John McClellan of Arkansas. According to the informants, McClellan was the enemy because his subcom-

mittee had eliminated a federal job-training program that
had been dominated by gang members. Humphrey and
McCarthy would be killed to embarrass The Mayor, or perhaps because Negroes also believe death comes in threes.

There was another assassination rumor that was not revealed publicly until almost six weeks later. Federal Bureau
of Investigation sources in California alerted the Chicago
office of the F.B.I. of the possibility that executioners had
been appointed by the Black Panthers to kill four prominent
Chicago Negroes who were marked as traitors by the Panthers' high command. Two were very close to The Mayor—
Federal Judge James Parsons and Alderman Ralph Metcalfe
of the Third Ward.

During the weekend of August 17–18, while hippie-Yippies and hippie-Yippies-watchers were moving into Lincoln
Park on the North Side, F.B.I. agents questioned the men
who supposedly were plotting against Humphrey, McCarthy
and McClellan. The F.B.I. wrote off the plot as wishful
thinking on the part of black Chicagoans who bombastically
willed McClellan dead but had no intention of pulling a trig-
ger or throwing a bomb.

There was cynical amusement for F.B.I. agents and Police
Department undercover agents in this cloak-and-dagger routine, because it was widely known that the leaders of a group
thought capable of trying to kill McClellan or anybody else
were planning to do more than go underground. Eight leaders
of the Blackstone Rangers, aware of the intense heat that was
to come, had decided to get out of town. The Rangers hierarchy had prevailed upon clergymen to arrange for work-
vacations on farms downstate. It is doubtful, however, that
the Blackstones or their sometime allies, the East Side Disciples, would have gone gunning for national figures if the
Ranger leaders had remained in the city. As is true of members of that most sophisticated of all Chicago gangs, the
Mafia, "soldiers" in the Rangers and the Disciples concentrate on killing troops in rival gangs, and sometimes members

of their own. They leave the murdering of political leaders to the twisted products of white society.

There obviously was a pressure campaign to persuade United States Attorney Thomas Foran that the "plotters" should be brought before the federal grand jury for questioning, but when the F.B.I. was unable to find a would-be assassin, Foran backed away. The city was sufficiently combustible what with the advance guard of the hippies and the Democratic party delegates on the scene, the inconveniences caused by a strike of telephone workers, and the threat of another wildcat strike by black bus drivers. Foran wisely felt that assassination rumors might touch off reactions that would be felt for months to come.

Even after the *Tribune* printed a story about the alleged plot in its editions of Tuesday, August 20, Foran continued to try to put down the rumors. Two days later he startled many legal experts with the announcement that the August grand jury would question the alleged plotters after all. Chicago lawyers and legal observers have become accustomed to reading of grand jury investigations in newspapers to which the information has been leaked, but it was hardly expected that the United States Attorney would make a public revelation.

Foran's unusual performance, which had to have Justice Department sanction, inspired a conclusion that was as blunt as it was inevitable. The Mayor had leaned on Washington, his critics decided. To be fair to Daley and to Foran, however, it should be remembered that Chicago was haunted by the murders of Robert F. Kennedy, Martin Luther King and John F. Kennedy. In the wake of April nobody in Chicago had the temerity to say, "It can't happen here." All that was left to say was, "We could not be guilty of the neglect that would permit it to happen here."

Eight leaders of the Blackstone Rangers came in from their downstate retreat on Friday, August 23, to testify before the grand jury. Jeff Fort, the twenty-one-year-old

Ranger chief, was asked about a location which he heard as "Forty-third and Austin." Because this location made no sense in the context of the inquiry, Fort's lawyer asked him if the question could have been about "Forty-third and Halsted." Fort said it might have been and then supposedly asked, "What's at Forty-third and Halsted?"

The International Amphitheater, which was to be the convention hall for the Democrats, is at Forty-third and Halsted. Two interpretations were put on Fort's supposed lack of knowledge of the Amphitheater. Those who thought Fort was being harassed cited it as proof of the cultural deprivation of the ghetto boy. Those who thought Fort should be locked up until after the Convention had ended shrugged it off as another manifestation of Fort's street-smart flair for making fools of persons in authority.

Warner Saunders, who knew as much as any man about the structure and the operations of the black gangs, because he had been a youth when the South Side gangs were in their ascendancy, might have told the grand jury and the city administration that Chicago had very little to fear from the Blackstone Rangers during this time of national political activity. "Black gangs, unlike white gangs, have not as yet been able to make the transition to political power," Saunders had explained on another occasion. "The stages of transition are from fighting among themselves, to fighting other gangs, to fighting the community, to fighting for complete reorganization as a political entity. The black gangs are unable to move to the final stage, because the door to the outside has been slammed on them. They could not break out and move into the Loop, as the Irish and Italian gangs did. Because the door was closed, their fury continued to be directed inward, on their own community."

The eight Blackstone Rangers answered the questions of the grand jury and quickly got out of town again. The Mayor concentrated on the business of the Convention. The eight Rangers would miss all the excitement.

43

Great Day

EARLY in his first term The Mayor began to practice mass psychology on a citizenry whose members either did not know what mass psychology was or were unaware that Dick Daley knew what it was. Over and over again The Mayor drummed into the consciousness of Chicagoans with variations on two simple themes. To all who accused him of being a politician, he would respond in a fatherly whisper, "Good politics is good government and good government is good politics." And each time that the good politicians who were under orders to give the citizens good government did something more than show up for their pay checks, The Mayor would smile paternally, puff out his cheeks and chest, and purr, "It's a great day for Chicago."

Students of what might be described by the coined word *politment* clearly understood that the new mayor was reiterating the policies of the Harrisons, Big Bill the Builder, and Ed Kelly. Good politics provided the services and the facilities that gladdened the hearts of the voters out in the neighborhoods and of the suburbanites who ran the business community downtown, and those voters and suburbanites provided the support, at the ballot boxes and in the campaign chests, that enabled the good-government representatives to get reelected, and that was good politics.

When this endless belt of cooperation and fulfillment produced a new expressway or a bridge or a fleet of trucks to

244

pick up the garbage, The Mayor was overcome by emotion.
Once he had recovered his composure, he would sigh, "It's a
great day for Chicago." Big Bill Thompson had put it another way during the Roaring Twenties. "Throw away your
hammer and get a horn," Bill had thundered. "Don't be a
knocker. Be a booster."

Booster Daley had a theme to live by, but it was expressed
in action, never in words. It was a modification of the pro-
found declaration that had become part of the image of a
baseball manager named Leo Durocher. "Nice guys finish
last" was the Durocher credo. The Mayor, whose sports heroes were more noble and majestic types than the flamboyant
and vengeful Durocher, would not go that far. Dick Daley
did not believe that nice guys finished last. What he knew
was that, in politics, soft guys finished out.

When Daley had taken Benjamin Becker off the Democratic
ticket less than a month before the election of 1955, those
who had not studied the man who was the Democratic candidate for mayor believed that Becker had been chopped
down because there had been no alternative. Daley was running against Merriam, a reformer always on the scent of
scandal. Daley was running scared and could not afford compassion. "Dick couldn't have done anything else," the City
Hall types said.

What the City Hall types would learn, as the Daley years
piled up, is that The Mayor wouldn't have done it another
way. He was a warm man in some respects, but he could be
terribly cold when he believed that the reputation of his city,
his party or himself was endangered. The first demonstration
of this came seventeen months after his first inauguration.

Herbert Paschen, an honorable and reasonably competent
public servant who was Cook County Treasurer, had been
slated to head the Democratic state ticket in 1956. Paschen
was to oppose the incumbent Republican governor, William
Stratton. Then somebody in the county treasurer's office

chose to talk about a form of kickback that was referred to as the "flower fund." The fund was sustained by "contributions" from banks that were holding county moneys in interest-free deposits. The official explanation was that the banks were chipping in—voluntarily, of course—toward purchases of flowers for deceased employees of the treasurer's office and for deceased members of the families of living employees. But what was left over—and a lot was left over—helped deserving Democrats get elected.

Paschen was running hard and uphill when the *Sun-Times* broke the story of the blooming scandal. Although it was generally conceded that Paschen had had nothing to do with the flower fund—the treasurer had dismissed two high-ranking employes for their involvement in the scheme—Daley did not attempt to extract the roses from among the thorns. The Mayor vividly remembered what "innocent until proven guilty" had done to the party in 1950, when Jack Arvey agreed to go all the way with Daniel Gilbert, the gambling man who ran for sheriff.

There were only two months until election day, but on September 4 the Democrats announced that suburbanite Richard Austin would replace Paschen. White-maned and strong-jawed, Dick Austin was a Superior Court judge who had served for seventeen years as an assistant state's attorney. Austin was not wild about going into the gubernatorial game as a second-string player and downstate Democrats were equally reluctant to let him carry the ball. The downstaters would have preferred one of their boys. But when Daley summoned him Austin went in, and although he had almost no time to mount a campaign, he ran very well. The voters gave Austin 2,134,909 votes. Stratton won his second term with 2,171,786.

This was a moral victory for Austin, who would be rewarded in 1961 with a seat on the federal bench, but it was a total victory for County Chairman Daley, whose action spoke more effectively to the voters than his words ever had. "See," the action said, "we Democrats would rather lose than offer a candidate who was even touched by scandal."

Then there was Freddie Romano, whose fedora brim wasn't necessarily the widest in The Hall but seemed to be the widest because he was so small. Beneath his hat Freddie looked like a small child viewing the world from under a porch. Or like the parody gangster types who were cast in movies that starred Edward G. Robinson or George Raft.

Freddie could have been described as a "party wheelhorse." A wheelhorse is a second- or third-string politician who works hard or has mastered the technique of giving the impression of working hard. As his reward for work or the illusion of work, Freddie had been made an assistant state's attorney.

He seemed to be doing well until a day in 1953 when the *Sun-Times* printed excerpts from a police captain's "little red book." The book offered rather broad suggestions that Assistant State's Attorney Romano was an associate, even a business associate, of Ross Prio, a wheelhorse in his own right. Prio was one of the coming stars of the crime syndicate. Romano resigned despite the protestations of his boss, State's Attorney John Gutknecht, who said that except for the company he kept, little Freddie was a dedicated public servant.

Freddie and his big fedora floated in obscurity for a while, and then early in 1955 he was slipped into the Probate Court of Cook County as an assistant judge. That was the accepted way to do things in those days. A party worker who got himself jammed up was benched while the heat subsided. As he did his penance, he continued to serve the organization until the leaders gauged the temperature of public opinion and decided that the unfortunate fellow could be put into another job. Romano's time was up and he could hide out now in the relative obscurity of Probate Court.

Under the old rules of operation Freddie might have spent

a useful lifetime adjudicating murky wills. Unfortunately for him the old rules had been changed. Assistant Judge Romano served exactly one day in Probate Court. The name of County Chairman Daley wasn't mentioned in stories of Romano's brief career on the bench, but nobody seriously wondered who had ordered the ax to drop. The word had come down. "Get him out of there." And Freddie was gone. It seemed so unfair.

Then there was Anthony DeTolve, who wanted nothing more than to be elected alderman of the historic First Ward. Tony, who had worked diligently in the Illinois state legislature for eleven years to acquire a reputation for buffoonery, felt certain that the citizens of the First would not look upon him unkindly simply because he was a nephew-by-marriage of one of the big men in the Syndicate, Sam (Mooney) Giancana. The citizens wouldn't have, either—DeTolve would have maintained the tradition of Bathhouse John Coughlin and Hinky Dink Kenna, who had been co-aldermen of the ward—but the late Sam Blair, an energetic young man who had a sense of humor and a sense of outrage, mercilessly lampooned DeTolve in the pages of *Chicago's American*. In his first attempt to interview the Democratic aldermanic candidate, Blair was told by DeTolve that Anthony was "busy, busy, all the time busy." In every story thereafter, Blair referred to his patsy as "Busy Busy" DeTolve. Other newspapers picked up the nickname.

On December 18, 1962, The Mayor was asked about the DeTolve situation and this was his response: "This is a matter for the people of the First Ward. I did not interfere in ward matters in 1955 or 1959 and I don't intend to now."

This was the sort of reaction politicians expected from a man who had not wanted outsiders to interfere in the affairs of the Eleventh Ward when he was committeeman, but those who had watched The Mayor for eight years were certain that DeTolve would have to go unless Blair stopped. Blair continued to ridicule DeTolve and soon "Busy Busy" announced that he was so busy he was compelled to withdraw from the aldermanic race. The absurdity was compounded after the election of Michael Fio Rito, the late replacement for DeTolve. Some unsportsmanlike citizen revealed that Fio Rito did not dwell in the First Ward but resided far away in a high-rent district. So the alderman of the First Ward had to be ejected from the City Council.

Ultimately the ward's bosses came up with a permanent alderman, and in time Sam Blair, a blithe and witty man, died of lung cancer. It will be noted that many of the severe critics of The Mayor, the men and women who often saved him from himself, have died in early middle age. Good health and longevity are important to a politician—he outlives most of his enemies—but the early death of Blair and other reporters of his stature was as much a loss for The Mayor as it was for the newspapers and the readers.

Then there was Benjamin Lewis, another candidate for alderman in 1963. Lewis, the most enigmatic and the most controversial of the Negro aldermen, had been reelected on Tuesday, February 26. The voters of the Twenty-fourth Ward, Colonel Jack Arvey's power base in an earlier day, had been so impressed with Lewis' first term they returned him to office with 12,179 votes. His opponent was given 888 votes. Even Arvey hadn't been much more popular than that.

At nine o'clock on Thursday morning, less than two days after the election, the body of the extremely popular Benjamin Lewis was found in his office in the new headquarters of the Twenty-fourth Ward, 3246 West Jackson Boulevard. The alderman had been shot in the back of the head three times.

The Mayor offered a $10,000 reward for the arrest and conviction of Lewis' slayer. The reward came from The Mayor's contingency fund. The police said the murder had been the culmination of "a personal matter," the sort of "what difference does it make?" remark that convinced Father Dan Mallette that black lives were not considered as important, by some in authority, as white lives were.

At the funeral in the Greater Gallilee Missionary Baptist Church, 1308 South Independence Boulevard, the former temple of Congregation Knesses Israel Nusach Sfard, the pastor asked The Mayor to come foward and say a few words. Some in the congregation thought the minister was trying to put The Mayor in a precarious position by compelling him to say something good about a black man, but Richard Daley also would seek reelection in April, and his edge over Republican candidate Benjamin Adamowski might be provided by black politicians like Ben Lewis and black voters like the men and women seated in the Greater Gallilee Church.

The Mayor was equal to the challenge, if challenge it was. In his tribute to the man who had been the first Negro precinct captain of the Twenty-fourth Ward, The Mayor said that Alderman Lewis had given himself for "this great community, this great ward, this great city." Relying, as he often did, upon Francis of Assisi to provide consolation, The Mayor concluded with "Lord, make us instruments of Thy peace."

Then there were Joseph Lohman, Steve Mitchell and Seymour Simon. Lohman, a sociologist on the University of Chicago faculty, had been the Democratic party's "reform" nominee for county sheriff on the first ticket picked under the supervision of County Chairman Daley in 1954. Lohman had won and he won again when the party slated him for state treasurer in 1958.

Mitchell, hand-picked by Adlai Stevenson in 1952 to be the national chairman of the Democratic party, had wanted to run for governor of Illinois against incumbent William Stratton in 1956. Richard Daley, only briefly The Mayor, first chose Herb Paschen and then turned to Dick Austin after Paschen had been pelted from his pedestal by flowers.

Although Cook County Democrats won eight of the ten Congressional seats available in 1956, Mitchell felt that the reelection of Republican Senator Everett Dirksen and Republican Governor William Stratton could be attributed to a lack of direction within the Democratic organization. On December 6, 1956, Mitchell wrote a letter to Daley charging that the Democratic party in Illinois and particularly in Cook County was suffering from "indolence and ineffective leadership."

Playing a rough political game, Mitchell went after The Mayor personally. Steve said that County Chairman Daley had been especially vigorous in promoting Mayor-candidate Daley in 1955. "When you received the full benefit of the party's resources in a primary contest with two other Democrats, many people felt this was unfair just as it would be unfair for a man to be both an umpire and a pitcher in a baseball game."

In 1960 there was another three-man primary. Lohman and Mitchell chose to enter the lists against The Mayor's preferred candidate, Judge Otto Kerner. In 1960 as in 1955 the organization candidate won the primary and the election. Lohman and Mitchell slid quickly out of the limelight.

Seymour Simon, he of the crew cut and the firm jaw, is the great mystery of Democratic party politics in Cook County. A fair-haired boy who had been spoken of as a potential candidate for mayor in the epoch after Daley, Simon had been chosen as the nominee for president of the Cook County Board in 1962. He won, as expected; but in 1966, when his reslating was taken for granted, Simon was dumped. There surely are party insiders who know why Daley didn't want Seymour any more. Simon himself may know why. But the voters do not. His hair longer and grayer, Simon was permitted to run for alderman in 1968. He won in his ward, which restored one fiftieth of the power that once had been his.

And then there was Bill Clark. And then there weren't young Adlai and John Stamos.

44

⠀⠀⠀⠀⠀⠀⠀⠀⠀⠀⠀⠀

One-Man Band

CONVENTION host. Party leader. Mayor. Commander in chief of the police force. Slatemaker. Those five tracks of activity lay ahead of The Mayor on Saturday, August 24, some twenty hours before the business of the Convention would begin. For five days and five nights he would have to operate on each of those tracks, incessantly switching back and forth, moving, moving, moving.

Five jobs and nobody seemed at all concerned that the responsibility might be too much for one man. Neither Ed Kelly nor Tony Cermak had burdened himself with so many things to do in so few days. Ed and Tony had been mayor and convention host and party leader and slatemaker, there could be no doubt about that, but they had had able, energetic co-workers. Pat Nash for Cermak and Kelly. And after Pat couldn't handle the jobs, Jack Arvey for Kelly. Even with those capable, tough assistants at their sides, Ed and Tony never dreamed of trying to maintain control of the police force during convention week. That weighty extra burden had been added to Richard Daley's shoulders when he took the police away from Jim Conlisk in April.

Nobody was concerned over the multiple responsibilities, because for thirteen and a half years, The Mayor had taken literally the "I" in "I Will." He had become everything to everybody. Settler of strikes. Eradicator of slums. Cleaner of alleys. Expediter of expressways. Salvager of neighborhoods.

Queller of riots. Adviser to Presidents. He was Hennessey, Fennesey and all the other Irishmen in McNamara's Band.

There may have been some friends who said, "Dick, for God's sake man, slow down. You are trying to do too much." But he had grown beyond the advice of friends, and the others, so many others, who should have been doing many of the jobs that devolved upon him, had grown accustomed to saying, "Let The Mayor handle it." He was the stern father clasping an entire city to his strutter's chest.

He had to be convention host, party leader, mayor, commander in chief. Those tracks were open and he must run on them. The slatemaking track should have been closed long ago, but this was the track on which he and his candidates would have to run until the first Tuesday of November, and the important events of the Convention would be the starting points for that ten-week trip.

The slate that troubled him on Saturday night was not President and Vice-President, but the close-to-home offices, the tickets for Illinois and Cook County. The movement on that track had been a series of false starts, missed signals, derailments and violent collisions. It had begun as a deadly serious race to maintain political power and it had deteriorated into something that might have been a script written by W. C. Fields for the Marx Brothers. Eventually it made the voters laugh, and the Democrats of Cook County were not accustomed to being laughed at.

The 1968 campaign had opened on January 4 with a trumpeting speech by The Mayor. In a mood that the press had described as "fighting," he had predicted a third term for Governor Otto Kerner, although Illinois political history reminded everybody that since the turn of the century governors had had no luck when they tried for a third term. On February 7 Kerner announced that the Democratic organization would have to proceed without him at the top of the state ticket. Kerner's withdrawal prompted a question from the voters. "Didn't The Mayor know what the Governor had been intending to do?"

With Kerner off the ticket The Mayor had five potential gubernatorial candidates, each certain that he would be as attractive to the voters as he was in his own eyes. Daley had to consider Samuel Shapiro, the lieutenant governor, who became governor when Kerner moved to the federal bench; Adlai Stevenson III, state treasurer; William Clark, state attorney general; Michael Howlett, state auditor; and Sargent Shriver, former president of the Chicago Board of Education.

In any other Presidential year The Mayor could have picked any of the five and billed his choice as a "blue-ribbon candidate." Any of the five could win. Four of the five had proved themselves as vote-getters. The fifth, Shriver, had the potential to be an outstanding candidate. He was a Kennedy son-in-law, the leader of the Peace Corps, and the general in the War on Poverty that had been begun by President Kennedy and continued by President Johnson. Each of the five had done things for The Mayor when Dick Daley had asked, just as The Mayor had done much for each of them.

45

Full Circle

NINETEEN-SIXTY, which had begun for The Mayor as the Year of the Song of Richie Morrison, improved greatly when the Democrats assembled in Los Angeles for their national convention. The Mayor's enthusiasm for John F. Kennedy, which had begun four years earlier during the convention in Chicago, swept the Illinois delegation at Los Angeles and, in time, swept the convention. In caucus the Illinois delegates voted to give 59½ of 69 votes to Senator Kennedy.

To assure this support for Kennedy, The Mayor had to do something else, which some characterized as desertion and others thought of as a double cross, but most regarded as political realism. He had to give Adlai Stevenson, former governor of Illinois, no votes from Cook County.

Stevenson, who twice had volunteered to be the Democrats' cannon fodder against the power of General Dwight Eisenhower, obviously thought he deserved a third campaign against a candidate who could, most Democrats believed, be beaten. Adlai tried to get through to Daley to ask, "What in the world is going on over there?" but The Mayor couldn't seem to bring himself to take the calls. Sentimentalists thought that Daley's sentimentalism had taken over and that he couldn't bear to speak the truth to the man who had done so much for him.

After Daley had forfeited his position in the Illinois Senate to make his ill-advised race for sheriff against Elmer Michael

Walsh in 1946, newly elected Governor Stevenson had recalled Dick from political limbo. Stevenson appointed Daley
to be director of revenue in 1949.

During the years of the growth of The Mayor's powers, his
admirers, his payrollers and his coat-tail riders insisted that
he would have made it even without Stevenson's helping
hand. They said that nothing could have stopped Dick from
becoming county chairman and The Mayor except an alive
and well Clarence Wagner. But all this was speculation.
What was known is that when Daley desperately needed re-
vival, Adlai Stevenson had breathed upon him.

Jack Arvey, who is widely thought to be more cynical than
The Mayor but probably has more soft spots in his heart than
Dick does, prevailed upon Daley to answer Stevenson's calls.
Bluntly The Mayor told the Governor that he had no support
in the Illinois delegation. Then Daley felt it necessary to add
that Stevenson had had no Illinois support in 1956, either,
but that he, The Mayor, had kept the delegation with Adlai.
Dick Daley had stopped payment on his political debt.

In 1968 there was another Adlai Stevenson and more trouble and more bitterness. This one, thirty-seven years old, was
as rumpled as his father had been well groomed, as hard-
bitten as his father had been forgiving, as rambling as his
father had been precise, as tough as his father had been gentle, as single-minded as his father had been vacillating. And
he wanted to be governor as his father had been.

On February 23 State Treasurer Stevenson walked into a
room in Springfield to make his presentation to the State
Central Committee and to be questioned by the committee
members. What must be understood is that this appearance
by a would-be candidate is a ritual and has no more meaning
than most ritual does. The oral presentation of the individual's qualifications is part of the show of democracy, but in
Illinois's Democracy the decision invariably is made long
before the potential candidates appear. Martin Kennelly
learned about that in 1954. Adlai Stevenson III must have

known that the decision was in, but for reasons that seemed mysterious at the time the Harvard graduate and former Marine Corps captain chose to bring the decision into the open.

Instead of going in with hat in hand as young aspirants are expected to do, Stevenson brought a typewritten statement. He told them he would be frank and blunt, and he let them have it in the third paragraph. "First of all, I believe I would win as a candidate for Governor," he read. "I base that conviction on all the polls which I have seen or heard about, my past record in running for office, and the widespread belief expressed by many people, including party leaders, labor leaders and responsible newspaper editors, that without my candidacy for Governor, the party would take a serious risk of losing. I would not like to see us lose both houses of the General Assembly and the offices of the Executive branch. I would not like to be the only Democratic officeholder in Springfield for the next two years. . . ."

He was being frank and blunt. He was telling them that he was the only candidate who could win for them. He was telling them, moreover, that without him, they might lose it all. Some had thought his father to be arrogant, but now they comprehended that arrogance can be measured by degrees. He was infuriating them, but more than a few suspected that his assessment might prove to be very close to the facts of the Democrats' Dilemma, State of Illinois version, 1968. Then he read another paragraph he did not have to read in that place, at that time. He read, and he provided them with words they could hit him with again and again:

"There is one last point I would like to make. I think you gentlemen should know that as a candidate for the Senate, I might feel obliged to take a stand in opposition to President Johnson on the subject of Vietnam. Although I would, of course, in any capacity do all in my power to support the whole ticket."

He knew that some slatemakers would not mind if he were

their candidate for United States Senator against Everett McKinley Dirksen, Republican minority leader and long-time friend of President Johnson. He was telling them that he didn't want to run for the Senate. This was family history come full circle. In 1948 his father had wanted to be slated for Senator and Paul Douglas had desired to be slated for governor, but Jack Arvey had not been charmed by the thought of the strong-willed, independent Douglas in the governor's mansion. Young Stevenson understood very well that he was expected to sacrifice his ambition. Perhaps he believed that the Stevenson family had been the lamb on the altar of Democratic expediency often enough.

There are reasons to doubt that Stevenson would have been given the nomination under the best of circumstances. From the moment of Otto Kerner's withdrawal the Democrats had an "incumbent" candidate in the pleasant person of Sam Shapiro. Mr. Sam, the gentleman from Kankakee, had fought beside The Mayor in intramural matches against downstate teams captained by Paul Powell. But Stevenson's allusion to the conduct of the war was sufficient cause to remove him from consideration. The Democrats of Illinois believed that their President knew best.

The slatemakers met again in Cook County Democratic headquarters in Chicago on Monday, and young Stevenson met again with The Mayor before that session. "The Senate was still 'in' as of that meeting, I felt," Stevenson said. "All I had to do was recant."

Adlai could not. When he walked into Suite 220 of the Sherman House, with its garish green-and-gold chairs and the picture of The Mayor looking benignly down upon the slatemakers, he felt he could do no more than explain his Vietnam position. Stevenson could not, would not, repudiate his position even after he felt a tug at an arm and looked down into the face of The Mayor, who was softly saying, "Does this mean that you will support the President on Vietnam?"

"I was aghast," Stevenson said as he reconstructed those few moments. "What I said was that I was reserving the right to make up my mind to do what was right. I wasn't at all averse to running for the Senate at that point, provided the Vietnam problem could have been worked out. If it could have been, there would have been opportunities for ideological confrontations with Dirksen."

Unfortunately, many Democratic slatemakers were much closer to Dirksen, ideologically, than to Adlai Stevenson III or II. Dirksen, like the slatemakers, endorsed the conduct of the war and was for Lyndon Baines Johnson. It did not take Adlai's idealistic or practical supporters long to decide that their man had been set up for a downfall, not necessarily by Daley but by party elder statesmen, such as folksy Paul Powell, secretary of state, and agile Joseph Knight, state director of financial institutions, old enemies of Adlai's father. Powell, who long has commanded great support in the southern end of the state, had sat out both of the elder Stevenson's campaigns for President.

46

Where's John?

WHILE the Democrats of Illinois were sweating over their slate with all the grace and dignity of two teams of Australian tag wrestlers, death brought them a haunting reminder of another dismal chapter in party history. Death had come for Scott Lucas, former United States Senator from Havana, Illinois. The mere mention of Lucas' name emphasized that disaster can be visited upon a party when it blunders in its slatemaking.

Lucas had been a candidate for reelection in 1950, the year that Colonel Jack Arvey suffered the major mistake of his political career. For the sheriff slot on the ticket, Arvey chose Captain Daniel Gilbert, a Chicago policeman on loan to the state's attorney's office, who modestly admitted to being the "richest cop in the world," and whose nicknames were "Tubbo" and "Fatso." Arvey was aware that Gilbert was an inveterate gambler, but the county chairman also knew that the policeman had invested shrewdly in the stock market and that his investments could be used to explain his great wealth satisfactorily.

What Arvey had no way of knowing was that Gilbert would insist upon testifying before the Senate Crime Investigating Committee when Estes Kefauver brought that body of relentless probers to Chicago. Gilbert did more than insist. He volunteered. Tubbo, who never lacked audacity, was gambling again. His hunch bet was that the public would be impressed by his willingness to talk to the Kefauver Committee. Gilbert probably would have won had it not been for Ray Brennan, a daring and imaginative reporter for the *Sun-Times*.

Brennan reasoned that the police captain would tell the whole truth, or almost the whole truth, to an investigative body representing the federal government, and that the truth would be damning. All that was needed was a transcript of Gilbert's testimony. Getting it was easy for a reporter of Brennan's skill. He learned the location of the stenographic service that was transcribing the testimony, posed as a member of Kefauver's staff, and was given a copy of all that the captain had said. It was all there—including Tubbo's admission that he had gambled heavily in ornate bookmaking establishments in the Loop. Gilbert, who wore a big white fedora as did most of the gangsters in town, told the Kefauver Committee that he bet on baseball, football, prize fights and elections. The detailed testimony in the *Sun-Times* so fascinated the voters of Cook County they turned out in record numbers for an off-year election.

John Babb, a World War II hero who had been the Republicans' eleventh-hour replacement after the death on August 25 of Sheriff-candidate Malachy Coughlan, swamped Gilbert by 400,000 votes. So anxious were Chicago-area voters to be rid of Fatso, many pulled the straight Republican lever. Senator Lucas carried Cook County by no more than 8,000 votes and Everett McKinley Dirksen, who had retired from the United States House of Representatives, was propelled to the United States Senate with a majority of 284,000 votes.

In less serious circumstances Dick Daley would have torn a candidate's name from the ticket, but Arvey allowed Tubbo to go all the way. Gilbert lost and brought down most of the Democratic ticket. Senator Lucas was a loser at the polls in November and Arvey was a loser in party councils. From that day forward the Colonel never was more than a figurehead. Years later Arvey would say, "In retrospect it was a mistake to slate Gilbert because that is what helped to beat Lucas."

Ray Brennan adds this footnote to Chicago's political history in his singular style:

"Well, Dan didn't really volunteer to testify. He was muscled into it by the *Sun-Times.*

"What happened was that Kefauver, Rudy Halley, chief counsel, and other Senate Committee people were at the Morrison Hotel the night before the Chicago hearings opened.

"Halley telephoned Gilbert at home after talking in private with Kefauver. Kefauver, a politically ambitious Democrat, was aghast at the peril of alienating the Chicago Democratic organization. Halley told Gilbert by phone, in effect: 'You are *invited* to testify at tomorrow's hearing. You are not under subpoena. You may accept the invitation or you may decline.'

"Of course, Gilbert declined. I listened in on the conversation on an extension phone, without Halley's knowledge. As a result we carried a Page One story and banner headline saying Gilbert was afraid to testify.

"Dan couldn't stand the heat from the *Sun-Times.* He made a deal with the committee. He testified but his testimony was behind locked doors, a most unusual thing, and the transcript was impounded.

"As for putting Dirksen in the Senate, it is a cross I will bear to my grave.

"Any credit for the story really should go to Marshall Field IV. He had the guts to print the story—about twenty columns of it—in the face of prosecution threats from the committee. Furthermore, after I was indicted in Washington and up against the possibility of six years in the pen, Field spent at least $50,000 on legal fees, court costs and other expenses to defend me.

"Incidentally, the story had beautiful timing—appearing on the Thursday before the Tuesday election."

On Monday, February 26, 1968, Democrats from all over the state ostensibly were striving to select a candidate to defeat Everett Dirksen, the Republican who had been the beneficiary of Gilbert's sabotaging of Lucas. They had to recess their slatemaking session, however, to attend Senator Lucas' funeral in Havana. During this mournful pause The Mayor had a respite to think of ways to bring together his rebellious slatemakers, but this was not time enough. After the committee had reconvened in Chicago for an extraordinary night session, The Mayor asked for adjournment until Tuesday morning.

Sleeping on the slate produced a ticket on Tuesday, but neither the sleep nor the slate sent Illinois's Democratic leaders back to their homes feeling refreshed. Tied to one another though they were by bonds of interparty acrimony, the Democrats of Illinois, even the old Democrats—especially the old Democrats—were shaken by the bitterness of those three days and one night in February. After any slatemaking the ill will that is generated continues for weeks or months or years. This time the animosity was brought out for public inspection almost immediately. Incredibly there was a defection from the ticket between the time the slate was picked and the moment for it to be announced officially.

In a matter of minutes John Stamos, slated for Illinois attorney general, had quit the ticket. "Joe Knight showed me the list," said Paul Simon, who had been chosen to run for lieutenant governor, "and John Stamos was there as one of the candidates. But as we walked from one part of the Sherman House to another, Frank Lorenz walked with us. Stamos was out."

Stamos was the most angry man in the party—even more so than Adlai Stevenson—and with reason. Stamos had been working hard as acting state's attorney for Cook County and thought he was doing an excellent job, a conviction shared by the press and the public. John had been expected to be picked to run for state's attorney on his own merits in 1968, but the men in charge tapped Edward Hanrahan, who had served with distinction and with much publicity as United States attorney for the Northern District of Illinois.

Attorney general is a prestigious position, but state's attorney of Cook County is a much more powerful position. His responsibilities are similar to those of a district attorney in other metropolitan areas. When the county's prosecutor makes news he makes it in Chicago, where the four major newspapers are located along with the powerful television channels and numerous radio stations. The state's attorney can be extremely important if the prosecutor happens to be a Republican and the mayor a Democrat, as was true when Ben Adamowski won the state's attorney's office on the Republican ticket in 1960. Fear of this occurring again inspired the shift of Stamos. The explanation was that John's national origin would not pull sufficient votes. Stamos is Greek, and the Democrats wanted an Irishman. Nobody in either party then anticipated that 1968 was going to be a very good year for Greeks.

Stamos declared that if the party didn't want him to be its candidate for state's attorney, he would not be the party's candidate for attorney general. Francis Lorenz, handsome director of public works for Cook County, was the last-second substitute for Stamos. Frank would be opposed by forty-one-year-old Republican Bill Scott, and Lorenz and his elders could envision unwanted disaster there. Potentially, Scott was the Republicans' best vote-getter and better than many Democrats. Additionally, Scott is even better-looking than Lorenz.

Without Stamos and young Adlai The Mayor didn't have an all-star team, but he did have big vote-getters at five positions—Bill Clark for Senator; Sam Shapiro for governor; Paul Simon for lieutenant governor; Paul Powell for secretary of state; and Michael Howlett for auditor of public accounts. Those five knew how to win. They had won before.

"They will carry the banner of Johnson and the entire

Democratic ticket to victory in 1968," The Mayor thundered.

With Lyndon Baines Johnson at the head of the ticket, everybody could win, including Bill Clark, who would be going against the President's old pal, Everett McKinley Dirksen. The experts accepted the premise that Johnson would need Dirksen on the other side of the aisle much more than the Democrats of Illinois needed a Democratic Senator, but nobody had expected Chuck Percy to win in 1966.

All the polls indicated that the President would not carry the county by 641,000 and the state by 890,000, as he had carried it against Barry Goldwater in 1964. The Democrats of Cook County, realists all, accepted that. They didn't expect a landslide. They didn't need a landslide. A nice, substantial Cook County victory for the President over the Republican nominee would be sufficient.

Then they started to run.

Five days later they came to a temporary halt along with the rest of the nation. On Saturday, March 2, the report of the National Advisory Commission on Civil Disorders was released. "Our nation is moving toward two societies, one black, one white—separate and unequal," the writers of the report concluded. This conclusion startled no one in Chicago, which had been, for generations, two societies, one black, one white—separate and unequal.

During his press conference on March 4 The Mayor criticized the report, but his objections were mild. Although he found flaws in the report, his tone seemed to imply that the men and the women who wrote the report did not understand the racial situation as he understood it. In his own conclusion The Mayor called the report "a good report" and told the newspapermen and television and radio reporters, "Put that at the top [of your stories]."

If The Mayor had not had sufficient time to read the entire report—581 pages, including appendices but not including charts—he had had time to comprehend it better than many who were applauding it. He understood the fact that really mattered: The report was not about Chicago. It was written to analyze and explain the racial disorders of 1967. It was about Tampa, Cincinnati, Atlanta, Newark, Plainfield, New Brunswick, Detroit. Chicago had been quiet in the summer of 1967. The report mentioned Chicago merely in passing.

There was another thing about the report that The Mayor understood. It was not a "good" report. Written by moderates, it momentarily edified liberals and infuriated conservatives. After liberals and conservatives had read the report for themselves, the conservatives were mollified and the liberals were disillusioned. Again. Again. Again. It was a "combat history" of the riots in Detroit, Newark, Tampa and the other cities that had been devastated, spiritually and morally, if not physically, by the terror of 1967. And it was a rehash of all that had been written before.

The most analytical and prophetic words in the report appeared at the "conclusion to the conclusion (summary)." They were a quotation from Dr. Kenneth B. Clark, "one of the first witnesses to be invited to appear before this Commission." Dr. Clark, a Negro psychologist, had told the panel:

> I read that report . . . of the 1919 riot in Chicago, and it is as if I were reading the report of the investigating committee on the Harlem riot of '35, the report of the investigating committee on the Harlem riot of '43, the report of the McCone Commission on the Watts riot.
>
> I must again in candor say to you members of this Commission—it is a kind of Alice in Wonderland—with the same moving picture re-shown over and over again, the same analysis, the same recommendations, and the same inaction.

In fifty years Chicagoans had learned nothing from those other reports of other riots. Wasn't it almost too much to hope that Chicagoans and other Americans would learn from the "Kerner Report"? That was what it was being called in the press and on the airwaves, and that was how it would be remembered by those who would read and reject it in the years ahead—the "Kerner Report," in honor of Otto Kerner, chairman of the Advisory Commission. That was another reason why Otto Kerner did not choose to run again in 1968. The Governor had run poorly in 1964, lagging more than 700,000 votes behind the plurality Illinois gave to President Johnson. The white backlash had helped to bring down Paul Douglas in 1966 and the Kerner Report's honest and obvious conclusion surely would have meant disaster for the Governor on the next election day. There was a plum in Otto's future—a federal judgeship.

When the Kerner Report was issued, Senator Eugene McCarthy, who didn't seem to understand the odds against him, was campaigning for votes in the Democratic Presidential preference primary of New Hampshire. The pollsters and the professionals thought McCarthy would be fortunate to receive 20 percent of the vote. "Somewhere between ten and twenty," they said of this modern Quixote, who was willing to tilt with the many arms of Lyndon Johnson. When the primary votes were counted on March 12, McCarthy had 42 percent. President Johnson had received 48 percent on write-ins.

Two men took fast, hard looks at New Hampshire. One was Senator Robert F. Kennedy of New York. The other was the President. On Sunday, March 31, the man for whom The Mayor and the Democratic candidates in Illinois were carrying "the banner of Johnson" announced that he would not carry his own banner. Lyndon Baines Johnson startled the world by taking himself out of the race.

47

⌁⌁⌁⌁⌁⌁⌁⌁⌁⌁⌁⌁⌁⌁⌁⌁⌁⌁⌁⌁⌁⌁⌁⌁⌁⌁⌁

A Nice Man

CANDIDATES everywhere started to run again, and in Illinois it was all so very much like the Barney Google race-track cartoons that the children loved to watch in "the show" on Halsted Street when The Mayor was a young politician during the Depression years. All the entries were running backward in dreamlike slow motion. Some went over the fence, hindquarters first, while others skidded sideways across the track.

The most puzzling contestant of them all was curly-haired Bill Clark, who immediately began to run as though he intended to beat Everett Dirksen whether or not anybody in the Democratic party of Illinois wanted Dirksen to be beaten. Almost to a man the professionals had accepted the theory that because the President needed Dirksen, The Mayor needed Dirksen, too. When Clark was slated in late February, he was thought of as a straw man put in place to be knocked down at the whim of Dirksen. Pollsters to the contrary, it looked then as though Lyndon Johnson would be around for a long time. Defeat for the incumbent President had seemed unlikely, and it was important that Johnson continue to think kindly of Chicago. There would be available approximately one billion dollars that the city could use for essentials such as antipoverty, schools, summer programs, urban renewal, the crosstown expressway and a third major airport. If Johnson did not get Dirksen because a strong Sen-

268

atorial candidate had emerged from the councils of the Cook County Democratic organization, Chicago might not get all of that billion dollars, and what it did get might come slowly. This was the real reason why young Adlai had been passed over for Senator. One argument went: He might have won, and Johnson did not want a Democrat to win.

Those cynosures of cynicism, the political reporters assigned to the Washington beat, saw the Democratic ticket for Illinois as an admission to defeat. Many wrote that Clark was not supposed to win. During a Washington press conference Dirksen was asked if President Johnson could be expected to campaign for Everett. The question did not ruffle Dirksen. The senior Senator from Illinois peered out from above the great bags under his bloodhound eyes and sleepily said, "I don't know. You'll have to ask him." By "him" the Senator meant Lyndon B. Johnson.

When asked about Clark at the same press conference, Dirksen said, "He must be a nice man." The Senator would not use the name "Clark" during the entire campaign. The orotund orator from Pekin conveyed to the electorate the suggestion that a man who was so busy helping Lyndon Johnson run the country and win the war did not have time to consider a person as unworthy as Bill Clark.

The Democratic candidate did not ignore what was going on around him. At a meeting of ward committeemen Clark referred to "charges this ticket was named to run and lose." Adlai Stevenson couldn't have put it better—or worse. "We're going to win on a high level," Clark continued, "with no personalities, and we'll wage a tough, vigorous, winning campaign."

The committeemen were not impressed by the platitudinous pledge of a race along the high road and they were moved to fury by Clark's daring to mention that the ticket had been named "to run and lose." The professionals understood the reality of the situations, particularly of the Senatorial situation, but they did not appreciate their candidate's bringing it out into the open for all the voters to read.

The professionals had reasons to wonder whether Clark, a fellow professional, gave a damn about their reactions to him. Bill was running hard and under a full head of fury. He had given a hint of things to come on March 4, when he told reporters in Washington that Mayor Daley at no time had demanded that Clark give unqualified support to the administration's policies in Vietnam. The reporters who heard Clark's statement found it hard to reconcile with their belief that Lyndon Johnson had not wanted Adlai Stevenson to run for the Senate for the very basic reason that Stevenson might have beaten Dirksen. Why would Daley "free" Clark on Vietnam, they wondered, after The Mayor had restricted Stevenson on the same issue?

(Much later John Dreiske of the *Sun-Times* was to report that Senator Robert Kennedy had said flatly that Mayor Daley had favored a change in Vietnam policy by the White House. "And it was confirmed," Dreiske wrote, "that Daley had suggested to Kennedy that a commission be formed to review President Johnson's policies regarding the fighting.")

It was no more than coincidence that the President announced his intention to withdraw five days after Clark's statement on the war, but the sequence of events revealed to many voters and to some politicians that the "no chance" Senatorial candidate from Illinois had read the mood of the people better than many of his elders had. Clark consolidated his gain by taking a trip that underscored the truth that he was not the lightweight some of his alleged allies made him out to be. Clark went to Vietnam and took with him his nineteen-year-old son, Bill. When they returned after a four-day tour of the war zones, the elder Clark expressed the opinion that the Democrats' best Presidential candidate was Robert Kennedy.

The Illinois picture still was not so clear in April that it could be easily read, but some who were peering thought the picture was coming into focus. With another Kennedy at the top of the ticket, all the Democrats in Illinois could win again. And with Lyndon Johnson lameduck-walking toward the exit, The Mayor would not need Everett Dirksen.

48

Closer in Style

THIS would be the fifty-sixth national convention staged by the two major parties since 1860, the year Chicago went into the political-extravaganza business, and The Mayor was pleased to note that his great city had been host to twenty-three of those fifty-six. No other city was even close. Philadelphia was second with seven conventions, which proved conclusively that The Mayor had history on his side when he fought for the delegates' right to meet again in Chicago.

Chicago had been a city for no more than twenty-three years when it bid for and won the 1860 convention. Ironically, it was the Republicans who pitched that one to start delegates looking toward the sprawling new town in the Midwest. That was one of the most significant conventions—perhaps the most significant. Abraham Lincoln was nominated in the wooden Wigwam that had been hammered up at Lake Street and Market (now North Wacker Drive). That first convention also set the tone for all that would follow, a tone that would be remembered and sounded again by the Democrats in the days immediately ahead.

This would be the fifth Democratic convention in Chicago since 1932, the year of Franklin Delano Roosevelt's first nomination. It had been Roosevelt again in 1940 and '44, and Adlai Stevenson in 1956. The 1956 convention had been the real beginning of things for Jack Kennedy and for Bobby. After Adlai Stevenson had been nominated for a second run at the invulnerable Eisenhower, The Mayor had supported the Presidential nominee's decision to permit the convention at large to choose Stevenson's running mate. The Illinois delegation, which wasn't especially enthusiastic about the Vice-Presidential aspirations of Estes Kefauver because of his decision to bring his Senate Crime Investigating Committee into Chicago at a time when the Democrats of Cook County were trying to win an election, went for John F. Kennedy. Kefauver won the nomination, but Jack received the national exposure he needed; and so, in a secondary but overpowering sense, did Bobby.

Those who followed the convention telecasts in 1956 would never forget Bobby's huddles with The Mayor and other Democratic leaders, maneuvering, maneuvering, maneuvering. The Mayor surely would not forget '56; or 1960 in Los Angeles, when pivotal Illinois pivoted toward Bobby's big brother; or the torchlight parade down West Madison Street to the Chicago Stadium on the Friday night before the 1960 election (Chicago's Democrats, who love round numbers, said 1,000,000 turned out for the parade); or the '60 election, in which Cook County delivered a 320,000 plurality for Jack to enable him to win Illinois by 8,858 votes—an average of less than one vote per precinct.

Although he kept his counsel as to his Kennedy preferences, as he did about everything else, The Mayor was closer in style and manner to Robert Francis Kennedy than to John Fitzgerald Kennedy. Boston, Cape Cod, the preparatory school and Harvard had not put the polish of aristocracy on Bobby. He was rough, tough and mean. He was capable of kicking a downed opponent, and he neither forgot nor forgave. The Mayor could be excused for preening—inwardly, never outwardly—when it was said, as it had been said so often, that it was he, more than any other, who had elected Jack Kennedy. The Mayor knew, however, that it was the slight man with the wild hair and the chilling arrogance who had forced his older brother upon the Pooh-Bahs of the party, starting at Chicago in 1956. The elders of the party hated Bobby. They made fun of him and they cursed him, but they recognized the power he wielded like a shillelagh, and they made deals with him. The Mayor had been a beneficiary of all that.

Bobby had known how to get his brother elected, and he would have known how to get himself elected. The staff and the cash were there. He would have run the best campaign money and loyalty could buy. When he came in, after New Hampshire, everybody conceded that the young would be with him. He was forty-two years old, but those who were waiting to vote for the first time were convinced that he was of their time and their generation. What nobody understood, then, was that this millionaire would have with him the impoverished blacks of the nation. Even later, when the Negroes' love for this tough—and, it was said, cold—man was out in the open for all to see, nobody could explain it. The words that were used—"chemistry" and "charisma"—were fancy but empty. Perhaps, although neither blacks nor Irish had cared to think about it, there always had been a bond of empathy between those who were brought to America in slave ships and those who had come in coffin ships. Perhaps those who had traveled "last class" in the hold and survived understood one another instinctively. But, no, that could not be. The blacks of Chicago had not loved The Mayor and other Irish politicians as blacks of the nation had loved Bobby Kennedy.

Whether Robert Kennedy could win the Presidency against Richard Nixon was a question that could not be answered on April 1, but it seemed likely that Bobby could win the nomination at the Convention in August. In Chicago—Catholic, Negro, violent, nostalgic Chicago—he would be overpowering. The Mayor would deliver for another Kennedy and this second Kennedy would deliver for The Mayor.

But first, there was the bloodstain spreading on the balcony in Memphis. Robert Francis Kennedy was campaigning that night in a Negro district of Indianapolis, and to him fell the task of telling those black Americans that their leader had been shot to death as his brother, Jack, had been shot to death. There was a New Politics in America, the politics of the assassin.

He told them without notes at midnight. He told them softly, sorrowfully, but hopefully. He told them from his heart and he held his heart in his hand as he spoke. They saw his heart, recognized it as having been broken even more often than the heart of a ghetto child, and they gave to him their hearts. They had given their votes to his brother; to this Kennedy they would give their beings.

Until that night Robert F. Kennedy had been the oldest surviving brother of the country's most prominent family. After his small voice had carried the spirit of Martin Luther King to the crowd in Indianapolis, he became oldest brother to a nation.

He calmed them with his wistful sorrow. He spoke to them of the futility of vengeance. He was needed in Chicago that night to dam the flood of violence, but Chicago was on its own. The schoolchildren of the West Side would do on the morrow what the man had done in the lobby of the Matteson House after another man had said that Abraham Lincoln had got what was coming to him. They would react to the death of their hero as Chicagoans traditionally have reacted. Violently.

And then there was the bloodstain spreading on the kitchen floor in Los Angeles. So deranged was this assassin he did not bother to find a field of fire that would afford him a route for escape. His fanaticism was such that he needed no high building, no rooming-house bathroom. He had escaped from the world long before. He was not frightened by the huge professional football player or by the massive

Olympic hero or by the forbidding Secret Service men or by the wide-eyed faithful who had volunteered to insure their candidate against harm. He probably did not see them.

Into the void created by the death of Robert Francis Kennedy a malaise came to Chicago. The hand of death was upon the city. It was as though all the violence of the past was closing in. In the summers of other years that could be divided by four, the imminence of a national political convention brought a carnival air to Chicago. In late August of 1968 there was the unspoken wish that the Convention, like a baseball game or a riot in the streets, could be postponed because of rain.

There were ghouls in the party who held out the hope to one another that the last of the Kennedy brothers would emerge, temporarily, from the mourning at which he had had such interminable practice to join the convention festivities. It seemed to them that it would be the least Senator Edward M. Kennedy of Massachusetts could do. It wouldn't be for them. May God strike them dead! Not for them, not to rescue the party from the threat of defeat, but for the memory of his dear, dead brothers. Jack and Bobby would want Teddy to pick up the torch and carry it forward.

To his credit The Mayor was not among those who, in the words of the "Irish wake" joke, would suggest to the bereaved that he "have the corpse stuffed and keep the party going." In early July The Mayor had talked about the possibility of Ted Kennedy running for Vice-President, but he made his references vague, something he did expertly. On July 24 Daley said he would be for Teddy, if and when, and the matter should have been ended two days later. The Senator said then that he wanted all his well-wishers to remove his name from consideration for Vice-President. Ten days before this opening date of the convention The Mayor had told reporters at his City Hall press conference that Lyndon Johnson and Edward Kennedy had told him they would not run.

Even the optimism of The Mayor, which he wore as though it were part of his "best-dressed man" wardrobe, seemed to be forced as he made ready for his Sunday trip downtown and the caucus of the Illinois delegation. Had he had time to riffle through the Sunday newspapers he might have seen a picture of a loyal Democrat named Nancy Stevenson, who, according to a picture caption, was "helping to arrange a fete for 2,000 and then some." Nancy is the wife of Adlai Stevenson III.

The Loop

From 1895, when Charles T. Yerkes and the "transit trust" began to replace the horse-drawn cars with trolley cars, until the 1950's, when the tracks were torn out to make way for bumpy and noxious buses, every little boy knew what it meant to "go downtown on the streetcar with mother." Downtown meant the Loop, the magic place where everything was. Toys, clothes, food, shows and buildings that had a thing that rode you to the sky. For Mrs. Lillian Dunne Daley and her little boy, Dick, there were so many ways to go. The Thirty-fifth Street car over to State Street and then to the Loop. Or the Halsted Street car to Finley Peter Dunne's Archer Avenue and then angling into the Loop on the Archer car which ran from southwest to northeast. Or the Halsted car straight down to Madison, through the excitement of the Maxwell Street flea market, and Madison east to the Loop.

Even if the swaying of the streetcar made a little boy so sick it would be necessary for the conductor to go to the box that was provided for this purpose and throw sawdust on the floor, getting downtown was worth the discomfort of going downtown. State and Madison! Everybody knew that this was the busiest corner in the world. Carson, Pirie, Scott and the Boston Store, two of Mother's favorite stores, were right there. And along State Street in opposite directions were Marshall Field's and the Davis Store. And the dime stores. And the drugstores. And the fancy restaurants. And Spalding's Sporting Goods. And the fancy poolrooms that were called "billiards academies." And the places where men went to bet on horses. And the big newsstands. And the cars, hundreds of 'em. And the people, millions of 'em. And the *clackety-clackety-sparkity-sparkity-clackety* of the "L road."

The L road was the elevated line that was the principal reason for all this excitement and prosperity. In 1895 when Yerkes, his cooperators and his competitors were hurriedly laying track and stringing trolley wire with one hand while they craftily watered stock with the other, a few dozen feet above them other transit kings had the "L Loop" to make their stocks soar in value. Thousands of Chicagoans who have lived a lifetime in the city are not aware that the familiar name for the business district, the Loop, derives from this rectangle of steel, wood and wire. The first of the L roads were railroads in the literal sense, their cars drawn by small, wood-burning locomotives. The purpose of the Loop was to provide a turnaround whereby the L roads serving the south, north and west sides could come into the downtown district, travel around it and return again to the distant neighborhoods. The north-south tracks were elevated above Wabash Avenue (50 East) and Wells Street (200 West). The east-west tracks were in Van Buren Street (400 South) and Lake Street (200 North). The L Loop "locked in" some of the most valuable real estate in the world and enhanced its value immeasurably.

Within the steel pillars of the Loop are the two buildings in which The Mayor works—City Hall and the Sherman House. Inside the Loop, too, had been the Morrison Hotel, renowned as the structural powerhouse of the Democratic party of Cook County until the building was razed to make way for the new First National Bank Building.

Most Chicagoans and many politicians, dazzled as they are by the glamour and the power packed within the girders of the elevated, think of the Loop as the heart of the city. The Mayor saw another truth that had eluded even the shrewdest of his predecessors, Ed Kelly. The Mayor understood, early in life, that City Hall is downtown. Kelly, Tony Cermak and the others had waged sporadic guerrilla warfare against the business interests of State Street and Wabash Avenue and the financial interests of LaSalle Street and Clark Street. There were two reasons for the war. First, it was the thing to do. The Protestant, Republican suburbanites were the "enemy" of the Catholic, Democratic politicians and therefore the enemies of "the people." Second, Kelly and the others did not need the support of downtown in their times. The revenues that kept the in-party's treasury filled and made the city move were available from the gambling and vice syndicate that ran wide open in the Loop and in outlying areas of the First Ward.

Big Bill Thompson, Protestant and Republican though he was, capitalized on reason No. 2, just as did the Democrats who came to City Hall before and after him. In his book *Barbarians in Our Midst—A History of Chicago Crime and Politics,* Virgil Peterson, then operating director of the Chicago Crime Commission, wrote in 1952:

> Early in Mayor Thompson's first term of office certain changes in the political vice setup should have served as a foreboding of evil times ahead—of the impending rise of gangster rule which was to give Chicago its well-deserved reputation as the crime capital of the world. In the first place, Thompson curtailed the power of the morals squad, which had been assigned to enforce the vice and gambling laws. Throughout the police department he shuffled officers like a deck of cards, to make certain that ward committeemen received personnel who would permit wide-open conditions. In the First Ward, Alderman Kenna designated his aide, Dennis Cooney, commonly known as the "Duke," to take charge of the disorderly hotels of the area, using the Rex Hotel,

2138 South State Street, as a base of operations. Cooney met with the full approval of Big Jim Colosimo, who now became the overlord of vice in the district.

That was Chicago almost forty years before Dick Daley became The Mayor. He had not been above renewing the war upon the Protestant, Republican suburbanites. Remember his words in the 1955 primary, ". . . let them be the State Street candidate. Let others be the LaSalle Street candidate . . ." What was not understood then was that Dick Daley also was far above permitting a resumption of gambling and vice. His sense of values would not allow the return of the opulent handbooks to the Loop.

He knew a better way to obtain the funds that would be needed to move the city forward. In 1955 he did not choose to be the candidate of State Street and LaSalle Street, but once he had taken office he determined to become The Mayor of State Street and LaSalle Street. He knew how to work with the men in that other downtown. His knowledge of finance, gained in the county treasurer's office, in the Revenue Department of the State of Illinois, and the county clerk's office enabled him to see a great truth. State Street and LaSalle Street needed City Hall more than City Hall needed State Street and LaSalle Street.

He would do for them if they would do for him. This was good for everybody and so much better than working with bookmakers and whorehouse directors. The political party that cooperated with the department stores and the banks and the brokerage houses did not have to be concerned with sending out police captains and ward committeemen as bag men. The Mayor would get clean money and he would get far more of it than his predecessors even dreamed of shaking out of Al Capone and Big Jim Colosimo.

Guided by his newspaperman friend Donald Walsh of the Chicago *American*, The Mayor worked out a liaison be-

tween City Hall and State-LaSalle Streets that was so effective no potential Republican candidate could be found to run
against Dick Daley in 1959. Republican County Chairman
Timothy Sheehan had to take the nomination simply because he couldn't find another man to accept it. After less
than four years of a Daley-directed city, many prominent
Republicans were so enchanted with his leadership they
were bumping into one another in their haste to become
members of the Non-Partisan Committee for Reelection of
Mayor Daley.

There was a newspaper advertisement that infuriated Ben
Adamowski, a Republican by then and a politician who
doesn't believe in loving his opponents until long after the
campaign is over.

"I asked Tim Sheehan if he had been a paper boy when he
was a kid," Adamowski recalled, "and when he said he had
been, I offered him a suggestion. 'Roll a bunch of papers that
have that so-called "Progress Before Politics" ad in it,' I told
Tim, 'and throw a paper on the desk of every big Republican
in this town who is helping to beat you by lending his name
to that ad.' "

This was the advertisement's message:

Thousands of Chicagoans are going to cross political
lines to vote for Mayor Richard Daley. . . . Many of
the people who sponsored and paid for this advertisement are among them.

This committee has no affiliation with any organized
political party. But Republican, Independent or Democrat, they know the Mayor has done a good job.

Please vote on April 7. And spend a thoughtful moment before you pull the lever. Chicago is a cleaner, better place in which to live and it's getting better all the
time.

The man mainly responsible is the Mayor. Give him a
chance to continue his work.

THE LOOP 283

Tim Sheehan didn't become a political paper boy as Adamowski had suggested, but neither did Tim forgive his fellow Republicans who had abandoned him when he needed help desperately. In 1962 The Mayor had suffered one of his few defeats when the voters rejected a bond issue for city improvements. This setback taught Dick Daley something about the white backlash, which was just beginning its swing into the darkness of ignorance and hate, but it also taught him something more about the political promotion of objectives in the realm of high finance. When The Mayor and his administration went back to the voters with another large bond issue in 1966, he was ably assisted by the Mayor's Committee on Economic and Cultural Development. Nobody knew precisely what that grandiose title meant, but the name of the chairman told everybody what the committee was to do. The chairman was David M. Kennedy, who is not one of *those* Kennedys. Dave, Utah-born, Mormon, and chairman of Continental Illinois National Bank and Trust Company, was such a stanch Republican he would be appointed, in time, to be Secretary of the Treasury in the Cabinet of President Richard M. Nixon.

Kennedy's devotion to Daley inspired Sheehan to do a little backlashing of his own in 1966. Tim told the late Ed Lahey of the Chicago *Daily News*, "Why, even these $195,-000,000 in bonds authorized in the June 14 primary are going to be patronage for Dave Kennedy and Dick Daley's other LaSalle Street friends. The six biggest banks in Chicago will market these bonds and—don't kid yourself—this is important patronage for City Hall."

Kennedy reacted more like a partisan of the Cook County Democratic organization than like a member of the loyal opposition. "That's stupid, ignorant," Dave said in response to the blast by the man who was the chairman of Kennedy's party organization. "Naturally, we supported the bond issues. All segments of the community supported the bonds. But anyone, including Sheehan, should know that these bonds will be sold at auction, to realize the best return possible."

The Mayor couldn't have said it better, and Kennedy missed the point almost as effectively as The Mayor does when he is embroiled in similar confrontations. Kennedy also said something more direct, something that revealed he shared The Mayor's understanding of where the power truly was. "Usually business fights City Hall," the banker said. "But business should work with City Hall."

In 1959 William Patterson, president of United Air Lines, said, "This is a two-way street. So, I as a Republican must owe a quality of leadership and loyalty to his [Daley's] program. Because he is a Democrat is no reason I should bury my head in the sand and be a good loser."

Dave Kennedy shared The Mayor's conviction that business should work with City Hall, and Bill Patterson understood, as The Mayor did, that all the streets in the Loop ran from City Hall to the business community and back again. What Kennedy and Patterson seemed unconcerned about was the two-party system in Chicago.

The Mayor, then, was a man of many hats and on the Saturday night before the 1968 convention nobody suggested to him that he should leave two hats at home for the next four days. He wore them all so well, his admirers and payrollers and stooges and lackeys agreed.

With his mayoral fedora firmly in place The Mayor met for ninety minutes Saturday with representatives of the three major television networks to ameliorate relations between television and the city. Daley sometimes is cast as the arbitrator in disputes to which he is a party and this was one of those times. Richard S. Salant, president of CBS News, emerged to say that he had detected "a spirit of total cooperation" from each side. The Mayor said that the differences between the networks and the city were a mere "misunderstanding" caused by "additional security requirements and labor problems in the transit field."

With his party-leader crown on dead center The Mayor entertained two Senators who paid a "surprise call" on him Saturday in the Sherman House. One was George McGovern of South Dakota, who wanted to be President. The other was Abraham Ribicoff of Connecticut, who wanted to help George become President.

With his slatemaker halo whirling around his head Saturday night, The Mayor prepared to deal with Senatorial candidate Bill Clark, who had announced his intention to speak for George McGovern at the Illinois caucus Sunday. A *Sun-Times* survey had concluded that Senator McCarthy probably would carry Illinois over Richard Nixon but that Nixon would beat Vice-President Hubert Humphrey.

With his convention-host paper hat at a rakish angle The Mayor waited eagerly Saturday for the festivities that would enable Chicago to prove again that it was the greatest city on earth.

With his blue commander-in-chief helmet under his left arm The Mayor did not concern himself too much about the first major confrontation of police and hippie-Yippies Saturday night in Lincoln Park. The police would handle that with ease. They would clear the park at curfew time without trouble. Eleven persons were arrested and only one newspaperman—reporter Larry Green of the Chicago *Daily News* —was assaulted.

Wearing all his hats, Catholic, Irish Dick Daley passed through and under the suspended portals of the Loop on Sunday, August 25, 1968. He would go to the Sherman House to keep safe the Amphitheater for the Democrats, the city for all of the people, and downtown for his Protestant, Republican friends.

Part Three

THE FINISH

50

Windy City?

> *. . . Let them be turned back in disgrace, who desire my ruin.*
> *—Introit Psalm of the Mass*
> *for Sunday in Convention Week*

HIPPIES, Yippies and the Mayor's own creation, the flippies, all were shunted to the background, where eccentrics belong, as the Democrats of Illinois assembled Sunday to send off the Convention with a flying start. The Mayor and his stanch friends from Illinois could be modest to a fault, when the situation demanded a shrinking-violet approach, but their experiences in 1964 and in 1960 had persuaded them that there couldn't possibly be a convention without them. Until they (an all-encompassing synonym for The Mayor) picked a candidate, there would be no candidate.

Almost everybody else believed that Hubert H. Humphrey, the Vice-President of the United States, would be the candidate. With Bobby Kennedy gone, Humphrey was expected to win by a virtual forfeit. With Bobby gone, the poetry had gone out of the campaign of Senator McCarthy. Kennedy and McCarthy had been like two semifinalists in a boxing tournament, battling each other for the right to meet the favorite, who had drawn a bye in the semifinals. After the semifinal bout, the championship fight would be an anticlimax. The winner of Kennedy versus McCarthy would have had a chance in the main ring at Chicago, but because there had been no winner, the survivor was given little chance for the nomination.

And the other candidate, George McGovern of South Dakota, had not come in, it seemed, until day before yesterday.

When the delegates strutted or shambled or tottered into the 300-by-60-foot Illinois caucus room on the mezzanine floor of the Sherman House, Humphrey looked to be a cinch. The Illinois delegation never has cared to jump on a bandwagon while it is rolling. The Illinoisans prefer to be aboard before the bandwagon begins to move.

The Mayor, continuing in his role as apostle of love, opened the program by saying, "We should and we must proceed without bitterness and without hatred." After those social evils had been exorcised, The Mayor said resolutely, "The man who is nominated here will be the next President of the United States."

"Humphrey," the delegates said, shaking heads sagely.

The ever-faithful Tom Keane, chairman of the City Council finance committee, nominated The Mayor to be chairman of the delegation. Keane said, among other things, that the United States "would be a better country if every city in our country had a type of Daley administration." Tom also said that The Mayor was "the greatest political leader in American history."

The ever-ever faithful George Dunne, member of the Cook County Board, said, among still other things, that The Mayor was "the embodiment of politics, of dedication, of energy."

Then Dick Mudge, two-time state's attorney for Madison County, was recognized by the chair. Mudge, a McCarthy-pledged delegate from downstate Edwardsville, got off on a humorous note. "In view of all the statements that have been made," he said, "I'm hopefully inclined, at this point, to nominate Mayor Daley for President of the United States."

That was more like it. The Illinoisans cheered for at least

thirty seconds, each applauder stealing glances toward The Mayor to make certain that he appreciated the appreciation. Mudge went on to deliver what Adlai Stevenson was to recall as "a funny little speech."

Then Mudge moved to the attack and the hurrahs dried up. He said he had thought of nominating "Mayor Daley to be national committeeman," and he expressed dissatisfaction with the state ticket. "Daley hand-picked it and I think it's a rather undistinguished slate," Mudge had told Don Sullivan of *Chicago's American* on Saturday. "I don't want to see the same thing happen with our Presidential ticket."

Mudge, who had gone behind the wire of a German stalag after his fighter plane was shot down during World War II, took note of Chicago's extraordinary security measures. "You know, we're holding this convention behind barbed wire. There's an implication rampant in Chicago that anyone who demonstrates is criminal. I think this is a sad commentary on free expression."

Mudge said he didn't want "barbed wire around our convention," and with that he pulled out his verbal wire cutters and started to snip-snip at the infallibility of The Mayor. Mudge didn't apologize. His credentials were in order. With pardonable regional pride he mentioned that not even Cook County had brought in a higher percentage of Democratic victories over the preceding twenty years than had his bailiwick in Madison and St. Clair counties. He emphasized that his district had not had a Republican sheriff since 1948 or a Republican state's attorney since 1938. But the Democrats down there could lose both offices in 1968, he warned, and "the polls show it."

Mudge then did what he had come to do. He nominated The Mayor to be national committeeman and nominated Senatorial candidate William Clark to be chairman of the delegation. This was the kind of thing that was bad for the blood pressure of elderly delegates who wanted nothing more than peace and quiet. Clark, Mudge said, would give the ticket an exposure that would appeal to students at the University of Illinois and at Southern Illinois University. "What's he talking about students for?" some older delegates wondered. "What have students got to do with it?"

Adlai Stevenson, a rare politician in that he has retained his sense of the absurd, described Clark's reaction. "Bill raced up to the rostrum to withdraw his name from consideration," Stevenson said.

Clark said the nomination was "as much a shock to me as to anyone else here," dutifully praised The Mayor and let down Mudge gently by calling the downstater "well intentioned."

After Mudge's attempt to break into the compound had been thwarted just inside the wire, the candidates came on. Hubert Horatio Humphrey was first, his lips pursing, his eyes popping, his chin jutting and receding, his arms waving. Not many thought of this at that moment in that room, but Humphrey's trouble was that he, an intrinsically nice man who wanted to be nice and tried to be nice, reminded millions of Lyndon B. Johnson, who was thought of as not nice at all. In the weeks that were ahead Humphrey would do things with his face that would make voters think of the things they had seen the President do with his face.

Humphrey, the Vice-President of the United States, almost outdid loyalists Keane and Dunne in their idolatry of the mayor of the second-largest city in the United States. Hubert described Daley as "one of the most determined, one of the most dedicated public officials in the United States."

This wasn't flattery, said the man who had an unprecedented political opportunity drop into his hands but didn't seem to know how to advance with it; and he added that he was sure The Mayor knew it wasn't flattery. It was flattery, of course, and it would get Humphrey what the flatterer usually receives. Nothing. Hubert addressed the caucus for twenty-seven minutes.

Next came Gene McCarthy, the former apprentice Bene-
dictine monk and recreational poet, who did not remind anyone of Lyndon B. Johnson. The trouble with McCarthy is
that he does not look like a first-baseman. Almost everyone in
the Illinois caucus knew that McCarthy had been a semiprofessional baseball player, an avocation that makes a fellow
politician better somehow in the eyes of Chicago's politicians, but nobody there could imagine Gene in the uniform
of the Hamburg Club, playing for a thousand dollars a side.
McCarthy spoke for twenty minutes.

That brought on George McGovern, Irish-American Protestant who looked like an amateur boxer who had turned to
other forms of physical conditioning before the gloves left
too many ineradicable marks upon him. He spoke for seventeen minutes.

Last came Lester Maddox, who reminded some Illinois delegates of what they remembered as a happier, more simple
time when anybody could get elected. Maddox spoke for
twenty-five minutes, almost as long as Humphrey had
spoken, and that said something about the state of the Illinois Democratic party in August, 1968.

It should have been cut and dried. The rest of the ritual
should have been routine. The Illinois delegates should have
voted, almost unanimously, to start Hubert H. Humphrey
moving in the general direction of victory in November. But
Tom Keane, whose cynical depth never has been plumbed
because there isn't enough string in the world, moved that
the caucus be adjourned. To commit a delegation to a candidate at that time, said loyal Tom, would "impair Windy City
hospitality." A thoughtful native Chicagoan who loves his
hometown never refers to it by that asinine designation,
Windy City, but nothing sticks in the throat of Tom Keane.
The polling of the 118 members of the Illinois delegation
would not begin until Wednesday at 11 A.M.

The Mayor offered this explanation: "Because of Illinois's

friendliness and hospitality and because Governor Shapiro and I are going to give welcoming speeches . . . Monday night, we decided to greet the delegates uncommitted and postponed our action."

Those who believed implicitly that consummate politician Daley always knew what he was doing wondered what he had in mind. Not *what,* his confident admirers confided, but *whom.* Kennedy. There was one left. Teddy, the baby brother. Surely, he would come out of mourning if he was told that The Mayor himself wanted the Kennedy name at the top of the ticket again. Could a Kennedy resist running for President, the ghoulish and the foolish inquired, from the depths of their callousness.

The Humphrey bandwagon, so colorful three hours earlier, still was standing there, a large ugly dent in its side. The Mayor had not put his broad shoulder behind it to give it that first little push.

But the thoughtful reflected upon the facts that Dick Daley had proclaimed the invincibility of Otto Kerner and Lyndon Johnson, long-distance runners who had scratched from the marathon before it began, and the thoughtful began to wonder whether The Mayor really knew, any more, what he was doing.

On the other end of downtown, beyond the south boundary of the Loop, Detective James Stampnick arrested a nineteen-year-old Milwaukeean, Thomas Peter Laine, on the roof of the Conrad Hilton. The youth was not armed, but a rifle with a telescopic sight was found in his car.

Up in Lincoln Park the hippies, the Yippies and Mayor Daley's flippies were preparing to give the details from the Chicago Police Department a long night of exercise.

51

Doves Flying

BILL CLARK, who had not been waiting for signals from his elders, thought it pointless to keep his constituents guessing until Wednesday. Clark, the "superdove" of the Illinois delegation, called a press conference for seven o'clock Sunday night. He announced his endorsement of Senator McGovern for President.

Three weeks after The Mayor and his slatemakers had chosen Clark to run for the Senate, instead of Adlai Stevenson, the forty-two-year-old candidate emerged as "an Adlai with curly hair." In a statement made in Springfield Bill expressed "grave concern" about the administration's Vietnam policy. This was the sentiment of the choice of the men who had sat on Stevenson for saying, "I think you gentlemen should know that as a candidate for the Senate, I might feel obliged to take a stand in opposition to President Johnson on the subject of Vietnam."

What did The Mayor have to say about Clark's audacity? What The Mayor said, during his press conference the day after Clark's statement, shook the resolve of Democrats everywhere who had brainwashed themselves into believing that the only course in Vietnam was the course the President charted for them. Mayor Daley said he did not disagree with Clark's expression of "grave concern." The Mayor also said that his Senatorial candidate had not consulted Daley about the statement.

"I think it was a statement of what the President is doing at the present time," The Mayor said in his critique of Clark's startling declaration. "Anyone realizes that the situation has to be reviewed time and time again."

Those who wondered about the improbability of Lyndon Johnson's informing Bill Clark as to what "the President is doing at the present time" (would he tell Clark when he could tell Dirksen?) now began to ask another weighty question. Was Dick Daley, maker of Presidents, using Bill Clark to tell Lyndon Johnson something? A few days later The Mayor gave the Clark statement the customary Daley doublethink, but the revisions were minor.

Bill Clark, who had the radiance of Brendan Behan about him, carefully removed the curl from the front of his haircut, as was noted by the late Virginia Kay, columnist for the Chicago *Daily News*, and kept a steady course on Vietnam. The Mayor didn't travel the course with his candidate, but the older man seemed to be following the voyage of the adventurer.

There had been a persistent rumor of an effort by Daley and Robert Kennedy to persuade the President to change administration policy in Vietnam, and that rumor led to another: Clark was Daley's stalking horse. Some insiders and some political analysts believed that Clark was the advance man for The Mayor's true sentiments on the war issue, while Daley was giving surface support to the President's program.

As of Sunday night in convention week nobody knew what to think. In a speech to Illinois college students August 4 at Loyola University's Marquette Center, Clark had called for a bombing halt. If The Mayor had meant to influence foreign policy publicly, he would have picked up Clark's Loyola pronouncement and advanced with it. Instead, The Mayor went to the Illinois State Fair just a week later and told the loyal Democrats attending the Governor's Day rally what he thought they wanted to hear. "Our Democrats are solidly behind Lyndon B. Johnson all the way," The Mayor said, with the message yet to come. "I know I am—one hundred percent." (That was the message.) "No man wants peace more than Lyndon B. Johnson. He has two sons-in-law over there. I don't care what the intellectuals or the university professors say."

That was one of The Mayor's rare descents into demagoguery. The intellectuals and the university professors did not doubt that Johnson wanted peace. Their concern was that he did not seem to know how to achieve peace, this side of complete devastation of Vietnam.

Six days later the Russians offered what seemed to be a simple solution of the Democrats' dilemma. A few minutes after 1 A.M., August 21, a Soviet fighter plane landed at Ruzyne International Airport near Prague to signal the Russian invasion of Czechoslovakia.

"Then came the Communist invasion of Czechoslovakia, and Daley used it to climb back on the Johnson program," John Dreiske wrote in the *Sun-Times*. The Mayor's reaction to the invasion was, "This will affect a lot of doves flying around."

Clark's endorsement of Senator McGovern, while the rest of the Illinois delegation was frozen in its watchful-waiting pose, revealed that The Mayor's most prominent dove still was flying. During the cocktail party that convention host Daley pitched for the delegates Sunday night the word was around that, during a get-together of party leaders reacting to Clark's unilateral action, The Mayor had referred to his Senatorial candidate as "that boob." The Mayor was very much in evidence during the party, personally, pictorially and pointedly. A gigantic photograph of Himself looked down upon the guzzling Democrats, and "Daley for President" buttons popped out on many lapels.

The photo and the buttons provided additional reasons for wonderment about the conduct of The Mayor. In the past he always had striven for dignity above all else. He had made a conscious effort to be several cuts above the clownish machine politicians of the caricatures. The photograph in itself would not have been bothersome, but the lapel pins were a bit too much. "He's just kidding," some apologists said; but if he was kidding, the gag was not in good taste. "He didn't know about the buttons," other apologists said; but if he was the innocent victim of his partisans' unsolicited enthusiasm, it was the first time.

There could be no doubt that this was not The Mayor so many national Democratic leaders had come to know and grudgingly admire, and that was reason for concern.

At 11:15 P.M., when many delegates were thinking of a night's rest for the tiring days ahead, the battle between police and hippie-Yippies resumed at Lincoln Park, three miles north of the Sherman House. There was an inevitability about this, as though Chicago were living out its Violence Wish. The city had not been visited by a plague of 100,000 hippie-Yippies, as advertised, but the five thousand or the ten thousand or the how-many-thousand were quite enough. And truth to tell, there were moments late Sunday night when the police thought that 100,000 were on the loose.

In early afternoon there had been a noisy but bloodless march of demonstrators from Lincoln Park south to the Loop. A police escort went along. The marchers did much shouting, but they made no attempt to confront the police; nor were they intimidated by the police. Interestingly, this group did not bother to go as far as the Conrad Hilton Hotel or, if the marchers had had that goal in mind, they were peaceably dissuaded by another detail of police, who met them at Wabash Avenue and Jackson Boulevard, a half block from the southeastern corner of the Loop.

The vile language and the clubbing did not begin until late afternoon, back in Lincoln Park, and they were touched off by a misunderstanding over a parking position for a flatbed truck that the Yippies wished to use as a stage for their musicians. Much of what went on during the rest of the night was rooted in misunderstanding or miscalculation. Either the police thought they were being surrounded or the demonstrators confused the orders that were given by their self-appointed leaders, or the police misjudged the aggressiveness of the crowd or the hippies read the patience of the police as indecision.

Nobody got it right.

The only thing clearly understood by one and all was that heads would ring at curfew time. Despite the efforts of National Mobilization marshals, who tried to persuade the demonstrators that they should clear the park, demonstrators' skulls and police clubs had their predestined rendezvous a few minutes after the eleven-o'clock curfew. In the major confrontation more than a thousand demonstrators went against police details that totaled 458 men. The demonstrators lost.

Forgotten in all the analyses of Sunday in the streets was weather, the differences between warmth and cold, between sunshine and darkness. During the early afternoon, when the sun warmed demonstrators and police, the processional to the Loop had been almost joyous. There had been insults, from one side to the other, but they had been good-natured to a large extent. Nobody seemed to be mad at anyone.

By the time the stragglers made their way back to Lincoln Park, Chicago's air pollutants had obscured the sun and a chill came into the air. Warmth drained from the body as well as from the spirit, and the participants began to feel miserable. Misery generated surliness, as it usually does, and when dusk came there were ugly men and women on both sides of the neutral ground that separated police from hippies and their allies. Darkness brought out the meanness in everybody, as any former infantry commander knows it does, as every cop should know it does.

The fatigue factor—policemen working long hours and the demonstrators going at top speed without adequate sleep— would be emphasized as a reason for the violence, but almost nothing would be said about the weather. Orlando Wilson would have known about that. Orlando Wilson knew about everything. But Orlando Wilson was no longer in charge of the Chicago Police Department.

While the hippies were fighting for what they considered their right to sleep in Lincoln Park, despite the contrary opinion of National Mobilization marshals, who wanted the demonstrators to seek shelter elsewhere, The Mayor and the delegates were sleeping the sleep of the just, unaware that another column of marchers, which had filled broad Michigan Avenue from curb to curb, had been turned back by police at the Michigan Avenue Bridge.

The Michigan Avenue Bridge. Down there on the North Bank, Fritz Etienne's ancestor Jean Baptiste Point Du Sable had brought humanity to Chicago. Over there on the South Bank had been Fort Dearborn, from which soldiers and settlers had marched on August 15, 1812, to be massacred on the nearby sand dunes by Kickapoos and Winnebagos.

52

A Hero Came

> . . . tend the flock of God which is
> among you, governing not under con-
> straint, but willingly . . .
> —Epistle from the Mass
> for Monday in Convention Week

WHILE Hubert Humphrey and the two Macs were scurrying around to call upon delegations Monday, The Mayor spent most of his day at his headquarters in the Sherman House. In midafternoon he went home to rest and refresh for the official opening of the Convention.

While The Mayor was passing what for him was an uneventful day, the platform committee acrimoniously hammered in a plank that endorsed Lyndon Johnson's conduct of the war in Vietnam. The majority prevailed, however, by no more than 62–35. Bill Clark was on the side of the minority, which had fought for a peace plank. During the day Jim Conlisk, the superintendent of police, ordered an investigation of the clubbing of newsmen by men of his department. Starting with the case of Larry Green of the Chicago *Daily News*, who was hit on the back late Saturday night, a total of ten reporters and photographers had been knocked around by police during a twenty-six-hour period.

Conlisk's general order, which was to be read at all roll

301

calls during the Convention days, included this paragraph: "Despite any personal feelings of individuals, department personnel should avoid conflicts with newsmen. It is in the best interest of the department and the City of Chicago that there be a harmonious relationship between the news media and our personnel."

Conlisk had put out the order, but he removed the stinger by using the unwarranted and unfortunate phrase "Despite any personal feelings of individuals . . ." He was saying that he understood and condoned the "personal feelings" of men who were duty-bound to enforce the law impartially. Orlando Wilson never would have hedged an order in that manner.

Just as Conlisk blurred responsibility and feelings, Michael Di Salle, former governor of Ohio, confused party loyalty and feelings in matters political. Ted Kennedy did not, at that time, want to be a candidate for anything and was willing to say so. He said so, in fact, during a phone conversation with Di Salle; Kennedy asked that his name be withdrawn from consideration. Di Salle listened and then called a press conference at which he offered the gratuitous and calloused opinion that the "Draft Kennedy" surge "could not be stopped at this time."

Meanwhile, the Concerned Transit Workers who had left their buses and elevated trains at 12:01 A.M., Sunday, to start a wildcat strike said they would ignore an injunction ordering them back to work. They claimed they had cut service to 40 percent of normal. The drivers for Checker and Yellow, the city's largest taxicab companies, also had left the driving to others, but neither of these strikes particularly bothered the delegates. They were taken to the Amphitheater in chartered buses, and their schedule was such that they had almost no time to go sight-seeing by public transit or in a cab. And The Mayor was not bothered at all—personally, that is. He could have walked to the Amphitheater to give his welcoming speech. Easily. Much more easily than he could have walked home from the Martin Luther King Jr. Drive dedication.

"Reject the language of conflict and despair," he urged the delegates after he had taken control of the rostrum.

"There is a dangerous political rhetoric in this land," he said sagely, alluding to the Republicans and their recently nominated Presidential candidate, Richard Nixon. "We Democrats will nominate a President of the United States, a chief executive—not a police chief."

He said there was a valid reason why the dissenters who had come to Chicago had not bothered to go to Miami. "Because they know," he said, "at this political gathering there is hope and opportunity."

The man, or men, who had written those lines for The Mayor understood the mood of August, 1968. With three or four speeches similar to the one he was making, The Mayor might become something more than a builder of expressways, settler of strikes and maker of Presidents. He might become binder of wounds, healer of divisiveness, and bridger of generation gaps.

Then his infuriating compulsion to be all things to all people betrayed him. The problems of the nation never would be solved, he said, "in rioting and violence in the streets."

He reiterated the promise that brought comfort to many and the chill of fear to many others. "And as long as I'm mayor, there will be law and order in Chicago," he said.

It was a shame, because it was so unnecessary. So much that he was doing those days seemed to be unnecessary. The delegates didn't need to hear any more about law and order. They had had all they needed of that if they watched the telecasts of the Republican convention. They knew that Hubert Humphrey had arrived at O'Hare Airport Sunday while federal troops were leaving their carriers nearby. They knew that the National Guard was standing by and that the

Chicago police had had leaves and furloughs canceled. They knew that the hippies and the Yippies had burst from Lincoln Park Sunday night. Knowing all that, they needed more than anything else somebody to reconcile them, to assure them, to make them truly welcome.

Although the convention planners had made a big thing of minimizing demonstrations on the Amphitheater floor, The Mayor's little talk was hailed by the Shannon Rovers, a bagpipe band, and by forty citizens who were inspired to march about carrying "Daley for President" signs. The political leader who had worked so hard to maintain an image of dignity was being made to look like a clown in his sixty-seventh year.

Gentle Sam Shapiro took time in his welcoming speech to pay homage to the late Adlai Stevenson, governor of Illinois, Presidential candidate and United Nations delegate. Out in the hall Stevenson's son pursed his lips and adjusted his glasses.

The Mayor, rather than the Governor, set the tone for Illinois's contributions, and the events of Monday night would not be writ large in the history of the state's national-convention delegations. Illinois voted with the majority to seat the regular Texas delegation, which did not include many Mexican-Americans or Negro-Americans. Illinois also voted with the majority that wanted the vote on credentials shifted from Tuesday to Monday night. This was a stratagem designed to steal time from the McCarthy people, who had very little support among the so-called "regular" delegations. The conduct of the Illinois delegates and their votes had not been influenced by Sam Shapiro's recollections of Adlai Stevenson.

Then came a hero, the kind of black man who makes white women admit that they are not as fearful about integration as they pretend to be. Julian Bond, tan, soft and dreamy, like Belafonte but better- and tougher-looking and without the

Belafonte insouciance that sometimes comes through as pure wise-guy.

Julian Bond and his people, the Georgia "outs," came down from somewhere or in from somewhere looking for the seats they said belonged to them as regular, loyal, black and white Democrats. Lester Maddox and his people had the seats, of course, and although each of the three major broadcasting networks had been limited to seven floor passes for television and radio—as compared to twenty passes at Miami Beach and thirty-one at Atlantic City for the Democratic convention four years earlier—the television crews captured the moment and in so doing gave immeasurable future help to the Democratic party.

The moment would be remembered as the instant in which the Democratic party finally won the battle that had been started in 1948 by those young radicals—a Minnesotan named Hubert Humphrey had been among them—and broke free from bigotry. The exchanges between Bond and his forty-one and the forty-one who were led by Maddox were "charming"—there could have been no other word. They graciously first-named and "sir"-ed one another and they showed the whites and the blacks of Chicago the meaning of the word *civilized*.

And while the television cameras were looking and the microphones were listening to Bond and his people search for seats that were filled, the delegates voted to abolish the unit rule for the '68 Convention. It was too dramatic for fiction.

The struggle against the unit rule, which required that all the votes of a given state be cast according to the will of the majority of that state's delegation, had been led by the McCarthy people, whose Presidential choice had asked in Chicago on the last day of June, "Is the Democratic party itself democratic? Is it to be governed by the will of the many or the few? Shall the people decide?"

The hero-worship of Julian Bond went on until long after midnight, long after the opening night should have ended. There was an impromptu rally then for the handsome young man from Georgia, and Senator Daniel Inouye of Hawaii, himself a member of a minority group, keynoter and temporary chairman, didn't seem to know quite what to do about it.

The Mayor told him with a little hand signal which clearly meant "The End." Inouye called for adjournment.

‖‖‖‖‖‖‖‖‖‖‖‖‖‖‖‖‖‖‖‖‖‖‖‖‖‖‖‖‖‖‖‖‖‖‖‖

53

To Make Some Witness

THERE was no way to know then that he would speak the most prophetic words about convention week. That was why a businessman, attempting to explain why the extra volume of sales that had been anticipated while the delegates were in town had not materialized, didn't get his name in the paper. "There's a kind of gray hanging over the city," he said.

Monday afternoon, light had been shone into the grayness by an alliance of ministers, priests and rabbis who called themselves the North Side Cooperative Ministry. They called a press conference and charged that Chicago had been turned into a "police state." The Reverend Carl Lezak of St. Sebastian Roman Catholic Church, 824 West Wellington Avenue, said that he saw police beat protesters "without reason." So often those days The Mayor was given his lumps by Catholic priests.

The hippie-Yippies continued to battle on two fronts—in Grant Park by day and in Lincoln Park by night. There was a spontaneity about everything that was done by the long-haired young people and their more conventional-looking allies, but by midday Monday the police had sound reasons to believe that the spontaneity was planned. These were the guerrilla tactics of organized confusion.

The Monday pattern carried over into Tuesday. Morning was quiet as the protesters, the love people, the clowns and the exhibitionists drifted in from the church basements and other shelters they had found after the retreat from Lincoln Park. The police came yawning back to duty.

In midafternoon police arrested two leaders of National Mobilization—Tom Hayden, twenty-eight, and Wolfe Lowenthal, twenty-nine—on charges of obstructing police, resisting arrest and disorderly conduct. The reaction to the arrests was almost gentle. Some five hundred hippie-Yippies decided to repeat their march of Sunday afternoon, but this time they would go to Police Headquarters at Eleventh and State Streets to let Jim Conlisk and other high-ranking officers know how they felt about the cops taking Hayden and Lowenthal away from their disciples. Again the processional was escorted by police and again it was peaceful—only three persons were arrested—which led to the conclusion that the police who were walking into and through the Loop with the demonstrators were not the same police who were banging heads in Lincoln Park after dark.

Perhaps because they had been lulled by the good-natured attitude of the marchers, the police miscalculated again and permitted the demonstrators to return north during the evening rush hour on a route that took them to Grant Park, across from the south end of the vast Conrad Hilton Hotel. Again the mood changed with the weather, and the hippie-Yippies began to chant of "Revolution!"

Into the park went the "revolutionaries" to parade around the equestrian statue of General John A. Logan, a Civil War hero who had been studiously ignored by generations of Chicagoans. Most citizens don't know that the Logan statue is in the park, and those who do know never look at it. Within a few minutes some adventurers climbed upon the poor general and his steed to wave Viet Cong flags and to shout obscenities at the police. Ultimately, the police charged. Cops were kicked, demonstrators were beaten and a young man who had soared to the shoulders of the bronze general suffered a broken arm. Numerous cameramen from press and television photographed the scene and only two were struck by police clubs. Both injuries were minor.

Peace, beautiful peace, prevailed in Lincoln Park during the early evening, but there was chaos in nearby Old Town, a synthetic community of taverns, restaurants and shops that trap tourists, newcomers to the city and those who are most appropriately described as "singles." Hayden and Lowenthal were released, each on $1,000 bond, not long after 8 P.M., and Abbie Hoffman, one of the founding fathers of the Yippies, a "party" he candidly described as a myth, was telling anyone who would listen, "If we are told to leave [the park], then leave."

Along about nine o'clock a phantasmagoric group did leave. (Its numbers were "estimated" at two hundred by some rational observers and at fifteen hundred by others who thought themselves equally logical, so perhaps somebody *had* put LSD into the water supply. Or into the air.) Whatever their ghostly number, these crusaders declared that they would parade down to the Sherman House to holler nasty words at The Mayor, which seemed especially pointless, because everybody knew that he was at the Amphitheater.

The pattern of Sunday continued to repeat itself. The major battle of Monday night occurred after the curfew hour. The Reverend Mark Miller, an assistant pastor of St. Paul's Church (United Church of Christ), was present in the park. These were some of the things he saw as he described them two weeks later in a message to members of his congregation:

I was personally involved with fifty other clergymen. We were there not as zealous evangelists. Rather, we were there hoping our presence would bring some levity and sanity to the situation. Of course, we failed. When the first scents of [tear] gas came, over two thousand kids left the park . . . orderly. Trying to determine their escape route, they lingered at one large intersection, chanting their "Hell, no, we won't go."

The police force then mobilized, and instead of being methodical and restrained, literally charged in groups of seventy into the throngs of kids, hitting anyone they could. One of the seminary students fell to a flurry of nightsticks (he was clearly identifiable by his clerical collar), ending up with a skull fracture and possible loss of one eye. Countless others, as you well know, received the same expression of law and order.

Still smarting from the gas and the unbelievable action of those who drive in cars which are labeled, "We Protect and Serve," I was standing on a corner with two other clergymen, trying to get the kids to disperse calmly rather than provoke the hordes of policemen. (And also let it be accurately clear the provocation was not singular, for it emerged from both the police and the kids assembled.)

A squad car drove up; someone hurled a rock through the back window, and immediately one of the policemen jumped out and fired his revolver into the air. Everyone scrambled like mad. The officer came charging into the three of us, screaming wildly, "Get out of here! You clergy don't belong here." We assured him we were leaving, but not in a sprint. Luckily he restrained himself at that point, choosing to leave rather than intimidate.

As the agonizing week ground on, many delegates and many more Chicagoans were infuriated by references to the hippie-Yippies as "kids" and "children," but Pastor Miller was young enough to make the distinction. In the eyes of the twenty-eight-year-old minister they were kids. Mark Miller is not the type of clergyman that cops dismiss as a "do-gooder." Rather he is a minister whom policemen and other active types usually identify with easily. During his high-school days Mark had been a baseball teammate of Pete Ward, who was with the Chicago White Sox in the summer of 1968, and it had been the future minister, not the future major-leaguer, who led the prep league in batting. At Stanford University Miller had been the star left-handed pitcher. The star right-handed pitcher had been Jim Lonborg, who pitched the Boston Red Sox to the American League championship in 1967. For three successive summers, while he was a seminarian, Miller pitched his team to a national amateur baseball championship. Many of the policemen would have liked him had they known him. In a fair fight, and perhaps in a foul one, he probably could have whipped most of the police on the details.

Pastor Miller was one of many residents of the Lincoln Park area who had argued, before the fact, against the city's imposition of the 11 P.M. curfew.

The week before the Convention, Frederick Trost, my senior pastor, and others negotiated with our Congressman, the assistant to Police Chief Conlisk, the head men at our Eighteenth Police District precinct, and the Mayor's office to bring to bear what pressure was necessary to reverse the Mayor's decision to close the Lincoln Park [the young minister recalled].

We knew the kids—Yippies, hippies, S.D.S. and the other people who participated—would be present Sunday evening and would be chased from the park. Sunday evening Pastor Trost made the decision that we would offer our church as a sanctuary for those who needed a place to stay.

So each evening, up to and including Thursday evening, the kids came in droves to St. Paul's. We have a large gymnasium that served as their crash pad. By the end of the week we had sheltered and fed about two thousand kids. The experience of meeting them and being able to help was ineffable.

They came with their blankets and their wounds and they needed help. Some of those who stayed each night knew something about treating gassed eyes, so they set up their own medical corps. Some were in more serious shape: the gal who had a miscarriage on State Street, the boy with the caved-in ribs, the boy with the concussion. For these we worked closely with a "Medical Central," which was set up for just such cases.

Each night we were fearful of getting "busted" by "The Man." One night a friend of mine, employed by the Police Department, came over in plain clothes to advise me that the police would be raiding us. I became very anxious about such a possibility so I checked each kid in, requesting from them any grass, acid or weapons they might have.

The surprising thing about this is that the kids gave us their stuff, which, of course, we either discarded or locked up. The police never did come to the church.

But the act of St. Paul's meeting this crisis is not the important thing. Neither is the fact that five other churches around us and, belatedly, McCormick Theological Seminary pitched in to offer places for the kids to sleep. Neither is the fact that all kinds of community people helped, from seminary students to nuns, to young marrieds offering themselves as kitchen help, to fathers of teen-agers offering their cars to transport kids from Michigan Avenue to St. Paul's, about four miles in distance.

The important thing [the Reverend Miller concluded] is for us to make some witness to the unbelievable brutality, which occurs every night of the year on many of our corners, and express our utter rejection of it. I am not sure how we do this. The kids themselves, so many of them innocent and gentle, did accomplish national exposure of our Chicago style of democracy. To get the issue to the Convention floor was no small accomplishment. And certainly the wanton flailing of night sticks and the irrational beatings only helped strengthen the designs of the power centers to have order without law and justice without love.

Horrifying though it had been, Monday night and early Tuesday morning had been a time of fulfillment for Mark Miller, a minor-leaguer among the men of the collar. The time had been something less than that for the Reverend Dr. Kenneth Hildebrand, a big name in the clerical big league of Chicago. Dr. Hildebrand, scheduled to give the benediction that would close the Monday session of the Convention, was left standing in the wings, a prayer on his lips, when The Mayor, stage-managing from out in the house, signaled "curtain" to Senator Inouye.

54

‖‖‖‖‖‖‖‖‖‖‖‖‖‖‖‖‖‖‖‖‖‖‖‖‖‖‖‖‖‖‖

Goodbye, Gene

*The mouth of the just man tells of
wisdom and his tongue utters what is
right.*
    —*Gradual Psalm from the Mass
    for Tuesday in Convention Week*

TUESDAY was the sixtieth birthday of the Texan from Stone-
wall, Lyndon B. Johnson. What a day this could have been
for the President and for The Mayor—if it hadn't been for
the war in Vietnam. Lyndon would have been sitting down
there in Texas in all his folksy regalia waiting for the people
of the Democratic party to summon him to Chicago to accept his second nomination. That part of the Convention that
was being conducted within the walls of the Amphitheater
would have been so much easier for The Mayor. That other
convention, the one out there in the streets, might have been
even more of a bother, of course, but who could be sure
about that?

Jim Conlisk certainly had his hands full. For the second
successive day the superintendent of police issued an order
to ask his men to, please, stop knocking the hell out of reporters and photographers. This order was occasioned by an
afternoon meeting with editors of Chicago's four daily newspapers and with officials of television networks, magazines

314

and wire services. The meeting in turn had been occasioned by the slugging of nineteen newsmen Monday night and early Tuesday morning. If Conlisk didn't do more than tap wrists there soon would be almost nobody physically able to cover the Convention, which may have been what some of the police had in mind.

The younger newsmen began to comprehend that very little sympathy was forthcoming from the public. Some young men and women go into the various branches of journalism with the idealistic notion that they will be admired, appreciated and even loved by the people they serve. Those who came back to their offices bloodied and bruised Tuesday morning, or checked into hospitals, began to understand that newsmen and policemen have almost everything in common. Neither group ever will be the "good guys" in the eyes of the public. They are in there together even when they are battling one another. The only time a citizen roots for a cop or a newsman is when the citizen needs one. The rest of the time they are a pain in the ass to the man in the street who doesn't want to be arrested or exposed in print.

After he had met with Emmett Dedmon of the *Sun-Times*, Roy Fisher of the *Daily News*, Lloyd Wendt of the Chicago *American* and Thomas Moore of the *Tribune*, Conlisk put out a three-point order. Uniformed men would be subject to disciplinary action if they removed star or nameplate, as some had been doing. Lieutenants would be assigned as "press officers" in the areas of confrontation. No policeman would demand that a newsman surrender his camera, recorder or other professional equipment.

The assaulted newsmen and photographers discovered that The Mayor was giving them the same diluted brand of sympathy that was being ladled out by the bemused public. "We ask that newsmen follow the orders of the police too." The Mayor said. "These men [police] are working twelve hours a day. If they ask a newsman and photographer to move, they should move as well as anyone else. How can they [the police] tell the difference [between a demonstrator and a newsman]?"

The Mayor was missing the point, and because he is a lawyer there had to be an assumption that his miss was deliberate. The point is that a policeman can ask a newsman to move, but that the choice to move or not to move is the newsman's. The policeman has no right to order a newsman out of an area simply because the policeman thinks the newsman should not be there. Freedom of the press is a much too precious right to be left to the discretion of an individual. The suspicion persisted that a few cops were slugging newsmen because those cops did not want their actions to be reported on newsprint, tape or film. And The Mayor's transparent argument that the police could not tell the difference between a demonstrator and a newsman surely would persuade some sadistic men that The Mayor approved of their actions. The man who had spoken to the Convention delegates about law and order had given a benediction to those who would take the Constitution into their own hands, no matter how little they might know of its meaning.

The Convention resumed, everything about it interesting except its primary purpose, the selection of a Presidential candidate. The Southern states were coming over to Humphrey, who had it all but won in the opinion of everybody except himself. There were hints that L.B.J. would show to take a bow and revitalize his people, and there were rumors that Ted Kennedy would come in to be drafted after all. But the hints and the rumors weren't inspiring anybody.

What little hope Gene McCarthy might have had was being buried in the blood and the excrement and the garbage and the sperm in Lincoln and Grant parks. Almost everything about the Convention, inside and outside, was touched with sickness, but this was a hallucination generated by those who sought imagery that only drugs could produce. McCarthy was the only candidate who understood the hippie-Yippies, who could sympathize with them, and they were killing him.

McCarthy's men in Chicago always had known which candidate would be hurt by clashes between the police and the hippie-Yippies. Twenty years before, Hubert Humphrey might have understood what the angry young people were saying, but not now. He could not hear them. McCarthy heard and understood. He understood best what they were doing to him.

"Because we could anticipate what was coming, we wanted our young supporters to stay away from Chicago," McCarthy man Martin Gleason said. "During a press conference on August 12, Senator McCarthy said just that. He mentioned the 'unintended violence.' We sent telegrams to all our McCarthy campaign headquarters around the country to emphasize the importance of the Senator's request.

"The Senator and Daley had talked about this when they got together on the phone," Gleason continued. "That was in late July. I had to talk to a lot of people to prevail upon the Senator before he would make the call to Daley. I had a feeling that their Irishness and their Catholicity could draw them together. And their sense of humor—that too. Daley does have a sense of humor in spite of what you read about him.

"All of us—the McCarthy people and the people in City Hall—knew what the radical groups were planning to do. There wasn't anything secret about it. We were all, frankly, very frightened of *provocateurs* and what might happen. Those of us who were with McCarthy were determined to do everything possible to keep the Yippies and hippies away from the Convention hall."

Many of McCarthy's young partisans had stayed away from Chicago, but the Senator was burdened by the "support" of others, who were walking back and forth between Lincoln and Grant.

A large black woman with a large voice, Fannie Lou

Hamer of the Mississippi Freedom Party, delivered an important speech to the delegates, many of whom were not listening. There was no applause at all for Fannie Lou from the Illinois delegation, which was sitting down front, close enough to hear. Perhaps the Illinoisans were tired. Up to that point they had applauded everybody else.

It was a night for black women at the Convention, just as Monday night had been. Aretha Franklin had soulfully opened the Monday session with the national anthem, and even those delegates who didn't want to listen to Aretha heard her. She was not "the woman who," in the eyes or the hearts or, surely, the souls of most in her audience. Those who would have preferred a more established and establishment black singer like Mahalia Jackson didn't dig Miss Franklin at all. They were mollified somewhat when Aretha got ahead of the musicians, as even the best of national anthem singers sometimes do.

It was a night for black men. The battle of the chairs ended with the "regular" Georgia delegation walking out when they were confronted with the reality of having to share their seats with Julian Bond and his dissidents. During the mild uproar that ensued Dan Rather, the CBS reporter who had become familiar to millions because of his splendid work in Dallas after the assassination of President Kennedy, was punched in the stomach.

Rather's leader, anchorman Walter Cronkite, consoled the slightly winded reporter with these words, heard by millions: "I think we've got a bunch of thugs there, Dan. . . ."

Senator McCarthy and all the others who had fought for an open convention won a significant victory when the delegates finished the wrecking job they had begun on the unit rule Monday night. By a vote of 1,350 to 1,206 the Convention upset the majority report and decreed that every vestige of the century-old unit rule system would be eradicated for the 1972 Convention. The minority report, written by a committee under the leadership of the dynamic Harold Hughes, governor of Iowa, prevailed without the help of Illinois. The Mayor and his men were not at all the progressives that Illinois delegates had been at other conventions.

Bill Clark continued his lonely fight for a strong peace plank, and newspaper headlines suggested that the "Draft Ted Kennedy" movement posed the possibility that Humphrey would lose the support of the state of Ohio and of Big Labor. But Illinois would get around to endorsing somebody Wednesday, and The Mayor was dropping hints that Humphrey would be the boy.

What with one thing and another, the Tuesday session dragged on past the hoped-for hour of adjournment, just as Monday's proceedings had done. All across the nation Convention watchers who had remained by their television sets to watch the great debate on Vietnam were dropping out or dropping off. Prime television time was long gone as the clock pushed into Wednesday, and there were indications that almost nobody would be around to watch the Democrats go to war over Vietnam. This would have pleased the Humphreyites, of course, because it would have been to their advantage to keep the minority viewpoint out of sight and sound.

New York and California would not permit the administration to control this aspect of the Convention. New York and California and like-minded delegations hollered that the session should be recessed until noon Wednesday, and they refused to stop hollering. New York and California had very poor locations in the Amphitheater, and the floor microphones assigned to them for purposes of communicating with the chair didn't always work; but New York and California had something superior, the microphones of television and radio. Much later it was written that this was the networks' way of punishing The Mayor for his lack of sympathy toward them, but that was a misreading of the fact. The mi-

crophones and the lenses were at the back of the hall because
that is where the story was. Whether one believed that The
Mayor and all the others who supported the majority view
on Vietnam were right or wrong, one had to concede that
The Mayor and the other pro-Johnson people were doing this
wrong at one o'clock in the morning Wednesday.

Good Democrats all, they continued to fight among themselves until the uproar became embarrassing. Democracy
was being wounded, and the Democratic party was suffering.
Finally, The Mayor attracted the attention of Senator Carl
Albert of Oklahoma, the permanent chairman. The Mayor
drew a finger across his neck, the signal that said, "That's all
for tonight!"

Many in the Amphitheater did not see The Mayor's direc-
torial gesture, but so many cameras saw it. This was the second night running that he, personally, had taken the Convention away from the delegates. Early Tuesday morning his
action had seemed eminently reasonable. Then he had been
one of the few rational men in the building. But on Wednesday morning, this was too much for all but his stanchest admirers. He had revealed for millions to see that he actually
believed that the Convention, as well as the Convention city,
was his.

55

Victory from Defeat

GENE MCCARTHY died in the Amphitheater and in the hotels where the delegations listened to him ever so politely. The young people who were killing him died out in the streets along with the adults who were supporting them. Tuesday was the day that the demonstrations that were to be became the demonstrations that never would be. Saturday, Sunday and Monday had given promise of meaningful actions to come, but Tuesday was a day of silliness. Tuesday was when the young people who might have done so much came apart.

The reasons? Exhaustion, surely; weary troops do not fight well. Leadership, surely; leaderless troops do not fight well. The people, all of the people out there in television land, and even the people of Chicago, the conservative people of Chicago, who had wondered whether the young men and women in Lincoln Park would make a meaningful, dramatic, historic contribution to this Convention, came to the conclusion that these young people were damn fools.

It was sad, completely sad. The young people had been given a great opportunity by Dave Dellinger—by Dave Dellinger, alone—and they had blown it.

On Tuesday the young people were as wrong in the streets as Mayor Daley was wrong in the Convention. And wrong—this, in a word of the day, was beautiful—for the same reason. Because they thought they were so right. The troops of Lincoln Park and their sympathizers split off into scores of platoons, each fighting its own battle, and the strength of the army was gone on the tear gas.

Everything they did was wrong. The ministers and the priests of the North Side Cooperative Ministry were reinforced by residents of the area, and a whole new unit was organized. They called it the Lincoln Park Emergency Citizens Committee. The Committee's mission was logical and necessary. It would ask the police to revoke the ban on sleeping in Lincoln Park. But the tactics designed for the attack were terrible. They asked the wrong police. They went to the commanders of the local police districts, who had neither the power nor the authority to do anything but talk.

In the early evening Jerry Rubin and Bobby Seale, a big man in the Black Panther party, harangued a Lincoln Park crowd of some fifteen hundred with a lecture in white and black. A revolutionary lecture that had no significance because the black people were out of this. The Negroes of Chicago were cooling it for reasons of their own—Jeff Fort and the Blackstone Rangers were long gone and gone long—and there weren't enough black people in the park to have a decent basketball tournament.

The motley little army went off in a half dozen different directions—some to picket a bus barn on behalf of the black drivers who were striking the Chicago Transit Authority and their own union; some to the Coliseum to "uncelebrate" the President's birthday ("Chicago is now known as the Prague of the Midwest," Dellinger told the three thousand who were there); some to join the prayer vigil conducted by the clergy in front of a crude eight-foot cross; some to make love; some to throw crap at the police; some to be tear-gassed again after curfew in Lincoln Park; some to demonstrate in Grant Park across from the Hilton.

The events of Tuesday convinced those who had been concerned about the potential power of the young that the young were not to be taken seriously. The young had earned that brushoff by not taking themselves seriously. They had a cause, a great cause, and the zeal and energy and fanaticism to make the cause felt, but they did not have what so many of them professed to hate. They did not have discipline.

The demonstrators had dissipated their strength in foolishness. As of early Wednesday morning theirs was a combat division that no longer existed. The troops were spent, all the fight gone out of them. And then, at three o'clock in the morning, Chicago made an astonishing tactical error. Chicago called in the troops of the Illinois National Guard to relieve the police in front of the Hilton. Chicago admitted defeat to a defeated enemy while The Mayor slept.

The war was on again.

56

ıllıllıllıllıllıllıllıllıllıllı

Coffee and Sandwiches

*For there will come a time when
they will not endure the sound doctrine . . .*

—*Epistle from the Mass
for Wednesday in Convention Week*

AUGUST 28 was the feast day of Saint Augustine, Bishop,
Confessor, Doctor of the Church, and self-proclaimed all-
time juvenile hell-raiser of Christendom. One wonders
whether Augustine was in the thoughts of The Mayor as he
knelt in Nativity of Our Lord or in the thoughts of the young
people as they straggled back to Lincoln Park. Imaginative
though they were, in their forays against the Establishment,
the Yippies and the hippies had not thought of some tactics
that had been born in the lively mind of Augustine the African.

The Mayor's official day began at breakfast with Hubert
Humphrey in the Vice-President's suite at the Hilton. The
reporters who watch such minor events without seeing them
said that the candidate and The Mayor spent an hour together and that the conversationalists ate scrambled eggs.
Only a smidgen of suspense remained on the plates, along
with the egg stains, when this breakfast had ended. Unless
Teddy Kennedy was waiting in Massachusetts to come
charging from the wings with his version of the white-knight

routine, Hubert Humphrey no longer needed Richard J. Daley. Without a Kennedy, 1968 could not be 1960. Without a Johnson, 1968 could not be 1964. The kingmaker had become just another elderly party leader. The Mayor had waited too long.

"Let's not be too hasty," the hero-worshipers cautioned. "The Mayor always knows what he's doing. He held back the endorsement because he had his reasons."

Not long after breakfast the hero-worshipers had reason to grin. Illinois delegates were together again in the Sherman House for the caucus that had been suspended since Sunday, and outside the doors of the caucus room more than one hundred young people were chanting, "We want Teddy."

As the voices of the chanters came through the door, Democrats exchanged the look of conspirators, the look that asked, "Who sent for them?" It might be said that The Mayor did not have complete control over demonstrations in lakefront parks, but it was illogical to suppose that all those young people would be allowed to demonstrate within the hotel that housed Cook County Democratic headquarters if The Mayor was not willing to put up with them. Had The Mayor sent for them? Were they there to tell the delegates that The Mayor also wanted Teddy?

In the room, though, nobody was fighting for Teddy. A voice was raised for a peace plank in the platform and for Senator McGovern. The voice of a dove, flying around. The voice of Bill Clark. Bill, who seemed to have been carried away by his antiadministration role to the point of self-mesmerization, wished to remind the delegates of his family's history within the Democratic party of Illinois. To mind came his father's reminiscence that surely never was very far out of mind. "When my father was finance committee chairman of the City Council," Clark said, "there was an assistant sergeant at arms who used to go for coffee for my dad and go across the street for sandwiches."

The candlepower in the narrow room rose to astonishing

intensity as so many red faces were turned on by Clark's audacity. It wasn't necessary for Bill to explain that the assistant sergeant at arms of happy memory had been the once and future mayor of Chicago. The punk! The *punk!* Who did he think he was? What was he trying to do? Show up Dick Daley?

The old-timers who reacted wanted The Mayor to observe that the "arrogance" of Clark had infuriated them, but Adlai Stevenson, who was there, felt that much of the fury was feigned. Those who had been looking for an excuse to get Clark had been provided with an unhoped-for opportunity by their intended victim. "Bill wasn't being arrogant at all," Stevenson remembered. "It was just a long, rambling, sentimental speech. What Bill was trying to do, and I felt it while he was speaking, was to reminisce about the long association his family has had with Daley."

Paul Simon, candidate for lieutenant governor, agreed with Stevenson's interpretation. Simon did not get the impression that Clark was demeaning Daley.

Much later, Clark would write, "I was referring to the sixty-five years in continuous elective public office of my grandfather, my father and myself, and restating my Democratic credentials, since there were some who believed my independent position concerning the administration of the war in Vietnam was disloyal to the administration of President Johnson. I told the delegates that a man first had to be loyal to himself, and I praised the Democratic party and the fact that when my father was chairman of the finance committee of the City Council there was a young man named Richard J. Daley, who worked for the Council in a ministerial position and that he had worked his way up to be mayor of the city of Chicago and the leader of the Democratic party in this state. I also referred to the fact that he was a man that Presidents, kings, queens and some of the world's most important people came to see. The remark was intended to be complimentary."

The compliment did nothing for the cause of Senator McGovern, for the cause of those who advocated a peace plank, or for the cause of Bill Clark. Possibly because he concluded that there was no turning back, Clark angrily gave a parting shot to his enemies within the delegation. "If there is anybody here who would question any position I have taken in my political life or in this campaign," Clark said, "stand up now and debate me. You have no right to sit around in the saloons on LaSalle Street and question my party loyalty."

Saloons? Democrats in saloons? Horrors!

The Mayor emerged from the caucus room, took his customary position on a temporary platform, looked at the twenty microphones arrayed in front of him, and said, "Illinois, in its usual winning tradition, has endorsed Hubert H. Humphrey, the next President of the United States, with 112 votes."

The automatic applause came on cue but there were boos and a boo never was written for this script. The raucous disapproval came from the "We want Teddy" chanters. They still wanted Teddy. Color came up through the wattles of The Mayor, pushed through the gelatinous jowls and tinted his cheeks. He paused to speak to the young people about good manners and then plunged ahead with the platitudes that the moment demanded. Quite obviously he had not sent for them.

Although The Mayor had spoken with his usual fervor of "winning tradition," Illinois wasn't doing this thing in the style of its tradition. Illinois had waited too long. Illinois had no meaning now for Hubert Humphrey, who didn't especially need those 112 votes.

And the Illinois delegates were not at all confident that they were endorsing the next President of the United States.

Wednesday, day and night, would not be a golden page in the history of Illinois's winning tradition. The Mayor—his person or his name or his picture—was everywhere that unfortunate day, but now the man who had intended to run the Convention was being run by the Convention. And being criticized for the way it was running.

Chet Huntley of NBC had started the verbal attack Wednesday morning when he told a national radio audience, "The news profession in this city is now under assault by the Chicago police."

One of Huntley's competitors was willing to fight back. The combative and abrasive Mike Wallace of CBS became involved in a convention-floor scuffle that led to a confrontation with Captain Paul McLaughlin, the police officer in charge of security at the Amphitheater. Accidentally or otherwise, Wallace struck McLaughlin on the face. McLaughlin responded with a blow to Mike's outthrust chin. Wallace was rushed through Vice-President Humphrey's command post on the second floor of the Amphitheater en route to a Police Department security van. The Mayor had much more disturbing events on his mind at that precise moment, but he dutifully scurried from the floor to the van for a meeting with Wallace, Richard S. Salant, president of CBS News, McLaughlin and Deputy Police Superintendent James Rochford. Urged by the Great Arbitrator, the television commentator and the police captain reacted like boys in a schoolyard. They shook hands and agreed to let bygones be bygones.

Criticism from "the media" was to be expected, but The Mayor surely thought he would be spared pressure from Lyndon Johnson's very own lame-duck Cabinet. A Federal Bureau of Investigation probe of the Police Department's handling of news personnel was ordered by Attorney General Ramsey Clark. Everything and everybody was turning in upon The Mayor.

A Happening

Two exhausted armies had faced each other across Michigan Avenue, in front of the Conrad Hilton, early Wednesday morning. The policemen, most of them on the job for fifteen hours or more, were drained by the monotony and the emotion of this strange kind of guard duty. The hippies, Yippies and flippies, energies spent by endless hours of pointless motion, had reached the point at which a man or woman collapses in a heap or begins to babble and scream. Battle fatigue was prevalent on both sides of Michigan Avenue, and out of the ennui came a kind of grudging understanding that bridged the wide boulevard.

Not *respect*, because these adversaries never would exchange respect. They had hurled four-letter insults at one another, in the manner of enemy infantry units confronting one another from holding positions, but these words had stung as the epithets of wartime never had. Policemen had not expected the language of the squad room from eighteen-year-old girls, and the girls had not expected to hear the words from men old enough to be their fathers.

Police Sergeant Thomas Ryan, a specialist in wry humor, said, "I didn't mind being called a pig, or even certain kinds of a pig, but when they called me a Nazi pig that hurt a little." During another turbulent time in history Ryan had known about the Nazis. He was a staff sergeant in the Second Rangers, the unit that had climbed the sheer cliffs at Normandy hours before the major landing on D Day, 1944.

329

At 1:35 A.M., Wednesday, police officials had made the long-awaited gesture of accommodation. Through the bullhorns came the announcement that the demonstrators could remain overnight in Grant Park provided that they were peaceful. This was a victory for the crowd, but it also was a peace offering by the police. The unexpectedness of it dissipated much of the bitterness. For the first time since Saturday night the tension was gone and the sullenness was replaced by a vacant-eyed numbness.

At 3:10 A.M. thirty National Guard vehicles emerged from the mist to the north. Nobody had said that the troops were coming. The bullhorns had not explained that the Guardsmen had been called as relief for the bone-weary police. The appearance of six hundred "soldiers," dressed for combat, sent a new charge of bitterness through the crowd, and the hippies and their allies were rejuvenated for the new day.

Warmed by a bright sun, the demonstrators rested Wednesday morning. Many left the area across from the Conrad Hilton to make room for cleanup crews assigned by the city. Chicago is very proud of its "front yard." At 9:45 a Police Department detail relieved National Guard military police, who had been on duty in front of the hotel.

The action picked up in early afternoon at the Grant Park band shell, three blocks south of the Hilton and a half mile to the east. National Mobilization, which had a permit for a rally, hoped to convince the crowd that a march should be made to the Amphitheater Wednesday night.

During the speeches a young man lowered an American flag to half-staff on the pole near the band shell. Police arrested the youth and then retreated under a barrage of objects thrown from the crowd. Somewhat later a group of six young men lowered the American flag and replaced it with a red object that was to be described by various witnesses as "a Viet Cong flag," "a black flag of anarchy," and "a bright red slip." A squad of police charged the area and removed the red banner but did not restore the American flag. The police lobbed a smoke bomb into the crowd; a hippie lobbed the smoke bomb back to the police; the police lobbed more smoke bombs, and a very active quarter hour was passed by all. The Police Department reported that thirty men were hurt in these melees. The hippie-Yippies did not count their injured.

At 7:57 P.M., in the intersection of Michigan Avenue and Balbo Avenue, the demonstrators, the police and The Mayor achieved what they had been building toward for five days. The Mayor was not present physically, of course—the evening program had begun at the Amphitheater—but his policies and his attitudes were represented by the police. It would be cruel to say that hippie, policeman and Mayor each got what was coming to him, but it is truth to say that each got what he was looking for so eagerly.

Only a few policemen forgot their training. Only a few demonstrators dared to antagonize authority. But the cameras of television and the news photographers were there to film the violent collision of the few. The blame for it and the praise for it were reserved for The Mayor.

It was much more grotesquely surrealistic than Pablo's rusting dog in the Civic Center Plaza. It was the thing that couldn't happen here happening here. Most Chicagoans never had seen anything like it. A few Chicagoans had not seen anything like it since Memorial Day, 1937, when Chicago police, unable or unwilling to cope with a mob of tough steelmakers, shot to death ten strikers outside the Republic Steel Corporation plant on the East Side.

In 1937 the citizenry had to wait for the newsreels to bring them moving pictures of the labor riots. In 1968 too there was a delay in the transmission of the moving pictures, the pictures of television which could not be delivered immediately into American homes because another labor problem had intruded upon this hour in Chicago history; the strike of the members of the International Brotherhood of Electrical Workers had made it impossible for television producers and directors to transmit live action from "remote" locations. The television networks' trailer studios in the vicinity of the Conrad Hilton were remote locations, and the best they could do was record the street riot on tape for transmission as soon as possible.

Ironically, the *Tribune* and the *Sun-Times* had reported Wednesday morning that Illinois Bell Telephone and the I.B.E.W. had reached an accord, but the settlement had come too late. Historians who study the last week of August, 1968, in the city of Chicago surely will ask why this embarrassment was visited upon The Mayor who had done so much for Labor and who had such devoted friends in the hierarchy of Labor. Will the historians decide that a political decision to harass the television networks by prolonging the strike was turned in upon the Master Politician?

The horrendous happening at Michigan and Balbo provided television with its hour of revenge and the knife was turned savagely. Television was getting even for all the indignities suffered by its reporters and photographers and the staff men of newspapers and magazines. The tactics of vengeance never are pretty, and they were not this time, but neither are the tactics of repression.

It was terribly unfair. First, pictures of blue-helmeted policemen careening through the early darkness to seize demonstrators and throw them in the general direction of patrol wagons and vans. Pictures of young girls being seized by arms and legs, their panties exposed to shock those who are sickened by sexuality but thrilled by violence. Pictures of young girls, reduced to human projectiles, striking the sides of police vehicles instead of flying through the doors that were the targets of the police. Pictures of clubs and batons flailing in the gloom and coming down upon heads, rib cages, arms, legs and groins.

Second, pictures of The Mayor back at the Amphitheater.

Pictures of The Mayor smiling. Pictures of The Mayor grin-
ning. Pictures of The Mayor laughing. Pictures of The
Mayor applauding. Pictures of The Mayor that made it seem
that he was laughing in reaction to what was happening in
those other pictures filmed at Michigan and Balbo.

Unfair, so terribly unfair. Sure, there were explanations
that the pictures from Michigan and Balbo had been made
much earlier but were being presented now because of
"technical problems," but these explanations were not heard
by millions or were misunderstood by other millions. The
laughter of The Mayor, so innocent and so coincidental,
seemed to be the ultimate madness.

From his suite in the Conrad Hilton Vice-President Humphrey gazed upon the carnage below and reportedly said, "I
don't feel so good tonight, with what's going on down there."
Senator McCarthy looked down from Olympus and reportedly said, "It looks like the Battle of Cannae." McCarthy's
allusion was to an action fought in 216 B.C. He might have
reached more souls if he had recalled the Battle of Bastogne,
but those who knew him—or thought they knew him—suspected that McCarthy chose Cannae because he had been
present at that battle.

News of the street riot reached the floor of the Convention
before the moving pictures did. Most of the delegates knew
that something extraordinary had happened. Some thought it
terrible. Others thought it justifiable. Donald Peterson, a delegate from Wisconsin, a state that McCarthy had won in the
primary, rose to demand that the Convention be adjourned
for two weeks and then moved to another city. Peterson
made a tactical mistake that lost him the support of many
who were furious and many who were frightened. He referred to the demonstrators as "children." Nobody saw them
as children. The furious saw them as courageous men and
women who were willing to be clubbed and kicked and
kneed and thrown through the air for a cause they believed
to be true. The frightened saw them as dangerous *provoca-*

teurs who were old enough and dedicated enough to over-throw democracy along with the Democratic party.

Peterson had the attention of the microphones and the cameras, but he did not have the attention of the chairman of the Convention. The roll call of the states had begun as a prelude to nominating speeches. Nominations were in order, but when "Illinois" was sounded, The Mayor rose and, then and there, cast his vote for Hubert Humphrey. Quite clearly the Convention had gotten away from Richard Daley. His enemies in the hall gleefully booed the *faux pas*. He stalked from the floor and disappeared through a rear door.

The unforgettable moment, the moment that will be re-membered long after the historical events of the 1968 Demo-cratic Convention have been filed in the archives of the scholars of politics, came during a speech for Senator Mc-Govern. It was provided by a man not renowned for a dramatic flair, Senator Abraham Ribicoff of Connecticut. The same Ribicoff who had called upon The Mayor as recently as Saturday.

Only two lines of what was an uninspiring speech would be remembered, and one of those was weak and anticlimac-tic. The lines read:

"And with George McGovern as President of the United States we wouldn't have those Gestapo tactics in the streets of Chicago. With George McGovern we wouldn't have a Na-tional Guard."

The streets of Chicago! *Gestapo* tactics in Chicago! That terrible word from a man whose name told of his spiritual kinship with six million Jews who died during the long night of the Nazis. *Gestapo* from the mouth of a Swede or a Pole or an Irishman would have been less hard to take.

The Mayor should have taken it. His political instinct should have said, "Dick, shrug your shoulders, put your head down and look at the floor until this passes. You can't win this one."

There is another instinct, though, that motivates men. The

Mayor of Chicago leaped from his chair to shout at Ribicoff and to gesture toward him. The ever-faithful George Dunne was at Daley's left. The ever-faithful Tom Keane was seated behind Dick. A sweet-faced young Daley son was there, shouting, too.

This was something between two men who had lost their man. Abe Ribicoff, a Kennedy man. Dick Daley, a Kennedy man. Abe and Dick in the vacuum now. Again most of the delegates on the floor did not see the exchange, but millions of television watchers saw it. And what many of them saw was not two old men in a vacuum, but the tragic thing between Catholic and Jew that has been so much a part of the history of our nation.

The Mayor's reaction provided Abe with an opportunity to seize the moment and make it his glory forever. "How hard it is to accept the truth," he said in the soft but positive voice of an order priest conducting a men's mission in a parish church.

After it was over, after Hubert Humphrey received the nomination that had been his as soon as Lyndon Johnson had assured the delegates, earlier in the day, that he had not changed his mind about defaulting this match, and as soon as Edward Kennedy had reiterated that he would not enter the tournament, more than five hundred delegates who had gone down with McCarthy and McGovern thought they might do something dramatic.

They would walk, in candlelight procession, from the Amphitheater to the Conrad Hilton. They would pass the nearby home of The Mayor, the only sound the shuffle of feet. The distance, portal to portal, is forty-four blocks, five and one-half miles. The delegates might have walked, but as was true of The Mayor of Chicago, earlier in August, they did not walk.

They walked only as far as the Amphitheater parking lot, where buses awaited. This was another absurdity worthy of W. C. Fields and the Marx Brothers. Somewhere an old liberal was laughing—a not altogether bad thing, because old liberals don't laugh much these days. The laughter was harsh and derisive. Old liberals would have paraded past the home of The Mayor, shouting their slogans, but liberal soles and wills had grown soft from disuse.

58

᠁᠁᠁᠁᠁᠁

Day of the Baptist

For behold I have made you this day
a fortified city, and a pillar of iron,
and a wall of brass . . .
—Epistle from the Mass
for Thursday in Convention Week

MANY of the triumphs of The Mayor were so close in time
and space, but on Thursday morning they were breaking up
and fading away like the shimmering landscape in a mirage.
Had not the people of Chicago preferred him to Ben
Adamowski in 1963 and to John Waner in 1967? The pattern
of Richard Daley's elections was tough-easy-tough-easy. Ben
Adamowski had been very tough, even more so than Bob
Merriam. John Waner had been too easy, even more so than
Tim Sheehan.

Waner, who made certain that he would have no chance at
all by denouncing Police Superintendent Orlando Wilson
during the 1967 mayoral campaign, received no more than
272,542 votes. The Mayor strolled to victory with 792,238, a
very real figure that must be seriously studied by those political Pollyandrews who have persuaded themselves that Richard Daley will be beatable in 1971. Tim Sheehan, first of the
Republican candidates to get the back of the hand from the
big money men of the party, managed to convince 311,940

voters that he should be mayor in the 1959 campaign. The Mayor ran up 778,612 against Sheehan.

Adamowski, the apostate Democrat, knew how to fight. Ben's first instinct was for battle. He had been fighting all his political life, sometimes when fighting was not necessary. He had the instinct for the jugular, and when he was knocked down, he got up. He rarely bothered to take the mandatory count of eight.

Ben caught one on his jut-jaw and went down hard. On January 8, 1963, the *Sun-Times* reported in a copyrighted story that during his four years as state's attorney Adamowski had spent $833,984 from a contingency fund as compared with $445,558 spent by his predecessor, John Gutknecht. "Benjamin S. Adamowski has said he spent major sums of the taxpayers' money as state's attorney without retaining the information he paid for," the *Sun-Times* story said.

Adamowski conceded that he had paid out $87,000 to informants who were aiding him in investigations of graft in City Hall and of the narcotics racket. The $87,000 had been spent in the fiscal year from December 1, 1959, to November 30, 1960. Ben said he had burned the information received from his secret agents, as well as the records of this cloak-and-dagger fund, before he left the state's attorney office in 1962. Adamowski had lost in the primary to John Bickley, and Bickley was defeated by Democrat Daniel Ward, the man who uncovered the material on the contingency fund. Ben said that he had burned the espionage reports and the financial records to protect his informants.

Ben got up quickly and tossed a few jabs, such as his revelation that even as his contingency fund was being questioned, the city government maintained forty-three contingency funds. He suggested darkly that somebody ought to look into the operation of those funds.

When the cobwebs had cleared, the pugilistic Pole started swinging with both hands. He hit Daley as hard as he had walloped the old champion, Ed Kelly, in earlier battles. And as is true of all capable street fighters, Ben wasn't careful about where the blows might land. The man who had compared Kelly with Hitler and Stalin now found parallels between The Mayor and Cuba's dictator, Fidel Castro. The Democrats had drafted "a political slave army by controlling the very food and housing on which the Negro depends," Adamowski charged.

Looking ahead to election day, Adamowski thundered, "The explosion April 2 will make the atomic bomb dropped on Hiroshima seem like a firecracker." He predicted a "searing, seething blast of votes." Ben also dared Daley to take lie tests to see how each measured up to the public trust.

At 7 P.M. on election night Adamowski told a radio reporter, "I think you're interviewing the next mayor of Chicago." At 9:14 P.M. Ben conceded to The Mayor with bitter remarks about the "Progress Before Politics" Republicans who had supported Daley with their money.

The Mayor's victory margin was 137,531 votes. The fourteen wards that were predominantly black or changing rapidly from white to black gave him a plurality of 138,769. Daley had only 49 percent of the vote in the white wards, but an overpowering 82 percent of the levers were pulled for him in the black wards.

"I had the feeling—and the proof is there if we could get a true count—that the community was looking for a change in 1963 and that I had a chance to win," Adamowski said. "I felt I could win. I further felt that support would come from the newspapers. Why it didn't come I can't explain, other than that advertisement, 'Progress Before Politics.' If I'd had the Polish vote against Daley I would have won. The *Polish Daily News* endorsed Daley against me in 1963 and against John Waner, another Pole, in 1967."

During the '63 campaign The Mayor listed the major accomplishments of his administrations. He was very proud of:

Reorganization of the Police Department after the Summerdale scandal.

Addition of men and equipment to the Fire Department.

Improved street cleaning.

Improved traffic safety, best among large cities for 1962.

Public improvements, the Dan Ryan Expressway, the
modernization of Navy Pier and the enlarging of O'Hare
International Airport.

Prime rating from Dun and Bradstreet on Chicago's
municipal bonds.

Lowest property taxes for any city of more than 500,000
population. Thirty-three of thirty-nine suburban communities near Chicago had higher tax rates than the
city did, The Mayor said modestly.

Then he had revived his familiar call to the voters. "The
guiding principle of my public life is that 'good government
is good politics and good politics is good government.'"

Had he not done all those wondrous things? Were not the
streets cleaner out in the neighborhoods? Was not the skyline of the Loop transformed? Did not the Dan Ryan take
South Siders to their homes in half the time they expended in
earlier years? Was not the O'Hare Airport a thing of beauty?

Yes, yes, yes, yes, yes, your Honor, said those to whom the
word *yes* came as a reflex action.

Why then must he justify himself? Could April and August of 1968 have undone all the good that was accomplished
in the months, the many months since April of 1955? Why
was it necessary for him to come, freshly groomed and tai-
lored, to the fifth-floor conference room at City Hall, the
room that had been the scene of so many press-conference
triumphs, to stand behind the lectern and offer an explanation?

"On behalf of the city of Chicago and its people and the
Chicago Police Department," The Mayor began, "I would

like to issue this statement and I expect that in the sense of fair play it will be given the same kind of distribution on press, radio and television as the mob of rioters was given yesterday.

"For weeks—months—the press, radio and television across the nation have revealed the tactics and strategy that was to be carried on in Chicago during the convention week by groups of terrorists.

"In the heat of emotion and riot some policemen may have overreacted, but to judge the entire police force by the alleged action of a few would be just as unfair as to judge our entire younger generation by the actions of this mob.

"I would like to say here and now that this administration, our administration, and the people of Chicago have never condoned brutality at any time, but they will never permit a lawless group of terrorists to menace the lives of millions of people, destroy the purpose of the convention, and take over the streets of Chicago."

That was it. This was a press conference without questions. "This is my statement, gentlemen," The Mayor said. "It speaks for itself." Moving, moving, moving, The Mayor turned quickly and disappeared into an inner office.

His statement spoke for itself, but it did not speak for everybody. Some Democrats and other Americans, disunited, were speaking for themselves. Senator McGovern said, "I saw American youths being savagely beaten by policemen simply because they were protesting policies about which they have had very little to say."

The mystic McCarthy came down from his mountain, passed through the protestations of the Secret Service men, crossed to the other side of Michigan Avenue and walked among his people.

Early runs of *The New World*, the weekly newspaper of the Roman Catholic Archdiocese of Chicago, revealed that The Mayor's fellow communicants would read strong criticism of the Police Department action when the newspaper was delivered Friday.

Dr. Edward Sparling, president emeritus of Roosevelt University, whose committee had issued the report on the April 27 disturbance at Civic Center Plaza, laid the blame for the Wednesday night riot upon the doorstep at 3536 South Lowe Avenue. Sparling said that The Mayor's policy decisions were directly responsible for the violence.

Unlike The Mayor, Judge Elmer Schnackenberg of the United States Court of Appeals did not make exceptions for some policemen who "may have overreacted." Judge Schnackenberg signed an injunction Thursday restraining all Chicago policemen from interfering with newsmen who were covering demonstrations and other convention events. Schnackenberg reversed the ruling of United States District Court Judge William Campbell, who had turned down a petition for an injunction. The petition had been filed by the American Civil Liberties Union.

The Police Department, still not willing to concede that a mistake or two might have been made, reacted to the injunction with this statement: "The Chicago Police Department, before it received the injunction, did not have a policy of harassing newsmen and it still does not have such a policy. Newsmen will not be harassed."

The statement consoled the thirteen newsmen who had been Maced or clubbed or arrested while on assignment near Michigan and Balbo Wednesday night.

The answer to all the questions asked by, of and for The Mayor may have been one that he would not want to hear. The answer very well might have been that he had been right during all those other weeks of his glorious administrations, but he had been very wrong during convention week, 1968.

Thursday was the feast of the beheading of Saint John the Baptist.

Honest, Abe

CHICAGO politicians had been packing convention halls for one hundred and eight years. The ancient art of "shoehorning" had been passed down to the Chicago Democrats of 1968 from the Chicago Republicans of 1860, and the techniques had been so thoroughly worked out for that pre–Civil War convention it would have been futile to attempt to refine them for the Vietnam War convention.

Chicago, ninth-largest city of the nation and closing in on Cincinnati and St. Louis, won the Republican convention for 1860, although everybody knew that Chicago belonged to the Democrats. The go-getters out in the wilds of the West outbid other would-be Republican hosts by promising to build a new jim-dandy convention hall right downtown. Even Dick Daley would have been dazzled by the way those Chicagoans moved. In April the city knocked down Mark Beaubien's historic Sauganash Tavern at Lake and Market (Wacker Drive). By May a two-story wooden hall called the Wigwam awaited the arrival of the Republican delegates. There were seats for five thousand in this simple, barnlike structure, but Chicago's Republicans knew something very important. They knew that the hall would hold ten thousand when the proper time came.

Thurlow Weed, the big Whig from New York, came in with his candidate, Senator William Seward. The New Yorkers, who had been working at national politics for a long time, would show the rubes out in Chicago a thing or two. When New Yorkers said they would march for Seward, their favorite son, they weren't using a figure of speech. Hundreds of Easterners spilled out of the trains, resplendent in the vivid uniforms of marching societies and bands. Seward couldn't miss. That strange man from Illinois, Abraham Lincoln, simply did not have a chance.

Herman Kogan and Lloyd Wendt tell what happened next, in their book *Chicago, A Pictorial History:* "The Illinois men waited. The first two days of the convention were devoted to routine business. On the third, Friday, May 18, with nominations scheduled, the Lincoln strategists issued thousands of bogus tickets to their followers. While Sewardites paraded, the Lincoln men packed the hall."

Seward's supporters tried to get into the Wigwam. They fought to get in, with fists and sticks, but the Lincolnites controlled the doors. After all, it was "their" hall. They built it, didn't they? Official delegates who supported Seward were permitted to enter, out of respect for the democratic process, but any Lincoln man, official or otherwise, was allowed to enter, out of respect for the republican process. This was the day the hall would hold ten thousand souls, and it was estimated that more than five thousand were in various Lincoln rooting sections. Lincoln men were everywhere.

Although the convention might have wanted Seward when nominations began, the New Yorker had no chance to prevail. Seward had 173½ votes on the first roll call. Lincoln had 102. Seward picked up only eleven votes on the second go-round and Lincoln gained seventy-nine. Lincoln had been nominated by a Chicagoan, Norman Judd, and during the third roll call, another Chicagoan, Joseph Medill, just happened to be seated with the Ohio delegation. As Lincoln closed in and his claques continued their thunderous cheering, Medill made a little deal. The Ohioans switched four votes to Lincoln and the Illinoisan was in. When the word of his victory reached Honest Abe down in Springfield, he was touched by the loyalty of his Chicago followers.

It is not totally unrealistic, then, to say that the bogus tickets, printed up to pack the Wigwam, changed the course of United States history. The art begins with tickets, and if a faction has the tickets it can do wondrous things. The Mayor and his loyal Chicago followers had the tickets on Thursday night, August 29, 1968.

The Mayor also had a cause. He didn't have a Lincoln to maneuver into the center stage of history. There were no Lincolns here. There were no Lincolns in the Land of Lincoln in 1968. He didn't have a Teddy Kennedy. He didn't even have a Hubert H. Humphrey, because he had waited too long to use his tickets on Humphrey's behalf. The Mayor didn't have a great cause, but he had something that must be done.

Packing the hall on Thursday night, 1968, was not quite the same as packing the hall on Friday, 1860. There really wasn't much wrong with bringing busloads of city workers to the Amphitheater Thursday night to whoop and holler during Hubert's acceptance speech and for the nomination of Maine's Senator Edmund Muskie, a good and gentle man. That was traditional. That was the thing to do. When the fourth night of any convention rolled around and the Presidential nomination was out of the way, a lot of delegates took time off to go out on the town. And Chicago was a good town to go out on even if the night might be filled with hippie-Yippies. The seats invariably were available after the nomination so why not bring in all the hard-working precinct captains—all the sewer workers, the water workers, the street workers, the forestry workers, the health department workers, the public-works department workers—all those who are willing to take menial jobs in exchange for the glamour of being "in politics"? Bring them down to the Amphitheater and let them participate in the Convention so that they would have something to talk about on their next trip to The Hall. "I saw The Mayor at the Convention and he said to me, 'Joe, . . .'" And because a precinct captain must work for each favor bestowed by the Cook County Democratic organization, the captains and their wives and children would be asked to whoop it up for the candidates, to generate enthusiasm that might be transmitted to the millions sitting in front of television sets.

Nothing wrong with that, is there?

But the signs, the nauseating signs. There was no other apt word for them. They turned the stomach. They were at least as offensive to the eye, the mind, the soul as Yippies giving a public screwing exhibition on the grass of Lincoln Park. There were thousands of them in the hall before the Thursday night session began. "We Love Daley" was the basic theme.

So this was The Mayor's cause. Not a Lincoln. Not a Kennedy. Not even a Hubert Humphrey, who would need all the help he could get this night. Himself, as the old Irish say. The Mayor's cause was The Mayor. He would show the nation that he was loved, in spite of all to the contrary that the nation had heard from Eric Sevareid, David Brinkley, Hugh Downs and the others from "the media."

How could The Mayor, this mayor, do this to himself? How could The Mayor allow this to be done to him? Where were the able lieutenants who would intercept the sign carriers and say with a snarl, "Who sent for you?"

Who, in God's name, had sent for them? Throughout his career The Mayor had fought to be something more than another shanty-Irish politician. He had not wanted to be a caricature—and now he was caricaturing himself. There was a cruelty in this that made those who cared about him wince. Unfortunately, those who cared about him in this situation were total strangers. They were far from the convention hall, watching the tasteless spectacle on television. Those who were with him in the Amphitheater, close enough to touch him, did nothing to protect him. It is charitable to suppose that they would have helped him if they had seen what the television audience was seeing.

But the signs would not have been there if The Mayor hadn't wanted them there. Could it be that this remote man —the man who "isn't close to anybody," in the words of an old friend—needed love now, even love that was bought in a printer's job shop?

Not a Kennedy. Not even a dead Kennedy. The Democrats held their quadrennial Kennedy Memorial Service Thursday night. In 1964 at Atlantic City they had remembered John Fitzgerald. In 1968 at Chicago they would remember Robert Francis. The movie about Bobby was incredibly beautiful. For the first time in four days decency returned to the hall. Many delegates understood that the mean, tough little man, who had made himself a decent tough man, had been the best the party could have offered in 1968—was the best in death. The movie made Americans cry.

More Americans wept after the movie had ended and the soft, dreamlike singing began. "The Battle Hymn of the Republic" started within the New York delegation and soon was picked up by hundreds. Whether or not the singing had been a spontaneous thing in its inception, the joining in was spontaneous. It was so tender, so haunting. It had the perfection of love in it for a few shining minutes. And then it was spoiled by the excesses typical of those who surrounded the Kennedys. Those who loved Bobby Kennedy were writhing very much as they had winced for The Mayor, whom they did not love.

The singing for Bobby, like the funeral for Bobby, went on too long. It was tragic that the Kennedys, the Kennedy brothers, who had so much class, magnetized family, friends and admirers who had so little. Kennedy people were never able merely to say, "Here he is and we loved him." After an

interminable time the leech and the jackal had to say, "Here
we are. See, we loved him."

Some of them had become like The Mayor, who had been
their ally and their tool when Jack was alive but now was
their enemy. Like The Mayor they no longer seemed to know
what they were doing. Their singing had begun as a huge
vocal wreath upon the grave of Robert Kennedy, but they
prolonged it as a protest against all that had gone on during
convention week. They twisted a hymn of love until it became a wail of bitterness and hate. They had meant to honor
his memory, but now they were profaning his memory.

For twenty minutes the singing went on, television record-
ing it and offering far too many pictures of Roosevelt Grier,
the large professional football player who had been in the
kitchen the night Robert Kennedy was mortally wounded,
and of Shirley MacLaine, the musical-comedy actress. The
singing went on until millions were shrieking silently, "Stop
it. Stop it."

The Mayor's claque in the gallery tried to stop it, not because they were offended by this exploitation of a good man's
memory, but because they were sure that The Mayor wanted
to get on with Convention business. "We Want Daley! We
Want Daley!" they chanted; but, of course, nobody wanted
Daley. The singing went on.

Finally, The Mayor sent for a man he had called upon in
the past. Dutifully, the ghost of Martin Luther King Jr. made
the walk from the statue of the Black Infantryman, up Thirty-
fifth Street and down Halsted, to bring calm to the Amphitheater as he once had brought calm to the West Side. Alderman Ralph Metcalfe, a black man, asked for a moment of
silent tribute for Dr. King. The night belonged to the dead.
Would Lazarus soon walk in carrying his "We Love Daley"
sign?

One wondered what the black precinct captains in the balcony thought when they heard the memory of Martin Luther

King Jr. invoked to shut off the memory of Robert Francis Kennedy.

He was doing this awful thing to himself, in his own back-yard, where one would expect him to be surrounded by true friends. On this night he needed men like lovable John McGuane and devoted Stanley Nowakowski, who had helped him in his first campaign for mayor and in all the bat-tles that had gone before. But John and Stanley and so many other neighbors who might have said, "No, Dick, for God's sake, no!" were dead.

The Convention moved on to balloting for candidates for Vice-President. The Mayor was given a vote by delegate Bull Connor, the former Alabama police chief. In the summer of 1965, when the little girls of Bridgeport were chanting, "Cuz if I were an Alabama trooper, I could kill the niggers legally," Bull Connor had been their great hero.

Television wanted The Mayor Thursday night and he wanted television. He had something to say. He had a need to tell the nation that he and the police and Chicago were right and that the hippies and the newsmen were wrong. He wanted equal time for Chicago but he did not want it so much that he would go on with Sevareid or with Huntley and Brinkley or with Chancellor or with Reynolds or with any of the others who might rip a man's flesh with a question. He would go on with Walter Cronkite, with sweet guy Wal-ter.

There was risk in this because Walter had said to Rather, "I think we've got a bunch of thugs there, Dan. . . ." two nights earlier after Rather had been punched in the stomach. The risk was there, but The Mayor was willing to run it. He went into the interview with very little to lose. After a few minutes he clearly realized that he could gain something. There were only two interpretations that could be put on the interview. Either ground rules had been worked out in ad-vance or Cronkite was being flimflammed. Cronkite, whose colleagues had been beaten and abused on the streets and on the convention floor, owed it to his profession, if not to his audience, to take the offensive, but The Mayor had the ball. He moved with it in the glorious tradition of the Hamburg Athletic Association. He revealed the "plot."

"Let me say something I've never said to anyone," The Mayor began, taking good old Walter into his confidence. "It's unfortunate and we can't say it, but the television industry didn't have the information I had. There were reports on my desk that certain people planned to assassinate many of the leaders, including myself, but I've had that constantly. So I took the necessary precautions."

The Mayor turned a beseeching look upon Cronkite and upon all those out there on the other side of the picture tubes, a look that said two things. It said, "What would you have done?" And it said, "I'm witchoo."

There was more. There were the pictures, The Mayor said, that television had not shown, of fifty-one injured policemen, and there was the revelation that some of the newsmen were "hippies" and "revolutionaries" who "want these things to happen."

The Mayor had finished. He had told them—the people— and he had told them off—the media. He seemed so sure that the citizens would agree he had done the right thing. He had protected three Presidential candidates from assassination.

At that hour on Thursday, The Mayor could not have known the results of interviews conducted that day by market-research teams from Sindlinger and Company. The researchers had questioned 1,194 adults to learn their reaction to what had happened Wednesday night. The security measures were justified, 71.4 percent said. Mayor Daley was doing a good job, 61.7 percent said. The demonstrations had been organized to disrupt the Convention and create riot conditions, 48.3 percent said. The police were overly violent, 21.3 percent said.

The Mayor did not know of this survey but he did hear the chants of "We Love Daley" when he returned to the convention floor after twenty minutes in the CBS booth with the mesmerized Cronkite. The Mayor turned an affectionate look toward the sea of waving signs, applauded lustily, and climbed upon a chair to wave to his kind of people.

In a nation that always had hated much more intensely than it had loved, 61.7 percent said they loved Mayor Richard J. Daley of Chicago.

EPILOGUE

Another Run

THE race was done on Friday morning, and all the marathon runners who had come to the end of the course wore the look of agony and anguish that reflects a hammering heart and near-bursting lungs. All of them—The Mayor, Hubert Humphrey, Eugene McCarthy, George McGovern, Julian Bond, David Dellinger, Jerry Rubin, Jim Conlisk, Bill Clark, Adlai Stevenson III, hippie, Yippie, flippie, delegate, policeman, newsman—all of them jogged in place, shook their hands convulsively and then trotted ever so slowly as each waited for body and soul to return to normal.

Chicago *Daily News* television critic Dean Gysel, who later died in a traffic accident, wrote, "The mayor has his city back, but the hippies won the battle."

Conlisk's Friday message for the Police Department teletype read: "I have received the following message from Mayor Richard J. Daley: 'The Democratic National Committee and the mayor of Chicago express their heartfelt gratitude to the men and women of the Chicago Police Department for their devotion to duty and a job well done.'"

Governor Philip Hoff of Vermont sent this telegram to The Mayor: "We and other members of the Vermont delegation are not yet home, but our arrival in New York City signified that we are free once again. We do not believe the people of Chicago or this country will long endure the police state you imposed on freedom-loving Americans, who came to your city to demonstrate the democratic process. We are pleased to be liberated from your streets, as well as from your Amphitheater."

In his newsletter for September 17, 1968, Illinois State Treasurer Stevenson wrote: "The events surrounding the convention have made the need for reform obvious. More than ever before, Illinois Democrats are restless within the confines of a feudal structure which exists by rewarding homage with jobs and favors. Chicago, the Democratic Party, indeed all our institutions, must open up to new ideas and forces, rewarding idealism and energy and innovation—either that or they will not command the allegiance of the people."

. Thomas Peter Laine, the "boy on the Hilton roof," was freed when he appeared in court. "I just walked into the hotel," Laine said, "took an elevator to the twenty-fourth floor, walked up a floor and onto the roof and stayed there for about fifteen minutes before I was discovered. I didn't think it was anything unusual." Judge Saul Epton said he was disturbed by the ease with which the University of Chicago student had penetrated the security cordon.

Endorsed by McCarthy, McGovern, Senator Kennedy and Jesse Jackson, Bill Clark went boating on the rivers of Illinois, in his Clark Ark, searching for votes, and found so many that he gave Senator Dirksen unexpectedly strong competition. Dirksen won in 99 of 102 counties, but Clark received 2,073,242 votes as compared to 2,358,947 for the winner. Still, Dirksen outdistanced every other candidate on the Illinois ballot.

• Clark suffered a heart attack in March, 1969, not long after he had become a partner in Colonel Arvey's law firm.

• Paul Simon, the bow-tied crusader, led the Democratic ticket with 2,222,331 votes, and thereby helped to provide a "first" for Illinois political history. Simon, a Democrat, was elected lieutenant governor. Richard Ogilvie, a Republican, was elected governor.

Simon's strength, not at all unexpected, convinced those Democrats who were not political jobholders that Simon would have beaten Dirksen. And that Stevenson would have beaten Dirksen.

Ogilvie promised to "dismantle the Democratic machine" in Illinois, but The Mayor heatedly retorted that the new governor would not make good that promise. When Ogilvie departed for Springfield, he left vacant the position he had held, the presidency of the Cook County Board of Trustees. The Democratic majority on the board quickly elected The Mayor's loyal and devoted supporter, George Dunne, to the presidency, and cynical watchers of the political scene smiled and said that The Mayor would much rather have a Democratic County Board president than a Democratic governor.

The Mayor would call upon Ogilvie at the governor's mansion, just as The Mayor had called upon Bill Stratton in 1955, to work out accords that would be mutually beneficial to the great State of Illinois and the great City of Chicago.

• Handsome Bill Scott, second only to Dirksen as a votegetter on the Republican side in November, defeated Francis Lorenz in the run for attorney general. John Stamos did not laugh publicly. There was a judgeship in the offing for John. The Democrat who had displaced Stamos on the Cook County ticket, Edward Hanrahan, was elected state's attorney, and The Mayor retained control of another important office.

• The National Commission on Urban Problems issued a report that contained so many pages they had to be packed in shopping bags so newsmen would be able to handle them. In the report the Commission rated the projects of the Chicago Housing Authority as excellent in "fiscal solvency, occupancy levels and property maintenance"—words certain to gladden the heart of The Mayor, who is so proud of his city's "programs." But the Commission had other words to say about the stewardship of the C.H.A. ". . . if weighed in

terms of human values, quality of family life or the development of community life, it may be one of the poorest programs," the Commission suggested.

Those few words were a summation of all the indictments
of the Daley Years. Maximum efficiency but very little humanity.

The chairman of the National Commission on Urban Problems was Illinois's greatest living liberal, Paul Douglas.

• A federal court ruled that the Chicago Housing Authority must cease practicing racial discrimination in choosing
building sites for the city's public-housing units and in assigning tenants to them. The decision was made by Judge
Richard Austin of United States District Court, the same
Dick Austin who had run for governor at the request of The
Mayor in 1956. Austin also told the City Council that it would
be bound by law to do precisely what he would say must be
done to end the discriminatory practices.

"No criterion, other than race, can plausibly explain the
veto of over ninety-nine and a half percent of the housing
units located on white sites which were initially selected on
the basis of C.H.A.'s expert judgment and at the same time
the rejection of only ten percent or so of the units on Negro
sites," Austin ruled. "The statistics on the family housing
sites considered during the five major programs (since 1954)
show a very high probability, a near certainty, that many
sites were vetoed on the basis of the racial composition of the
site's neighborhood."

Elizabeth Wood, who had been fired for saying virtually
the same thing, resisted the impulse to say, "I told you so,
gentlemen of the City Council."

The suit, filed by the American Civil Liberties Union, began with a complaint by Father Dan Mallette and his partner in the bottom of the West Side pit, the Reverend Shelvin
Hall. Although he had been exiled to New York, Danny
Mallette was still touching the life of The Mayor. "In my

eleven years on the West Side, and in my lifetime in Chicago, one of the most obvious ironic cruelties was that public housing, intended as a means of escape from poverty, was degraded into a system almost as rigid as the reservations of South Africa. Chicago just might be able to reverse the trend toward an apartheid society," Father Mallette told *The New World*, the newspaper of the Archdiocese of Chicago.

• Hubert Humphrey, conducting a postmortem on his defeat by Richard Nixon, a defeat that clearly could have been averted if the Democrats had worked together, said, "Mayor Daley didn't exactly break his heart for me."

The Mayor peevishly responded by pointing out that Chicago had brought in a plurality of 419,000 for Humphrey. John Fitzgerald Kennedy had won Chicago by 456,000 votes in 1960. And The Mayor, a skillful player at "Can You Top This?" archly suggested that a Democratic Presidential candidate stronger than Humphrey would have had "the name of a former President."

Those who knew that Senator Kennedy had refused to run and that there were no Trumans or Roosevelts prominent at the 1968 Convention speculated that The Mayor had Orlando Wilson in mind.

• Abe Ribicoff, still not ready to throw his arms around The Mayor in the Democrats' traditional gesture of affection for an old foe, could not resist an opportunity to say that Richard Daley had given no support whatsoever to Senator Kennedy. "I was in those smoke-filled rooms," Ribicoff said. "From personal knowledge I can say that Mayor Daley was not for Ted Kennedy for President either before, during or after the convention in Chicago."

• In March of 1969 the Supreme Court of the United States unanimously reversed Dick Gregory's conviction for disorderly conduct. He had been charged for leading a march in front of The Mayor's home in 1965.

• The Shannon Rovers and all the other members of the

official cheering section showed up on April 23, 1969, to help The Mayor celebrate his 5,117th day in office. The old record had been held by the first of his predecessors from the Eleventh Ward, Big Ed Kelly.

Alderman Ralph Metcalfe was confirmed as president pro tem of the City Council. He would be the first black man in Chicago history to preside over Council meetings when The Mayor could not be present.

During the spring of 1969 Richard Ogilvie, Governor of Illinois, asked for a revenue program that would include an income tax of 4 percent on individuals and corporations. Thirty years earlier Senator Richard Daley had proposed that the legislature pass a similar bill with a 2 percent levy on personal and corporate income, but in 1969 The Mayor was not wildly enthusiastic about Ogilvie's idea. After a lot of haggling and great trumpeting in the headlines, The Mayor and the Governor compromised on a package that would tax individuals at 2½ percent and corporations at 4 percent.

The next summer, a car was driven off a bridge on Chappaquiddick Island, off Martha's Vineyard, Massachusetts, and a few hours later Adlai Stevenson III became a potential Democratic candidate for a Presidential election sometime in the Seventies.

Everett McKinley Dirksen's voice was stilled by cardiac and respiratory arrest in his seventy-fourth year. The Senator died full of honors. On the same day in the autumn of 1969, The Mayor made a totally unexpected appearance at a picnic for five thousand Democratic liberals in Libertyville, Illinois. The picnic was on a farm that had been owned by the late Adlai Stevenson. His son, Adlai III, was the official host.

The Mayor went over to the Federal Building on January 6, 1970, to testify at the federal conspiracy trial of the "Chicago Eight Minus One." Black Panther leader Bobby Seale, one of the eight charged with conspiracy to incite riots during the Democratic Convention in 1968, had been sentenced, during the trial, to prison for contempt of court.

The Mayor was called as a defense witness. Some among the defendants considered this a clever ploy, but The Mayor went into his "pillow defense" that has confounded so many aggressive opponents. He spoke in the voice barely above a whisper, smiled now and then, and seemed to enjoy every moment of what the defense thought might be Daley's ordeal. The Mayor had help. Every major objection entered by the government's attorneys was sustained by Judge Julius Hoffman.

These are examples of dialogue involving The Mayor, Judge Hoffman, Defense Attorney William Kunstler and United States Attorney Thomas Foran:

KUNSTLER (questioning Daley): Were you there during the nominating speeches for Senator McGovern?

FORAN: I object to that.

JUDGE HOFFMAN: I sustain the objection.

KUNSTLER: Mayor Daley, on the twenty-eighth of August, 1968, did you say to Senator Ribicoff—

FORAN: Oh, your Honor, I object.

KUNSTLER (continuing): "You, you Jew ———, you lousy ———, go home"?

FORAN: Listen to that. I object to that kind of conduct in a courtroom. Of all the improper, foolish questions, typical, your Honor, of making up questions that have nothing to do with the lawsuit.

KUNSTLER: That is not a made-up question, your Honor. We can prove that.

FORAN: Oh, they can? That is so improper. I ask that counsel be admonished, your Honor.

Hoffman admonished Kunstler.

The relentless defense attorney attempted to have The Mayor declared a hostile witness, a designation that would have made it possible for the defense to put into the record many questions that the judge was ruling to be irrelevant, but Judge Hoffman blandly responded that The Mayor wasn't a bit hostile, but was downright friendly. And he was. During his testimony three spectators were dragged from the courtroom by federal marshals. Somebody had hissed.

After four and a half months the comitragic "Carnival in a Courtroom" that had been the Chicago Seven conspiracy trial came to a surprising end. The ten men and the two women of the jury, which had been expected to come in quickly with a guilty verdict, deliberated into a fifth day before they hammered out a decision. None of the seven was guilty of conspiring to cross state lines with intent to violate the antiriot section of the 1968 Civil Rights act, the jury decided.

Five of the seven—David Dellinger, Jerry Rubin, Rennie Davis, Tom Hayden and Abbie Hoffman—were guilty of crossing state lines as individuals with intent to violate the federal antiriot law. Two of the seven—Lee Weiner and John Froines—were cleared of all charges.

The verdicts were as inexplicable as the trial had been ridiculous. Nobody could have been satisfied with the verdicts, particularly not the man who professed to be satisfied, The Mayor. His argument, the argument that he had compelled Chicago to wear like a hairshirt, had been that the riots of convention week were the result of a conspiracy. No conspiracy, the jurors said. There was no satisfaction in the verdicts for those defendants who had wished to become political martyrs.

Hoffman, Rubin, Davis, Hayden and, to a lesser degree, Dellinger had done all that they could to be found guilty. They had made a burlesque hall of a federal courtroom and they had chosen as their straight man the seventy-four-year-old judge. Hoffman, who can ham it up with the best of them, went along with the act. And as a final irony of the time, each of five men had been found guilty of individually "doing his thing." The Mayor was asked if he regarded the verdicts as vindication of his position. He piously said, "I look no place for vindication." He looked no place and as the appeals were processed it seemed inevitable that there would be no vindication for him or for Chicago. A few days after each of the five had been sentenced to five years, the Associated Press revealed that some lawyers within the criminal division of the Justice Department had recommended against federal prosecution of the Seven. Those lawyers were convinced that (1) the trial would become a travesty and (2) the federal antiriot law as applied to individuals crossing state lines was of dubious constitutionality. After the verdicts many thoughtful Americans on both sides of the issue began to question the limitations of conventional politics.

Father Bill Hogan, who had been hopeful that the Archdiocese of Chicago would permit St. George Church to continue to operate the parish school, was told that the entire plant would be razed. Church and school were knocked down and the bulldozers and the graders of the Archdiocese left a vacant lot just as neat and smooth as the lots that the city had made on the West Side after the April riots of '68. Some St. George parishioners said that they would not cross the expressway to worship at another black parish, but would enroll in the parish to the immediate west, The Mayor's Nativity of Our Lord. Bill Hogan, the portable priest, was transferred for the sixth time in six years.

Four black families from St. George did transfer to Nativity of Our Lord. Christmas Eve, 1969, two young black parishioners attended midnight Mass at Nativity and took with them a friend from another community. Two boys and a girl, they left the church before Mass had ended. According to their report to police, they were accosted, not far from the church, by three young white men. The girl suffered the loss of a tooth when she was struck in the face by a chain, she alleged, and one of the white youths spit in the face of one of the young black men. The black youngsters returned to the steps of the church and sought help from the policemen who had accompanied The Mayor to midnight Mass.

The marathoners were beginning to move out again, ever so slowly, for another agonizing run.

For more than fourteen years, going on sixteen, The Mayor had been Chicago. Almost everything accomplished within the city, for good or for ill, had his name or his imprint upon it. Almost nothing had been done in Chicago that he had not wanted done. When Richard J. Daley took office in 1955, he saw himself as the city. In 1970 those who had studied him through his years in City Hall realized that he had understood Chicago, in 1955, far better than his critics had.

The Mayor's vision had not been dramatic or poetic. It was realistic. Chicago had been his "subject" for a lifetime, and he had pursued his research assiduously. The once and future mayor had been twelve years old on November 1, 1914, when Chicagoans who cared about such things read that *Poetry Magazine*'s first prize of $200 had been won by a citizen named Sandburg, who lived at 4646 North Hermitage Avenue. The poem written by Sandburg was titled "Chicago," which wasn't a bad start, and the city seen by the Chicago newspaperman was the one that natives expected a country boy to see. Sandburg came from Galesburg, Illinois, and as Eleventh Warders of that day put it in their patronizing Big City manner, "Once a rube, always a rube."

Sandburg wrote of Chicago as "Hog Butcher for the World . . . City of the Big Shoulders." During his boyhood and young manhood Dickie Daley's neighbors had been the broad-shouldered men who stuck the hogs in the nearby Union Stock Yards. The man who became mayor was certain that the Chicago of 1955 no longer was the Chicago that had been brought alive by the imagery of the man from Galesburg. And The Mayor had been right.

As the city waited for The Mayor to decide whether he would run for a fifth term in 1971, the question that many citizens were asking was whether The Mayor comprehended that the Chicago of the Seventies no longer was the Chicago of 1955. Nobody could be certain of the answer.

So many have said so often that he is "the best mayor" or "the greatest mayor" in Chicago's history, the accolade has come to be taken for granted, although it does not necessarily withstand examination. To bestow such superlatives is as easy as to argue that Chicago's baseball shortstops of 1970, Don Kessinger of the Cubs and Luis Aparicio of the White Sox, are "the greatest" the teams have had. Nobody can say for certain, however, that Kessinger and Aparicio are better baseball players than were their illustrious predecessors Billy Jurges and Luke Appling, who performed in a different time and in different circumstances.

Has Richard Daley truly been a better mayor than Edward Kelly, who brought Chicago through the Depression and built the subway under the Loop and accommodated the bookmakers and the vice bosses and had such magnetic appeal to the black residents of the city? Has Dick Daley truly done a better job than William Hale Thompson, who was the first of the great builders and who also won the hearts and the minds of the black voters?

John Dienhart, the venerable newspaper editor, who has seen them all come and go, says of Daley, "I like him as a man and as a public official. He's a clean man. The politicians didn't trust Dick, in the beginning, because he never has been reachable, even by inference. I can't conceive of him doing anything wrong." Dienhart puts comparisons into historical perspective when he says of Big Bill Thompson, "Despite all his damn foolishness, he did a lot for Chicago. It was he who pushed through the Burnham Plan and that saved the lake front for future generations."

Nick Bohling, the Republican alderman who remained in

his neighborhood until his was one of only two white families in a city block of high population density, says thoughtfully, "I don't think there's any doubt that he'll go into history as the greatest mayor Chicago has had."

As to the Chicago of tomorrow, Bohling says, "Much is dependent upon how long Daley will be around. He has the ability, and thankfully so, to run a tight ship. What will happen when he's gone [long pause] I just don't know. In another generation this hatred and resentment we have on the basis of color will be gone. Chicagoans of the future will look back and laugh at us just as we now laugh at some of the things that our predecessors did because they thought they were right."

Will Chicago or any other major city be able to afford the luxury of waiting a generation before the hatred and resentment blow away upon the winds of progress? One year after the release of the Kerner Report, which was a best seller in Chicago, the National Advisory Commission on Civil Disorders concluded its anniversary report with these words: "A year later, we are a year closer to being two societies, black and white, increasingly separate and scarcely less equal."

The overpowering question, the question being asked in every metropolis of the world, was one that frightened men. "Can the city of the 1970's be made to work?" John V. Lindsay, the mayor of New York, had the gift that Daley was denied—the instinct that enabled him to get into the hearts of the citizens—but New York was falling apart before Lindsay's eyes. Richard Daley, the mayor of Chicago, had the talent that Lindsay lacked—the ability to get things done—but Chicago was being sundered while Daley worked so energetically. Daley and, to a lesser extent, Lindsay knew how to play the political game by the rules of the Sixties and the Fifties, but by now the game itself had changed. The strategies of conventional politics were failing everywhere.

To paraphrase the words written more than fifteen years

earlier by Meyerson and Banfield for their book on the Chicago Housing Authority, ". . . whether one liked it or not and whether one ignored it or not, The Mayor's problem and the race problem are inseparably one."

If the man who vowed to be "the mayor of all the people" should decide to run again, he will have an opportunity to do something now about bringing together all the people. The motto of the Daley Clan is "Faithful to God and King," a rather contradictory battle cry for a family which sprang from a land whose patriots never hesitated to shout "to hell with the King" for the honor and glory of God.

During recent years this common man from a common background has so often revealed that he does not have the common touch. He has been much more at home with the kings. It is time for this king to learn more about his people, and the most dramatic way for him to communicate his willingness for contact would be to leave behind forever the castle at 3536 South Lowe Avenue. He has done enough for Bridgeport. His children are old enough now to permit him to do what Ed Kelly did, to move away from the old neighborhood and dwell on neutral ground in a high-rise luxury apartment east or north of the Loop. From that distance he may more clearly see that the good people of Bridgeport are much better than he thought them to be.

It is time for him to listen to those who say no. It is time for him to understand that Dan Mallette, Warner Saunders, Jesse Jackson and even Dick Gregory are on his side, as he has come to comprehend that Martin Luther King Jr. and he were on the same side.

"In modernizing the political system, Daley surrounded himself with bright young men who submerged their talents in order to exercise their talents telling him what a great gift he is to the people of Chicago," Father Mallette says with typical bitterness. "Daley's office is either modeled on, or is a model for, Archdiocesan chancery offices, where bishops surround themselves with handsome young monsignors whose main talents are their Irish names, handsome faces and ability to remain unfrustrated rubber stamps and soothsayers."

If he chooses to give of himself for four more years, The Mayor must leave the buildings to those who will come after him and concentrate on the people. Should he do this he will be remembered not as Chicago's most efficient mayor, not as the mayor who made State Street and LaSalle Street work with City Hall, but as the mayor of all the people, the greatest mayor Chicago ever had.

If he cannot do this he will be memorialized by the epitaph that this man would detest more than any other. He will be remembered as just another political boss.

SELECTED BIBLIOGRAPHY

BOOKS

BANFIELD, EDWARD C., and MEYERSON, MARTIN, *Politics, Planning and the Public Interest*. New York: Free Press, 1955.

DREISKE, JOHN, *Your Government and Mine: Metropolitan Chicago*. Dobbs Ferry, N.Y.: Oceana Publications, 1959.

DUNNE, FINLEY PETER, *Mr. Dooley in Peace and War*. Boston: Small, Maynard, 1898.

KOGAN, HERMAN, and WENDT, LLOYD, *Big Bill of Chicago*. Indianapolis: Bobbs-Merrill, 1953.

———, *Bosses in Lusty Chicago* (originally *Lords of the Levee*, published in 1943). Bloomington, Ind.: Indiana University Press, 1967.

———, *Chicago, A Pictorial History*. New York: Crown Publishers (Bonanza Books), 1958.

PETERSON, VIRGIL W., *Barbarians in Our Midst*, a history of Chicago crime and politics. Boston: Little, Brown, 1952.

Report of the National Advisory Commission on Civil Disorders. New York: Bantam Books, 1968.

Rights in Conflict, the official report to the National Commission on the Causes and Prevention of Violence. New York: New American Library (Signet Books), 1968.

SPEAR, ALLAN H., *Black Chicago: The Making of a Negro Ghetto*. Chicago: University of Chicago Press, 1967.

WAGENKNECHT, EDWARD CHARLES, *Chicago*. Norman, Okla.: University of Oklahoma Press, 1964.

369

WALDROP, FRANK C., *McCormick of Chicago.* Englewood Cliffs, N.J.: Prentice-Hall, 1966.

ZORBAUGH, HARVEY W., *The Gold Coast and the Slum,* a sociological study of Chicago's Near North Side. Chicago: University of Chicago Press, 1929.

BOOKLETS

Chicago Lawyers for McCarthy, *A Delegate's Guide to an Open Convention,* edited by Peter Barnes and Thomas Moffett. 1968.

Cook County Committee, Illinois Sesquicentennial, *The Story of Dan Cook.* 1968.

Facts About Chicago. Chicago Municipal Reference Library, 1968.

News from the Office of Adlai Stevenson III, Illinois State Treasurer, 1968.

REX, FREDERICK, *Historical Information About Chicago.* Chicago Municipal Reference Library, n.d.

ROBERTS, ALAN, *The Paul Simon Story.* Simon for Lieutenant Governor Committee, 1968.

WOLFERT, RICHARD J., *The Government of the City of Chicago;* revised by Joyce Madden. Chicago Municipal Reference Library, 1966.

UNPUBLISHED

WOODLOCK, DOUGLAS P., "The Chicago Mayoralty, 1955—An Urban Machine Chooses and Elects Its Man." 1969.

INDEX